POLITICAL ENTREPRENEURS

Political Entrepreneurs

The Rise of Challenger Parties in Europe

Catherine E. De Vries and Sara B. Hobolt

PRINCETON UNIVERSITY PRESS

PRINCETON AND OXFORD

Published by Princeton University Press
41 William Street, Princeton, New Jersey 08540
6 Oxford Street, Woodstock, Oxfordshire OX20 1TR

press.princeton.edu

All Rights Reserved
ISBN 978-0-691-19475-2
ISBN (e-book) 978-0-691-20654-7

British Library Cataloguing-in-Publication Data is available

Editorial: Sarah Caro, Hannah Paul and Josh Drake
Production Editorial: Jenny Wolkowicki
Jacket design: Carmina Alvarez
Production: Erin Suydam
Publicity: Kate Farquhar-Thomson and Kate Hensley
Copyeditor: Maia Vaswani

Jacket image: Shutterstock

This book has been composed in Adobe Text and Gotham

Printed on acid-free paper. ∞

Printed in the United States of America

10 9 8 7 6 5 4 3 2 1

To Mila, Noah, Elliot, and Alexander

CONTENTS

This book is the result of a long conversation between two colleagues and friends. It is the outcome of our personal experiences with as well as our research on political change in Western Europe. This conversation started about 16 years ago when we were both completing our doctoral research on ruptures in European politics. We met at a conference held at the Johns Hopkins University School of Advanced International Studies in Bologna, Italy. Born Danish and Dutch, we were perhaps not as taken aback as others by the rise of the populist far right in Europe. We were familiar with the successful political entrepreneurship of Mogens Glistrup, founder of the Progress Party in Denmark, and Pim Fortuyn, founder of the List Pim Fortuyn in the Netherlands. The permissive electoral rules in Denmark and the Netherlands had allowed electoral breakthrough of such challenger parties long before they succeeded elsewhere. At the same time, a comparison of our Danish and Dutch experiences presented us with an interesting puzzle about the timing of political change. The landslide election that shook up the political mainstream in Denmark occurred in the early 1970s, whereas Dutch mainstream parties remained resilient for much longer. This raised questions about why the pace and nature of political change were so different in countries otherwise so similar.

In our search for answers, we both noted an apparent schism between the scholarship on political parties and political change in Europe and that in the United States. Each of us had spent time at an American university, the University of North Carolina at Chapel Hill and the University of Michigan, and we were struck by the differences between how "Americanists" and "Europeanists" would explain political change. As students of politics in Europe, we were well-versed in sociological theories of political parties as expressions of societal divisions rooted in big historical divides. Yet, our exposure to scholarship on American politics presented us with another, equally compelling, image of political parties as an organizational vehicle for the strategic interests and actions of political elites. Our intellectual journey to understand political change, which is documented in this book, started with Seymour Martin Lipset and Stein Rokkan and their cleavage theory, and was enriched by classic books on American politics, such as *The Semisovereign People* by Elmer Schattschneider, *Liberalism against Populism* by William Riker, *Why Parties?* by John Aldrich, and *Issue Evolution* by Edward Carmines and James Stimson. Our theory of political change that is at the heart of this book fuses insights from the pathbreaking work on party competition in both Europe and the United States.

As such, this book is inspired by the work of incredible scholars of European politics, including James Adams, Lawrence Ezrow, Mark Franklin, Liesbet Hooghe, Ronald Inglehart, Orit Kedar, Herbert Kitschelt, Hanspeter Kriesi, Peter Mair, Gary Marks, Bonnie Meguid, Cas Mudde, Pippa Norris, and Robert Rohrschneider (and many others), as well as the seminal work on American politics by John Aldrich, Edward Carmines, Tom Carsey, Robert Erikson, Michael MacKuen, William Riker, Elmer Schattschneider, James Stimson, and many others. Another critical source of inspiration has been the work on political parties and electoral politics in developing democracies by scholars like Kevin Deegan-Krause, Tim Haughton, Noam Lupu, Beatriz Magaloni, and Joshua Tucker (and many others). This book is the result of us being able to stand on the shoulders of these intellectual giants, many of whom we had the pleasure of exchanging our ideas with in person.

Our own ideas have developed over a number of years. They build on our previous work on challenger parties and issue entrepreneurship that was published in *European Union Politics* in 2012, the *European Journal of Political Research* and the *Journal of Politics* in 2014, and *Comparative Political Studies* in 2015. We wish to thank our coauthors on two of these articles, Jae-Jae Spoon and Marc van der Wardt, for their important contributions to our thinking. We are also grateful to Julian Hörner and Mariken van der Velden, who worked with us on the research presented in chapters 6 and 8, respectively. Originally, we set out to write a book about just challenger parties, but we soon realized that the story of postwar European politics is just as much about the resilience of mainstream parties as it is about the rise of challengers.

In this book, we wish to tell a story of European party politics that is not simply focused on the last decade of turmoil, but that can help us understand decades of both stability and change in party systems across Europe. We adopt a long-term and comparative perspective to explain the nature of political change in Europe, combining quantitative evidence with qualitative case studies. The book is designed to be accessible to a broader audience of readers interested in understanding the changes in politics that we have been observing over the past decades. This more accessible format has presented us with some difficult choices, however. The book relies heavily on descriptive inference using observational data and case studies, rather than on causal inference and experiments. This is not because we think that causal identification is not important, but because the questions this book aims to cover often do not lend themselves to more narrowly focused causal inference research designs. In our view, the ability to causally identify political phenomena should not limit the questions we aim to address as political scientists.

Our analyses of long-term and cross-national patterns of political change and stability in Europe have been possible only because of the vital data collection efforts of teams of scholars over many decades. The analysis presented here relies on data from the Chapel Hill Expert Survey (CHES), the Comparative Study of Electoral Systems (CSES), the European Election Studies (EES), the Manifesto Project Database (MARPOR/CMP), ParlGov, and national election studies, among other data sources. These collaborative data collection projects provide an invaluable public good for scholars of European politics, and we are grateful to all the individuals who have contributed to them. We are also very fortunate to have worked with some amazing research assistants: Philipp Dreyer, whose help with data collection and data analysis has been invaluable, as well as Diane Bolet, Julian Hörner, Pia Nagl, Pit Rieger, and the many coders of antiestablishment rhetoric at the Vrije Universiteit Amsterdam, who all performed excellent work. We are grateful for the generous funding by the European Research Council (ERC GA 647835, EUDEMOS, PI: Sara Hobolt) and a VU Interdisciplinary Centre for European Studies (VICES) research grant (PI: Catherine De Vries), which gave us the necessary time and resources to work on this ambitious project.

This book has not been just a conversation between us as coauthors. We have been fortunate to have been accompanied by many wonderful and insightful colleagues and friends along the way. Over the years, we have shared and discussed our ideas with many colleagues in different settings, from conference presentations to talks to informal conversations over coffee. We are not able to mention them all by name, but we are grateful to everyone who has engaged with our ideas. We owe very special thanks to our colleagues Tarik Abou-Chadi, Lawrence Ezrow, Simon Hix, Robert Klemmensen, Toni Rodon, Petra Schleiter, Moritz Osnabrügge, and Julian Hörner, who all attended a book workshop at the London School of Economics and Political Science (LSE) in January 2019. They provided invaluable input on our book manuscript. Drafts of chapters were presented at faculty seminars, workshops, and conferences. Specifically, we thank the hosts and attendees at the LSE, University of Cologne, University of Essex, University of Konstanz, University of Mannheim, University of North Carolina at Chapel Hill, University of Oxford, University of Texas at Austin, Vrije Universiteit Amsterdam, WZB Berlin Social Science Center, and at panels during the meetings of the American Political Science Association, the European Political Science Association, the European Union Studies Association, and the Midwest Political Science Association. Their constructive comments have helped us to improve our arguments and evidence. At these conferences and workshops, we are grateful to have received valuable input from Ryan Bakker, Daniel Bischof, Lisanne de Blok, Bruno Castanho Silva, Russ Dalton, Elias Dinas,

Jeremy Ferwerda, Florian Foos, Ken Greene, Dominik Hangartner, Tim Haughton, Silja Häusermann, Liesbet Hooghe, Seth Jolly, Mark Kayser, Orit Kedar, Thomas Kurer, Heike Klüver, Gary Marks, Sergi Pardos-Prado, Jon Polk, Oli Proksch, Robert Rohrschneider, Jan Rovny, Jon Slapin, Zeynep Somer-Topcu, Jae-Jae Spoon, Rune Stubager, Marco Steenbergen, Jim Stimson, James Tilley, Markus Wagner, Stephen Whitefield, Chris Wlezien, and Chris Wratil. We are also grateful to Princeton University Press, and especially our editors Sarah Caro and Hannah Paul, who supported the project from the outset and encouraged us to find our voice.

We also wish to thank Hector Solaz, who mentioned in passing that we should read *The Theory of Industrial Organization* by the Nobel laureate in economics Jean Tirole, because the questions and patterns we were discussing sounded much like the issues that dominant and challenger firms face. This suggestion opened up a whole new world for us. It provided us with an intellectual frame to clarify our theoretical ideas. We are grateful to Hector for engaging with our ideas and reading drafts of our chapters.

Finally, we thank our husbands, Dominik Mattmann and Hector Solaz, for all their love and support while we were writing this book. We dedicate this book to the most wonderful disruptors in our own lives, our children. As British-Danish-Dutch-Spanish-Swiss citizens of Europe, they will bring their own unique perspective to these times of change.

Introduction

Truth is found neither in the thesis nor the antithesis, but in an emergent synthesis which reconciles the two.

—GEORG WILHELM FRIEDRICH HEGEL, GERMAN PHILOSOPHER[1]

The reason why it is so difficult for existing firms to capitalize on disruptive innovations is that their processes and their business model that make them good at the existing business actually make them bad at competing for the disruption.

—CLAYTON CHRISTENSEN, AMERICAN ACADEMIC AND BUSINESS CONSULTANT[2]

The familiar patterns of European politics are undergoing radical change. Stable party systems, dominated by mainstream parties of the center left and center right, are fracturing. In recent years, we have witnessed the steady electoral decline of mainstream parties and the rise of political outsiders. The 2017 presidential elections in France are a case in point. Neither the candidate of the center-left Socialist Party nor the candidate of the center-right Conservative Party made it to the final runoff. Instead, the election became a contest between two challengers: Emmanuel Macron and his newly formed La République En Marche! (The republic on the move!)

party and Marine Le Pen of the radical right-wing National Rally (previously National Front). France is not the only country where traditional parties have been losing ground recently. In Italy, the ruling center-left Democratic Party was beaten to the top spot in 2018 by the radical right-wing League, led by the charismatic Matteo Salvini, and the new populist party, the Five Star Movement, founded by the Italian comedian Beppe Grillo. In the Netherlands, electoral support for the traditionally strong Labour Party shrunk to single digits in the 2017 parliamentary elections. Even in Sweden, where the Social Democratic Party has dominated politics since the introduction of universal suffrage, the party received its lowest share of the vote for almost 100 years in the 2018 elections, while the far-right Swedish Democrats strongly gained in popularity.

The decline of mainstream parties has been accompanied by the rise of political outsiders, on both the right and left sides of the political spectrum. These political entrepreneurs gained electoral traction through their attacks on the political establishment and their mobilization of new issues. In the 2019 European parliamentary elections, three national populist parties—the newly formed Brexit Party in the UK, the League in Italy, and the National Rally in France—topped the polls. On the left of the political spectrum, green parties also did well. In Germany, the Greens outperformed the traditional center-left Social Democrats with a whopping 20 percent of the vote. Green challengers also performed well in several other West European countries.

What explains these upheavals in European politics? Political commentators and scholars provide a series of different interpretations. Much of the commentary has focused on the rise of right-wing populism,[3] and many have pointed to structural changes to the economy, increasing globalization, and economic downturns as the root cause of this upsurge.[4] Such explanations have drawn attention to the anger of the "left-behind" communities,[5] as well as the "cultural backlash" against multiculturalism and immigration.[6] While these factors no doubt are important, they do not provide a complete picture of what exactly has changed in Western European politics over the last few decades and why. The focus on right-wing populism fails to acknowledge that not all challenges to the existing political order have come from the right; some have also come from the left, like Syriza in Greece, and the center, such as La République En Marche! in France. Moreover, the emphasis on structural changes to the economy is difficult to square with the fact that challenges to the existing political order are not a new phenomenon, and nor is the trajectory of challenger parties uniform across countries. It also does not explain why challenger parties successfully entered the political arena in some countries as early as the 1970s and 1980s, while they are still marginal in others to this day. Importantly, the recent focus on the rise of populist parties tends to ignore the relative stability of mainstream parties. Other recent studies have focused explicitly on mainstream parties and their decline.[7] As with the work on the rise of the populist right, this literature takes as a starting point structural changes to voter demand that have led to changing electoral fortunes of traditionally mainstream parties. But existing scholarship rarely seeks to explain both continuity *and* change in West European party competition. By focusing on the recent electoral losses of mainstream political parties and the successes of challenger parties, it is easy to overlook the fact that the story of postwar Western European politics is predominately one of the resilience of the traditional party families. Moreover, while it is tempting to focus on the uniformity of the disruption to the system, "the rise of populism," "the decline of social democracy," and so on, there is in fact considerable variation in the timing of challenger-party success across countries. This implies that common shocks or structural changes can only partially account for what we are observing.

This book argues that in order to understand change in European politics, we need to account for the drivers of both the political upheavals we have observed recently and the decades of relative stability and dominance of the traditional mainstream parties. Rather than simply asking why political outsiders have been so successful recently, we also need to query why mainstream parties have been able to maintain their grip on power for so long. These questions are intrinsically interlinked. Moreover, we need to be able to account for the differences in timing and degree of electoral success of political outsiders. In order to do this, we have developed a theory of political change.

Political change, we argue, evolves around two competing political forces, those of *dominance* and *innovation*. These are the forces that also shape economic change and shape the fate of companies. By drawing on an analogy of how firms compete for market share, we argue that party politics is the struggle between mainstream parties trying to keep hold of their market power and political entrepreneurs aiming to chip away at mainstream dominance. While structural changes to societies provide an important backdrop to our argument, our approach focuses on the strategies that parties employ to succeed in the political market. Political change is the result of a tug-of-war between mainstream parties seeking to protect their dominance and political entrepreneurs with innovating strategies to break this dominance.

The decades-long ascendancy of the traditional mainstream parties has been possible because the political marketplace is not a free, fully competitive market, but rather one that favors dominant parties. Dominant parties are those parties that have government experience, while challenger parties are those who have not held office. It is difficult to break through as a challenger when many voters are attached to the dominant parties, whose office experience lends them additional credibility. As a result, many challenger parties fail to make any real impact on politics. Yet, some succeed and dramatically change the political landscape. The question is *why*. This book suggests that as the bonds between dominant parties and their voters have loosened in recent decades, it has become more difficult for those parties to protect their market power and easier for challenger parties to challenge and disrupt the existing political order through innovation. It also suggests that the challenger parties that succeed have done so by combining a specific set of policy and rhetorical innovation strategies. In time, as these political challengers become more electorally successful, they may become the new dominant forces in politics.

The Argument in Brief

To explain why Western European party systems have remained so stable for most of the postwar period despite major economic and cultural change, but are now facing disruptions by challenger parties, we introduce a theory of political change. It borrows key insights from the literature on *industrial organization* in the field of economics. Industrial organization studies markets that are characterized by imperfect competition. That is to say, markets in which a limited number of firms compete.[8] Our theory of political change allows us to explain both the resilience of dominant parties and the pathway to success of challenger parties. Our argument has four core elements:

The political market is an oligopoly: The market for votes and political office is an example of imperfect competition, because the rules of the game favor dominant parties and voters are attached to dominant parties. This makes it difficult for challenger parties to become dominant. Dominant parties actively attempt to safeguard their market power by adopting positions that appeal to a wide electoral base and focus their campaigning on issues where they are competitive.

There is weakening of this oligopoly: We are witnessing a weakening of the conditions that advantage the dominant parties. Voters are becoming more like critical consumers and less loyal to established parties, which makes it more difficult for dominant parties to safeguard their market power. The center-seeking catchall strategies of dominant parties are more likely to backfire as voters feel that parties look too similar and perceive that there is not a real political choice. Also, it has become more difficult for dominant parties to control the political agenda as wedge issues that do not fit nicely into the traditional left–right dimension in politics have emerged.

Challenger parties act as political entrepreneurs: The market power of dominant parties is constantly under attack from challenger parties that act as political entrepreneurs. Successful political entrepreneurs employ a twofold innovation strategy: (1) they introduce issues that can drive a wedge between coalitions of and within dominant parties, and (2) they use antiestablishment rhetoric to weaken the competence advantage of established parties. As voters become less loyal to dominant parties, these strategies are more likely to be electorally successful.

The party system is fragmenting: The weakening of the oligopoly and the success of challenger parties leads to market fragmentation. Market fragmentation increases the choice available to citizens, but also makes electoral outcomes more unpredictable and complicates government formation and stability.

Let us illustrate the rise of challenger parties in the political marketplace through an example from the world of business: the rise and fall of Nokia. In 1987, Nokia introduced the world's first handheld cell phone, the Mobira Cityman 900. This iconic phone was nicknamed "the Gorba" after the then president of the Soviet Union Mikhail Gorbachev was seen using it the same year. However, it took a few more years before Nokia's cell phones gained mass appeal. In the 1990s, the company started focusing solely on the telecommunications market, and developed smaller and cheaper cell phones accessible to a mass market. Their 2100 series phones became best sellers, with around 20 million handsets sold worldwide.[9] This was the beginning of Nokia's dominance of the cell-phone market.[10] Nokia had become the market leader with mass appeal and a distinct brand. Most people who lived through the 1990s will remember the iconic Nokia Tune ringtone and the classic Snake game. When Nokia launched the Nokia 3210, with an internal antenna, in 1999, it sold 160 million units worldwide, making it one of the most popular phones in history. Nokia continued as the world leader in the cellphone market into the early 2000s, but was not able to take advantage of the innovation in wireless and internet technologies to the same extent as some of its competitors. Most notably, Apple launched the first-generation iPhone in 2007, and the touch-screen phone grew in popularity. While Nokia introduced its own all-touch smartphone in 2008, the company was no longer the prime mover in the field. Apple was able to successfully present the introduction of the iPhone as a "revolution" in cell-phone technology. The iPhone was more than simply a phone: as the App Store was launched in 2008, the iPhone was enhanced as a minicomputer with personalized capabilities that could transform it into a music player, a television screen, a piano keyboard, a torch, or a compass. With this new revolution in the smartphone world, Nokia became yesterday's news. The company's cell-phone market share fell rapidly: from 49 percent in 2007 to 34 percent three years later. In 2011, Apple overtook Nokia in smartphone sales, and by 2013 Nokia's market share had slipped to just 3 percent.[11] Apple and Samsung had become the new market leaders, with their own distinctive brands and loyal consumers.

The story of the rise and fall of Nokia illustrates what the Austrian economist Joseph Schumpeter has referred to as "creative destruction."[12] This is the idea that innovation creates new companies while simultaneously destroying old ones that fail to adjust after their initial innovation has run its course. Schumpeter identifies innovation as critical for economic change. According to this view, economic change is fundamentally shaped by two forces: innovation revolving around entrepreneurs, who are doing new things or doing things that are already being done but in a new way, and dominance, which is the market power that dominant market players aim to protect.[13] We argue that these same forces also shape change in the markets for votes, seats, and political office in Europe. Political change is as much a story of the ability of challenger parties to innovate as it is of the inability of dominant parties to respond.

Dominant and Challenger Parties

Political entrepreneurship has a long-standing tradition in Europe. Think of the rise of social democratic parties in the late nineteenth century, leaders of political student movements in the 1960s, and green parties in the 1980s, for example. What might be different today is the <u>relative weakness of dominant parties in protecting their core market power</u> and the resulting fragmentation of the party system. To understand the success of challenger parties today, we need to study <u>the inability of dominant parties to adapt to a changing political environment</u> in which critical voters are much less loyal to the major parties, as well as the capacity of challenger parties to adapt to this environment. We also need an account that can explain why challenger parties were able to disrupt mainstream dominance decades ago in some countries, while the mainstream parties have retained their dominance in others.

To illustrate this interplay between dominant and challenger parties, we borrow insights from how firms compete. Analogous to the classic economic model of party competition, we assume that parties, similarly to firms, compete for their voters by offering policies that appeal to the average voter. In the classic spatial economic model of the American economist Harold Hotelling, ice-cream vendors try to attract customers on a hot summer's day: people who want to buy ice cream from the nearest ice-cream stand.[14] Since the product, ice cream, and the associated prices are likely relatively uniform, it makes sense for beachgoers to save time and energy by walking only to the nearest seller. From the vendors' point of view, it is sensible to locate centrally on the beach so they can attract more customers. If there are just two ice cream stalls, and the beachgoers are spread relatively evenly along the beach, then each of the ice-cream sellers will sell ice cream to half of the consumers. This principle of minimum differentiation in economic theory inspired the spatial models of party competition of the American economist Anthony Downs.[15] Instead of a beach, we have a unidimensional political space, where the ice-cream vendors are political parties and the location is their political position. The assumption is that each voter will vote for the candidate or party that is closest to his or her political position. So, when a candidate takes a position to the right of the other candidate, he or she will get the votes of everyone to the right of that position. As with the ice-cream vendors on the beach, political parties will choose a political position that is virtually the same as their opponents'. Furthermore, the parties will be driven to select the political position of the median voter.

While this model can explain the strategies adopted by many mainstream parties in Europe, converging on the political center and adopting similar "catchall" policies to appeal to a large segment of the electorate, it cannot explain the development we have witnessed in recent years with parties seemingly on the political extremes gaining significant electoral ground. We argue that to explain the patterns of party competition in postwar Western Europe, as well as recent disruptions, we need to go beyond the model of perfect competition where all ice-cream vendors, or parties, are on an equal footing.[16] There are barriers to entry that protect the dominant parties in the arena. But disruption can happen. And when it does, it is not driven by parties adopting the most centrist position on the left–right dimension, but rather by political entrepreneurs introducing new or previously ignored political issues that disrupt the political equilibrium and give the issue entrepreneur a strategic advantage. We also assume that voters, just like ice-cream consumers, care about not only the location of the party, but also the competence and integrity of the seller. As long as mainstream parties are seen as the most trustworthy and competent, it is difficult for challengers to make significant inroads. However, if that trust in the competence of the dominant parties erodes, challengers can exploit that with a powerful antiestablishment message.

We argue that understanding party politics in Western Europe requires us to explore the interplay between the two competing forces that maintain it: *dominance* and *innovation*. Dominance concerns the power of the dominant parties in the system to protect their positions. Innovation concerns the process through which political parties introduce a new or previously ignored issue, and where they use rhetorical innovation to challenge the competence of dominant parties. If the political entrepreneurship of challenger parties is successful, this may lead to a transformation of the political system. The most obvious change that successful challenger parties can bring about is to the composition of the party system as they capture a greater share of the electorate. But there are more subtle underlying changes that occur alongside such changes to the party system; namely, that voters begin to prioritize different issues in line with the issue entrepreneurship and antiestablishment strategies employed by challenger parties. Challenger parties bring about greater choice and may increase feelings of representation. Yet, the rise of challenger parties might also have disruptive effects. A more fragmented and polarized party system and the presence of challengers make it more difficult to form coalitions and also tend to make government arrangements less stable.

Plan of the Book

We develop and empirically test our argument in the remainder of the book. Our empirical focus is on Western Europe, as this region is traditionally home to some of the most stable and established party systems but has recently witnessed considerable changes. Yet, the timing and extent of this change is not uniform across countries in Western Europe. Our theory of political change, based on the strategies that dominant and challenger parties employ, allows us to account for these differences. In chapter 1, we explain our distinction between challenger and dominant parties in greater detail and look empirically at the changes to West European party systems since the introduction of universal suffrage. We then discuss our definition of challenger parties and look more closely at what unites these parties. In chapter 2, we outline our theory of political change. As discussed above, the main tenet of our argument is that the dynamics of party competition in Europe can best be understood as a tug-of-war between dominant and challenger parties, with dominant parties aiming to protect their pivotal positions in the system, while challenger parties aim to chip away at this dominance through innovation. After presenting our theory, we delve deeper into the interplay of our three main conceptual building blocks: *dominance, innovation,* and *transformation.*

In chapters 3 to 8, we outline a set of precise mechanisms that allow us to understand the dynamics underlying mainstream-party dominance, the innovation efforts of challengers and the conditions under which party systems will be transformed. We do so by providing a wealth of empirical data, which compares over 200 parties in 19 countries in Western Europe. This allows for a thorough understanding of the continuity and change in party systems in Europe. We also draw on specific country examples to give an in-depth picture of the causes and consequences of change. Chapter 3 examines party loyalty as a barrier to entry, showing how the ties between voters and mainstream parties have declined in most Western European countries, as voters have become less attached to political parties. In chapter 4, we explore the strategies that mainstream parties employ to remain dominant, through distinctive convergence, issue avoidance, and competence mobilization. We examine these strategies empirically by analyzing manifesto and survey data. We then move on to the innovation of challenger parties. Chapter 5 focuses on the policy innovation of challenger parties, which we call "issue entrepreneurship." It refers to the mobilization of new or previously ignored issues that cut across dominant ideological dimensions and are a core aspect of challenger parties' electoral appeal and political influence. The strategy is to appeal to voters and potentially cause a rift within dominant parties. We examine issue entrepreneurship empirically by analyzing manifesto data. Chapter 6 explores the antiestablishment rhetoric of challenger parties, which also sets them apart from the mainstream. Using state-of-the-art computerized content analysis and a wealth of data, including party manifestos and expert data from across Western Europe, this chapter examines the evolution of challenger-party strategies.

The final chapters of the book explore the transformation of party competition and electoral politics in Europe. In chapter 7, we examine changes to electoral behavior. Analyzing rich individual-level surveys and party-level data, we investigate what types of voters challenger parties appeal to, and how these voters respond to the innovative messages of challenger parties. Chapter 8 examines how the rise of challenger parties has led to increased fragmentation and polarization of choice, again using individual-level surveys and party-level data. The rise of challengers has resulted in a tension between the positive effects of greater choice for citizens, which mobilizes them and enhances their sense of representation, and the negative consequences for government efficiency and stability. Most challenger parties never enter government, but they can nonetheless have a profound impact on the ability of governments to form coalitions and to implement legislation, and on their survival chances. The concluding chapter of the book, chapter 9, summarizes the key arguments and findings of the book. It also discusses the normative and policy implications of this study, focusing particularly on the issue of the changing nature of representation and democracy in Europe.

PART I

Political Change in Europe

1

The Rise of Challenger Parties

This is the art of politics: to find some alternative that beats the current winner.

—WILLIAM RIKER, AMERICAN POLITICAL SCIENTIST[1]

Innovation distinguishes between a leader and a follower.

—STEVE JOBS, COFOUNDER, CHAIRMAN, AND CEO OF APPLE[2]

Politics in Western Europe has become more unpredictable and volatile in recent years. The electoral successes of populist parties across the continent have led commentators to proclaim the end of politics as we know it and the collapse of the political mainstream. Populist parties are tearing up the conventional rule book of left–right politics by mobilizing identity politics and taking aim at the political establishment as a whole. Yet, this is not the first time we have witnessed the breakthrough of political challengers in European party competition and the exploitation of new political cleavages and issues. Indeed, the most mainstream of party families, the social democrats, were challengers when they first emerged in the late nineteenth century across Western Europe. They campaigned on a radical platform of universal suffrage for the working classes and a promise of a brighter socialist future, and it was only later, once they had achieved widespread electoral success, that they became the catchall parties of parliamentary and executive dominance. The 1970s and 1980s saw the rise of a different kind of challenger in the form of the green, left-libertarian parties. These were movements that rebelled against the classic left–right politics of economic growth and centralized decision making. They mobilized new issues of green politics and criticized the established political elite for restricting democratic participation to the bargaining that took place between centralized interest groups and party leaders, emphasizing instead individual autonomy and popular participation.

We have witnessed parties seeking to disrupt the established ways of doing politics before. Some were very successful, others less so. But why does it feel so different this time? One reason for this is that change always feels more significant when you are living through it. Also, there is a temptation to focus on the developments that break with the past rather than those that remain the same. In this book, we adopt a long-term perspective to understand the magnitude and nature of current changes to party politics in Europe and to place them in the context of the overall evolution of European party systems in the postwar period. This long-term perspective allows us to develop a theoretical framework for understanding when, why, and to what extent challengers are reshaping European politics.

In this chapter, we first discuss how to define challenger parties, focusing on their lack of experience in office. We then give three examples of "waves" of challenger parties over the past century (social democratic parties, green parties, and populist radical right parties) and explore the commonalities in the strategies these parties have pursued, despite their very different ideological outlooks. Finally, we consider the evolution of party competition in postwar Western Europe, demonstrating both the remarkable degree of stability the established party families enjoyed for much of the postwar period and then the increasing fragmentation resulting from the strengthening of challengers on both the right and the left.

Who Are the Challengers?

Seeing the recent electoral successes of challenger parties, many political scientists and sociologists have tried to define them. Numerous labels have been used in the literature, such as niche parties,[3] populist parties,[4] "new politics" parties,[5] and challenger parties.[6] In this book, we conceive of political change as the result of a struggle between the innovation of the challenger parties and the power of the dominant parties. Challenger parties are therefore those parties that have not yet held the reins of power: the parties without government experience. To distinguish between parties, we focus on each party's position within the political marketplace, as either dominant or challenger. But how does that relate to other ways of classifying party types? There are three main ways of distinguishing between challengers and mainstream parties in the existing literature. One focuses on the historical origins of the parties, another focuses on the specific issues they mobilize, and the third focuses specifically on populism as a distinguishing feature.[7]

The first approach takes as its starting point the concept of a *party family* and argues that parties originating in the traditional party families are "dominant" whereas those that do not are "challengers." The notion of a party family was already evident in the classic work on party systems by American political scientist Seymour Martin Lipset and Norwegian sociologist Stein Rokkan.[8] They argued that macro developments—such as national revolutions, the Reformation, and the Industrial Revolution—produced enduring lines of conflict that continue to shape political structure, political organization, and the substantive character of conflict. These ongoing lines of conflict are called "cleavages" and arise out of structural social characteristics such as class, religion, and geographical location. People's class status, religious affiliation, or place of residence determines their political preferences and partisan allegiances. Cleavages produced the major party families that have dominated West European politics for decades: the conservative, liberal, Christian democratic, socialist, and communist party families. These "traditional" party families are classified as mainstream parties. New party families arise as a result of changes in the electorate's composition and preferences. Citizens respond to rapidly changing social and economic conditions by demanding new political offerings. The relative prosperity and security of the postwar period encouraged individuals coming of age during those years to care more about values such as sustainability, equal rights, and democratic engagement. As a result, new value-related cleavages emerged in voting behavior that crosscut or superseded older cleavages and gave rise to new types of party family—the green and new left parties.[9] Socioeconomic changes in the last few decades, associated with changing class structure and increasing globalization, have created new sets of "winners" and "losers," which in turn are closely tied to the rise and success of radical right parties.[10] Parties that emerged in response to this realignment, and that of the 1970s, are described as niche parties.[11] Education has been shown to be an important driver of the vote for such parties, as the highly educated are more likely to vote for green and new left parties, and the less educated more likely to vote for the radical right.[12]

Party families are a useful way of classifying political parties.[13] Yet, there are problems when using the party family typology to classify challenger parties. One issue is that it is a static definition that does not take into account the fact that, for example, while green parties may have been conceived of as "challengers" in the 1970s and 1980s, most of them have now become part of what we would consider the mainstream. Any cutoff point to divide "new" parties from "old"—for example, prewar or postwar origin—is inevitably arbitrary.[14] Even the social democratic parties that are now classified as mainstream were once "challengers" to the bourgeois order after the extension of the franchise to the working class.[15] Also, there is no agreement as to which party families are "mainstream" and which party families are "niche."[16]

This leads us to the second approach to classifying challenger parties, which focuses on their programmatic strategies—that is to say, the types of issues they mobilize. Challenger parties are those that address "noncentrist" or "new" issues. The most systematic attempt at classifying parties into "mainstream" and "niche" using this approach was developed by American political scientist Bonnie Meguid.[17] She classifies niche parties as those that reject the traditional class-based orientation of politics, <u>mobilize issues that do not coincide with existing lines of political division, and focus on a limited set of issues</u>. On the basis of this classification, "niche parties" are mostly green and radical right parties, as well as some single-issue parties. This rigorous classification, based on the appeal of non-class-based (economic) issues, such as green or regional issues, has many advantages and has been applied and extended by other scholars.[18] The focus on the issues that parties strategically choose to campaign on, rather than their historical origins, has several advantages, not least in that it allows greater precision and flexibility when classifying parties. However, if one of the aims of a research endeavor is to explain the *strategies* adopted by challengers to upset the political mainstream, it becomes somewhat circular to also define the parties by those same programmatic strategies. Given that in this book we are interested in examining what strategies challenger parties use to disrupt the dominance of mainstream parties, the programmatic strategies of these parties cannot also form the basis of their classification.

A third approach is one that focuses on the distinction between <u>"populist" and "nonpopulist" parties.</u> The literature on populism has burgeoned over the last two decades, as populist parties have gained in electoral strength. No firm consensus has emerged on how to define populist parties, but the most influential conceptualization of populist parties was put forward by the British political theorist Margaret Canovan and Dutch political scientist Cas Mudde, and rests on the understanding of populism as what is known as a <u>"thin-centered" ideology.</u> Populism separates society into two homogeneous and antagonistic groups, these authors say, "the pure people" and "the corrupt elite," and holds that politics should be an expression of "the general will" of the people.[19] Since populism is a thin-centered ideology based around a binary distinction, it is extremely malleable and can easily be integrated into another more complex host ideology, such as socialism or liberalism. This means that populist parties can be found on both the left and the right, or indeed in the center, of the political spectrum. Much of the literature on populist parties in Europe, however, has focused on those on the right and has included *nativism* as a key element of populism.[20] Such definitions of populist parties include an emphasis on expressions of nativism and xenophobic nationalism. When nativism is included as a core element of populism, the parties classified as populist are often more narrowly confined to the "populist radical right." Both the narrow and the broader definitions of populist parties take as their starting point the ideology of these parties, while our approach, as stated above, is different. By focusing on the position of parties within the system, as either challenger or dominant parties, we are trying to understand what types of party are more likely to employ strategies such as adopting anti-elitist rhetoric (see chapter 6) or anti-immigration positions (see chapter 5). Hence, our argument about challenger and dominant parties enriches the debate on populism by explaining why a certain type of party employs populist messages, and places the recent wave of populist parties in a much broader perspective.

Our book therefore presents a new approach to the conceptualization of challenger parties that focuses on their lack of dominance within the political system. Building on the industrial organization literature, we conceive political change to be the result of a struggle between dominant market forces, or parties, who wish to maintain their market power, and disruptive political entrepreneurs or challenger parties who want to unseat the dominant players through innovation. Dominant parties are those that control the political marketplace, while challenger parties are those parties that do not (yet) have dominance within the political system. Given the nature of the political marketplace, the delivery of the product (bundle of policies) is restricted to those parties that control the provision of public policy—that is, those that are in office. Parties in opposition may have some influence over the design of public policy through the legislative process, but ultimately parties in government and the executive branch control the provision of public policy. As a consequence, the dominant players in the marketplace are not only those who have a large market share—that is, a large share of the vote—but also those with a good chance of controlling government, and thus being able to implement their policies. Hence, in our conceptualization of market power we focus on the parties that have *government experience,* since these are the parties that control the provision of policies.[21] We label these the *dominant parties* in the party system. In contrast, the *challenger parties* are those that have not had the opportunity to control policy or government. There may be several reasons why parties have not had a controlling role in office. They may be newly formed or too small to enter into a government, or they may be unwilling to make the necessary compromises to join a coalition government, or be seen as too extreme to be part of government by mainstream parties. Such challenger parties have every incentive to challenge the dominance of existing players through political innovation.

In our empirical analysis, we thus operationalize challenger parties on the basis of their office-holding experience. Parties that have not held office in the postwar period are classified as challengers.[22] This is a flexible and dynamic conceptualization of challenger parties, rather than a static, inflexible one. Challengers that have risen to power, such as France's En Marche! (On the move!) party, Greece's Syriza (Coalition of the Radical Left), or Italy's League (previously the Northern League), can become dominant parties. They need not remain challenger parties forever. By focusing on the position of a party and its dominance or otherwise within the system, rather than on its ideology and programmatic strategies, we are also able to study what strategies challenger parties employ to appeal to a broader voter base and acquire a larger market share.

A binary classification can of course conceal important nuances within each of the broad party types that we have identified. It raises questions about whether parties that only enter coalition government for a short period of time, such as the radical right-wing Austrian Freedom Party, should be classified as dominant parties. And if one does set a minimum time in government to be considered dominant, how long should that be? Equally, questions may be asked about whether parties that never formally join government but enter in confidence-and-supply agreements that allow them to influence certain policies in return for their parliamentary support, such as the Danish People's Party, should also be considered "dominant," as they have some say over policy. Or what about parties that join coalition arrangements at the regional level, while being in permanent opposition at the national level, such as the United Left Party in Spain? Our argument is that there is a qualitative difference between holding office nationally and simply influencing policy through parliamentary influence or local power. Parties in national government are both constrained by their record and coalition agreements and empowered by the tools that executive office brings. Our distinction therefore focuses on parties with office-holding experience at the national level. However, when it comes to the length of government experience, we recognize that some parties can be considered more dominant than others. For example, the German Christian Democrats are clearly more dominant within the party system than the German Greens. Nonetheless, the fact that the Greens entered into coalition with the Social Democrats in the late 1990s, and have their hopes set on future coalition arrangements, makes them distinct from challenger parties such as the Alternative for Germany. Our conceptualization of challenger parties has the further advantage that it can be applied either as a dichotomous variable (challenger vs. dominant party) on the basis of office-holding experience, or as a continuous variable on the basis of the degree of dominance a party has within the system, measured as years in government in the postwar period. In most of this book we focus on challenger parties mainly as one side of a dichotomy, because we do think that they can be conceived of as a *type* of party, given their distinct role within the party system as outsiders in contrast with those who have traditionally held the reins of power. Yet, we recognize that dominant-party traits are likely more pronounced for parties with extensive office experience, while parties that have held only a brief spell in office may be more likely to resemble challenger parties. Hence, we replicate many of our core analyses with a continuous measure (see, for example, chapter 5).

Waves of Challenger Parties

Are challenger parties on the rise? Media coverage of challenger parties, especially those on the radical right in countries such as Austria, France, Italy, and the Netherlands, may have given the impression that the traditional European party systems have almost entirely imploded. Yet, a closer empirical examination of this claim suggests that patterns of party competition are more stable than a focus on recent events would suggest. If we plot the vote share by party family over the last 100 years we can see that the "traditional" party families, the conservatives/Christian democrats, the socialists/social democrats, and the liberals, still dominate West European party politics. This is illustrated in figure 1.1, which displays the shares of votes in democratic national parliamentary elections of the classical party families from 1918 to 2019.[23]

The picture that emerges from figure 1.1 is one of the dominance of the three major party families, the Christian democrats/conservatives, the social democrats/socialists, and the liberals, but with increasing party fragmentation from the early 1980s and especially over the last decade. The overall trend is a picture of continuity—one that illustrates the resilience of the three large party families that have dominated West European politics for a century. But there are signs of change.

Even within this picture of relative stability, we can observe shifting patterns. The 1920s and 1930s saw the rise of the social democrats and, in some countries, of the far right. In the postwar 1940s, stronger radical left parties emerged and the liberals went into decline. The 1980s can be characterized by the emergence of the green party family along with the radical right. In the 2010s, the radical left and the radical right grew stronger as the social democratic party family weakened. Each of these shifts represents a "wave" of challenges to the dominant political order, which has important parallels with recent developments. We discuss these three significant waves of disruption of West European party politics over the last century as an illustration of how challenger parties can sometimes contest the

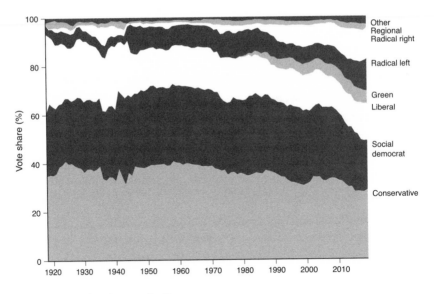

FIGURE 1.1 Vote share by party family

Note: Party vote shares 1918–2019 from Benedetto, Hix, and Mastrorocco, Dataset of Parties and Elections

dominance of the major party families. We focus on challenger parties that work within the confines of broad democratic norms, rather than those that seek to overthrow democratic institutions, such as some fascist and communist challenger parties.

THE SOCIAL DEMOCRATIC WAVE

The modern social democratic party family emerged as a serious force in Europe at the close of the nineteenth century. It grew out of the division in the socialist movement between those who insisted upon political revolution as a precondition for the achievement of socialist goals and those who maintained that a gradual or evolutionary path to socialism was both possible and desirable. Social democratic parties represented the faction of the socialist movement that put aside the principle of revolutionary violence in order to seek power, and committed to parliamentary democracy and even cross-party cooperation.[24] Once established, social democratic parties grew quickly in electoral support.[25] As figure 1.1

shows, by the early 1920s they had emerged as a serious force in European politics and their average vote share was close to 30 percent.

Today, we think of the social democrats as the quintessential mainstream party family. Yet at the close of the nineteenth century they were still very much challenger parties. The dominant parties at the time were liberal, conservative, and Christian democratic parties. The social democratic parties employed many of the political entrepreneurial strategies that we see challenger parties using today. Firstly, social democratic parties were issue entrepreneurs. They had radical objectives involving a complete restructuring of the economy and society through social revolution and the abolition of classes. But they campaigned for more intermediary goals, focusing on the rights and conditions of the working class. The extension of suffrage was a primary aim for the early socialist movement, and one that social democrats hoped would lead them to one day achieve their ultimate socialist objectives.[26] The struggle for better conditions for workers, through state intervention in the economy, a defining feature of left–right politics in Europe, was thus mobilized as a salient issue by these new challenger parties, the social democrats.[27] The dominant conservative/Christian democratic and liberal parties found it more difficult to credibly appeal to the growing working class on this class dimension of politics, as they were associated with the old establishment and the bourgeoisie.

Social democratic parties were also innately antiestablishment in their rhetoric. As long as workers did not have full political rights, the social democratic movement was inherently at odds with the political establishment. It used both parliamentary and insurrectionary methods to achieve its core goal of workers' suffrage, including general strikes. The rhetoric was aimed at attacking the establishment. Indeed, in the early years, social democratic parties were considered a danger to the established political and economic system. In Germany, for example, Chancellor Otto von Bismarck attempted to outlaw the social democrats in 1878 for their prorevolution, antimonarchy sentiments, but that did little to curb the increasing popularity of the party and the legislation lapsed in 1890.

The proworker, antiestablishment policies adopted by the social democrats were popular with the growing manual working class. As a result of these strategies, and the introduction of universal male suffrage, social democratic parties became a dominant force across Western Europe in the late nineteenth and early twentieth centuries. The Social Democratic Party of Germany won about 20 percent of the vote in 1890, after universal male suffrage had been introduced in 1871. Its share of the vote had grown to about 35 percent by 1912, making it the largest party in German politics, and it was part of the coalition government in 1918, with the party's leader, Friedrich Ebert, becoming chancellor in 1919. The challenger had become the dominant party. Other social democratic parties emerged a little later as powerful electoral forces, but the patterns are similar. The Swedish Social Democratic Party gained just short of 15 percent of the votes in 1908, the first elections after universal male suffrage was introduced. By 1911, it had jumped to about 29 percent of votes, and in 1917 it entered government for the first time as part of a coalition. From then onward, the Social Democratic Party has dominated Swedish politics, and has been in government for the majority of the time.

As social democratic parties became more dominant, they also evolved their political strategies. From being outsiders who had helped to define a new political battleground, they were now the insiders trying to defend the status quo.[28] As universal suffrage became a reality and social democratic parties entered office, their antiestablishment rhetoric became muted. They had committed to parliamentary democracy as a way of achieving incremental political change. Many social democratic parties also formed coalitions with other parties, which had a moderating influence on their own policies and rhetoric. Moreover, the American political scientists Adam Przeworski and John Sprague have argued that even as social democratic parties entered office, they faced a dilemma: the working class was not sufficiently numerous to guarantee electoral victory.[29] As a result, they were forced to appeal to the broader electorate and dilute their original class-based policies. As we will show in chapter 4, dominant social democratic parties became catchall parties that converged on the median voter. By the 1970s and 1980s, the erstwhile challengers were preoccupied with protecting their own dominant position in the system against new challengers, on both the left and the right.

THE GREEN WAVE

In the early 1970s, the American political scientist Ronald Inglehart argued that a "silent revolution" was taking place.[30] A new generation was coming of age that had grown up in a postwar era of relative prosperity and peace in Western Europe. For this generation, issues of economic hardship, redistribution, and security were less pressing. Instead, the postwar socioeconomic transformation allowed successive generations to prioritize different values. There was a shift toward "postmaterialist values," with an emphasis on environmental protection, gender equality, greater tolerance toward minorities, and alternative forms of democratic participation. Inglehart's seminal work focused on the rising demand for a new form of politics. But these shifts in values and politics were not just due to structural changes in the socioeconomic context in which postwar generations were growing up, but also due to the mobilization of postmaterial values. To understand the rise of "new politics" in Western Europe, we must look at a new set of challenger parties; namely, the green and new left parties.

The new wave of social movements and parties that emerged across Western Europe in the 1970s and 1980s campaigned on a "new politics" agenda of ecology, disarmament, and self-determination. The first green party in Europe was the Popular Movement for the Environment, founded in 1972 in the Swiss canton of Neuchâtel. The same year, another green party, the PEOPLE Party, was founded in the United Kingdom, the political predecessor of the Ecology Party and later the Green Party. By the mid-1980s, most West European countries had established viable green parties. Some of these parties were relatively electorally successful in the 1980s, gaining 6–9 percent of the vote in Belgium, Germany, Luxembourg, and Switzerland. The most prominent among them was the German Green Party, founded in 1980, known for its opposition to nuclear power, as well as the expression of anticentralist and pacifist values. In other West European countries, including Denmark, Greece, Spain, and the United Kingdom, the green parties remained very marginal and often failed to gain representation in their national parliaments.[31]

Despite their varying degrees of electoral success, these political parties shared a common emphasis on "new politics" issues. First among them was of course an ecological orientation and opposition to uncontrolled economic growth. Other shared programmatic concerns included an emphasis on equal rights, solidarity with developing countries, and demands for disarmament. Green parties were therefore issue entrepreneurs: seeking to mobilize issues that did not neatly fit with the dominant economic left–right politics—that is, issues with a level of what we term "high appropriability" (discussed in chapters 2 and 5).[32] They also shared another characteristic that is common among challenger parties; namely, their attacks on establishment politics. Green parties were not about just different issues, but also a fundamentally different way of doing politics. Their party organizations tended to be less centralized and hierarchical than mainstream parties, and to focus on the autonomy of local organizations, providing opportunities for grassroots influence and alternative forms of democracy, such as direct democracy. The German greens even described themselves as the "anti-party party" in the early 1980s.

These messages were popular among the younger and better educated segments of the electorate. As green parties became more electorally successful, there were often tensions between the radical party activists who wanted to stick to a fundamentally different, "green" model of democracy and economy and the more moderate elements that sought policy influence through compromise with other parties and to appeal to a broader set of voters that were often less radical than the party activists.[33] The best-known example of this is the "Fundis-Realos" conflict in the German Green Party, which played out in the 1980s and 1990s.[34] While the Realos were in favor of moderate policies and cabinet cooperation, the Fundis, more ideologically radical greens and ecosocialists, were opposed to compromise and cabinet cooperation. In 1985 came the first partial victory for the Realos wing of the party, as the Greens joined their first regional coalition government with the Social Democrats in Hessen, with Joschka Fischer as minister for the environment. As the party accepted the more traditional forms of parliamentary democracy and cooperation, some of the more radical elements left the party. In 1998, the German Greens completed the journey from a radical anti-party party to a dominant party: they joined the federal government with the Social Democratic Party in a so-called Red-Green alliance that lasted until 2005. Elsewhere in Europe other green parties have also joined cabinets at the national level, including the Finnish Green Party (Groen!, formerly Agalev), Ecolo in Belgium, les Verts in France, and the Green Party in Ireland. While the emphasis on green, left-libertarian issues is still a feature of these parties, the more radical antiestablishment, antisystem elements of the early green movements are much less pronounced in the green parties that have taken part in government. While green challengers did not reshape party competition in the 1980s and 1990s in the way that social democratic parties had done 100 years before, they did play a significant role in bringing important new issues on to the political agenda, including those of the environment, equality and human rights, and disarmament. In terms of their values, therefore, green parties represent the polar opposite of another set of challengers; namely, the radical right-wing parties. Yet, they share some important commonalities.

THE POPULIST RADICAL RIGHT WAVE

While green parties may have represented the silent revolution, the rise of the populist radical right in the 1980s and 1990s, and more significantly since the 2010s, has been described as the "silent counterrevolution."[35] Rather than embracing the internationalist, tolerant, and progressive agenda of "new politics," this recent wave comprised populist radical right-wing parties that have defined themselves in opposition to these views.[36] Of course, the rise of the radical right is not a new phenomenon in European politics. The rise and dominance of fascism in parts of Europe in the interwar period—notably Hitler's National Socialist German Workers' Party (Nazi) Party in Germany, Mussolini's National Fascist Party in Italy, and Franco's fascist regime in Spain—still cast a long shadow over Europe today. After 1945, with the defeat of fascism and the victory of liberal democracy, increasingly stable political structures and electoral systems developed across Western Europe. In this emerging postwar order, extreme right-wing forms did not totally disappear, but radical right-wing parties were marginalized. Since the 1980s, however, a new crop of radical right-wing parties, such as the French National Rally (previously National Front), the Belgian Vlaams Belang (Flemish Interest, previously Flemish Bloc), the Austrian Freedom Party, the Italian League (previously the Northern League) and the Danish People's Party, among several others, have established themselves as a significant force in West European countries. Hence, the rise of the populist right is not a recent phenomenon, although, as shown in figure 1.1, the popularity of these parties has accelerated since the Great Recession that followed the financial crisis.[37] The rise of these radical right-wing challengers has sparked serious concern about the future of liberal democracy on the European continent (a topic we will return to in chapters 8 and 9).

However, while the populist radical right parties of this new wave share elements of the nativist, authoritarian, and populist ideology that also characterized the earlier fascist movements, they generally distance themselves from the explicitly racist and antidemocratic ideology of fascism. Indeed, radical right parties that resort to openly racist language and celebrate their links with historical fascist movements have tended to remain marginalized in terms of electoral success.[38] The Norwegian political scientist Elisabeth Ivarsflaten has argued that the most successful radical right parties tend to have a "reputational shield"—a legacy that can be used to fend off accusations of racism and extremism.[39] Examples of radical right parties with reputational shields that were successful in the 1970s and 1980s include the Progress Parties of Scandinavia, originally established as tax-cutting movements in the 1970s, and the Freedom Party in Austria, which was a similarly neoliberal tax-cutting party. A different kind of reputational shield was adopted by the Northern League in Italy and Flemish Block (Vlaams Blok, now Vlaams Belang) in Belgium, both of which were originally established to pursue regional interests. These parties all adopted anti-immigration and nativist policy platforms, but avoided being tarnished with the same brush as the fascist and neofascist movements.

Despite variation in their origins, these new radical right-wing parties share an ideological core, which is a combination of nativism, authoritarianism, and populism.[40] Nativism, or ethnonationalism, is an emphasis on strengthening the nation by making it more ethnically homogeneous and by returning to traditional values. Non-nativist, or foreign, elements, whether people or ideas, are seen as fundamentally threatening to the homogeneous nation state.[41] This ideological core of nativism is embedded in a form of authoritarianism that stresses themes such as law and order and family values, as well as a focus on strong, charismatic leaders.[42] Radical right parties tend to be populist, emphasizing the division between the people and the corrupt elite, and their antiestablishment rhetoric is one of their defining features. One of their key electoral strategies is their opposition to the political elite, at both the national and international levels.

In addition to the strategy of populist antiestablishment rhetoric, most radical right-wing parties are also successful issue entrepreneurs. The core issue they promote is an anti-immigration platform. At the heart of their message is the idea that immigrants are a threat to national and cultural identity, but this is also linked to arguments that immigrants are a major cause of criminality, steal jobs from native workers, and are abusers of the generosity of European welfare states. At its core, the radical right has mobilized the cultural backlash against the impact of globalization, immigration, and European integration, and centered it around its ethnonationalist view of the nation.[43] Immigration is highly effective as a wedge issue.[44] It is not easily aligned with the dominant economic left–right dimension, and the dominant center-left and center-right parties have often found it difficult to respond effectively to the anti-immigration rhetoric of the radical right. Parties on the left are often torn between the preferences of their traditional working-class base, which is often skeptical of immigration, and the better educated middle-class partisans who favor liberal immigration policies. For example, in Denmark a successful anti-immigration party, the Progress Party, and its successor the Danish People's Party, emerged as early as the 1970s. On the cultural dimension the party is clearly to the right. Yet, the party's economic position has evolved from one on the right (anti-tax) to a more center-left position. Established parties have struggled to respond to the popular anti-immigration policies of the Danish People's Party. The Social Democrats in Denmark have increasingly adopted more restrictive policies on immigration, in part to hold on to their traditional working-class voters, while the Social Liberals, to the right of the Social Democrats on the left–right dimension, advocate far more tolerant immigration policies.[45] This is a good illustration of the fact that immigration cannot easily be subsumed into the left–right dimension. While the radical right has successfully mobilized its anti-immigration stance, it is far more ambiguous as far as economic policies are concerned. Most of the radical right-wing parties backed neoliberal economics of one sort or another during the 1980s, often manifested in campaigns for radical tax cuts.[46] However, during the 1990s, most of the new radical right parties shifted to a position in favor of greater government intervention in the economy. Their support for the welfare state can often be described as "welfare chauvinism," protecting social spending, but only for the true, "native" population.

The strategies of antiestablishment and anti-immigration rhetoric have been highly successful. The most electorally successful among the radical right-wing parties are the Freedom Party in Austria, which achieved over a quarter of the votes in 1999 and again in 2017; the Swiss People's Party, which also comfortably won more than a quarter of the votes to parliament since the early 2000s; the French National Rally, whose leaders have made it to the second round of the presidential elections in both 2002 (Jean-Marie Le Pen) and 2017 (Marine Le Pen); and, most recently, the Italian League, which won

17 percent in the 2017 election. Other radical right parties, such as the Danish People's Party, Flemish Interest in Belgium, and the Party of Freedom in the Netherlands, also regularly attract more than 10 percent of the vote.

As a party family, these parties have thus performed far better electorally than their counterparts in the green party family. However, they have generally struggled to gain dominance through office, as they have been seen as less palatable as coalition partners. Most of the radical right parties have thus remained challengers, but there are notable exceptions.[47] There was outrage when the Austrian Freedom Party formed a government in coalition with the center-right People's Party. The Freedom Party had experienced a steady increase in electoral support throughout the 1990s and was the second-most popular political party in the 1999 elections. Yet, European leaders objected to the inclusion of a xenophobic and populist party in the governing coalition of an EU member state and even levelled sanctions against the Austrian government, but these were quickly dropped. In 2001, the radical right-wing Northern League and National Alliance formed a government with Berlusconi's Forza Italy (Forward Italy), but with the Northern League as a minor coalition partner. Fast-forward 17 years, and the League obtained a resounding success, becoming the third-largest party in Italy with about 17 percent of the vote, and formed a short-lived government coalition with the populist Five Star Movement. The challengers had become dominant. What is noteworthy is that it was not classic economic policies that brought the coalition together, but rather a Euroskeptic, populist, and anti-immigrant stance. As challengers become successful, and even dominant, the issues they promote also take center stage in the political agenda and the process of government formation.

The Rise of Challenger Parties

These examples of three "waves" of challenger parties, the social democrats, the greens, and the radical right, illustrate how challengers can emerge from different corners of the political spectrum, and in some cases eventually become dominant parties. Of course, many other challengers exist that do not neatly fall into any of these categories. As discussed above, we define party types based on their government experience. While dominant parties are those that are currently in government or have had government experience in the recent past, challenger parties are those that have never been in government in the postwar and immediate prewar periods.[48] If a challenger party enters government, it becomes a dominant party in our binary classification. Our classification of dominant parties includes most parties belonging the traditional conservative, Christian democratic, liberal, and socialist party families, while far-right, far-left, green, or single-issue parties are more likely to belong to the challenger category.

In figure 1.2, we show the proportion of vote share by party family, focusing just on challenger parties, in the period between 1950 and 2017.[49] The figure shows that there is a great variety of challenger parties. Not surprisingly, the radical left and radical right parties have a larger proportion of the vote share among challenger parties than the more mainstream centrist party families. The figure shows that while there have been radical right challengers for the entire period, they have grown stronger in the last few decades. Since the mid-1980s, we also witness the rise of green challengers. But challengers are found not just on the fringes; we can also see challengers emerging from within the three major mainstream party families. Some of these quickly become dominant (such as President Macron's En Marche! party in France), while others remain challenger parties for longer. Certain challengers, such as the various pirate and single-issue parties, are not easily classified and have been grouped in the "other" category.

We can also look at how challenger parties, as a party grouping, have evolved over time in Western Europe. Figure 1.3 shows a gradual increase in the electoral support of challenger parties, but also illustrates the continuing electoral weight of dominant parties overall. Interestingly, it shows a much more gradual process of change from the 1950s to the present, compared with the picture that emerges based on a party family distinction.

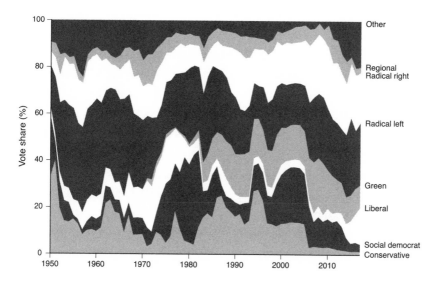

FIGURE 1.2 Challenger parties across party families

Note: Vote shares of the parties in each party family that are classified as challenger parties, 1950–2017, based on the authors' own data using Döring and Manow's Parliaments and Governments (ParlGov) database

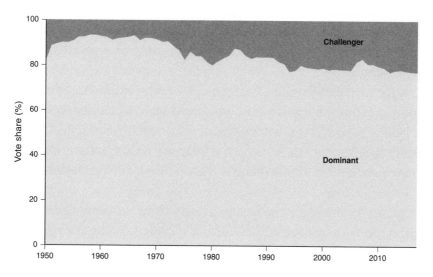

FIGURE 1.3 Dominant and challenger parties' vote shares

Note: Vote shares 1950–2017, based on authors' own data using the ParlGov database

Taken together, figures 1.1 and 1.3 suggest that European democracies are undergoing a transformation, albeit a very gradual one. The major parties of the right and the left that have dominated politics for decades are losing both members and electoral support. Yet, the evidence presented in this chapter also shows that, although societal and scholarly attention to the demise of dominant parties and the rise of challengers has spiked in recent years, especially in the wake of the Great Recession, this development is by no means new.

Are these developments uniform across countries? Figure 1.4 shows that there is significant cross-country variation in the decline of dominance of mainstream parties. In some countries, we find that the mainstream has been able to successfully maintain or even regain its dominance, for example in Malta or the United Kingdom until recently, whereas in others, such as Belgium, Denmark, or the Netherlands, the fragmentation of party politics began some decades ago. Moreover, the success of challenger parties is far from linear within an individual country—as in Finland or Greece, for example. These divergent patterns raise the question of *why* we see an early decline of electoral support for dominant parties in some countries, whereas in other countries dominant parties have been able to hold on for much longer, and challenger parties have only emerged in the last few decades.

The evidence presented in figures 1.1–1.4 leads us to three important questions that this book aims to address. First, since the rise of challenger parties is neither uniform across countries nor linear over time within individual countries, explanations that focus on changes in the socioeconomic structure, which are broadly uniform across Western Europe, cannot fully explain the variations we are observing. This calls for greater focus on variation in the *supply side*—that is, the activities and agency of political parties. Second, the evidence clearly shows that it is just as important to seek to explain the *stability* in the dominance of mainstream parties as it is to explain change. If we focus solely on the recent rise of nonmainstream parties, especially populist parties, we miss the equally important story of why mainstream center-left and center-right parties have been able to

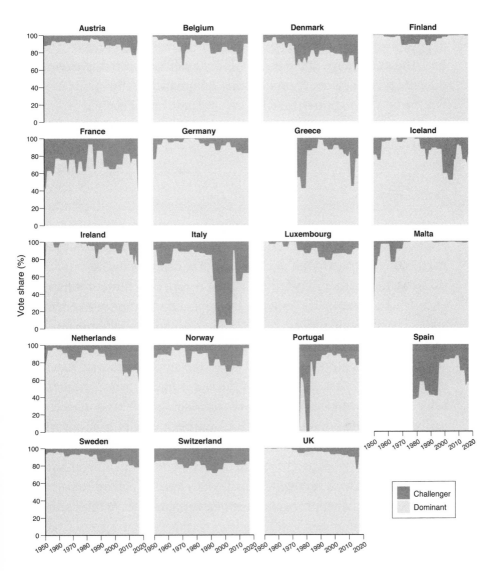

FIGURE 1.4 Dominant and challenger parties' vote shares by country
Note: Vote shares 1950–2017 by country, based on authors' own data using the ParlGov database

so successfully dominate party politics in Western Europe for so long. Finally, we do see evidence of challenger parties breaking through and this has become more prevalent in recent decades, which raises the question of why mainstream-party dominance is now waning.

We suggest that in order to deal with these challenges, we need a theory of change in European party systems that is sensitive to both the dominance of the mainstream as well as the strategies employed by challengers to disrupt that dominance. Only in this way will we be able to understand the general patterns of change within European party systems, while also being sensitive to specific national developments.

Conclusion

This chapter has provided an overview of challenger parties in Western Europe over the past century. Rather than classifying challenger parties on the basis of the party family origin or specific issue positions, we define them as parties without recent government experience. This definition has the advantage that it is dynamic rather than static—parties can go from being challengers to being dominant—and that it does not define parties on the basis of their programmatic strategies, thus allowing us to explore the similarities between a range of parties that seek to upset the status quo of party competition. We have argued that the rise of challenger parties is not necessarily a novel phenomenon, and that dominant parties have always faced attacks from challengers. We have also demonstrated that, while the mainstream party families of social democracy, liberal, and conservative/Christian democratic parties have remained remarkably resilient, challenger parties are clearly on the rise. While mainstream parties in most West European countries have by and large been able to maintain their dominance by protecting their market power—through institutional advantages, long-standing voter loyalties, and specific party strategies—their ties to voters have been weakening gradually. This has created opportunities for challenger parties that aim to disrupt the political system through political entrepreneurship. Firstly, they have acted as issue entrepreneurs that mobilize new political issues. Secondly, they have engaged in rhetorical innovation by challenging the "brand" of the mainstream using antiestablishment rhetoric. In this chapter we have illustrated the strategies used by the challengers by discussing the rise of social democratic parties, green parties, and populist radical right parties. In the next chapter, we will develop our argument about the interplay between dominance and innovation more systematically, to explain why West European party systems have remained so stable for decades, but also why they are now under so much strain.

2

A Theory of Political Change

By their very nature, all party alignments contain the seed of their own destruction. The various groups that make up the party may be united on some issues, particularly on those that gave rise to the alignment in the first place. But lurking just below the surface a myriad of potential issues divides the party faithful and can lead to the dissolution of the existing equilibrium.

—EDWARD CARMINES AND JAMES A. STIMSON, AMERICAN POLITICAL SCIENTISTS[1]

The point is, you can't keep doing the same thing and expect it to keep working.

—MICHAEL DELL, FOUNDER AND CEO OF DELL[2]

In 1984, Michael Dell started a computer company from his dorm room at the University of Texas. The company he started would become one of the biggest success stories in modern business and a source of inspiration for new entrepreneurs. By the late 1990s, Dell had generated over 800 billion dollars in cumulative revenues, according to its annual reports.[3] Dell's stock price outperformed that of its closest competitor by a factor of 20 between 1991 and 1999. In

1992, Michael Dell entered the Fortune 500 lists, making him the youngest CEO on the list.[4] Dell was "the stuff of a business-school legend."[5]

Dell achieved its staggering success by disrupting the computer industry through an innovative direct business model. By cutting out distributors and resellers, the company sold computers directly to its customers over the phone, and later over the Internet. The company's disruptive innovation and early adaption to e-commerce allowed it to obtain the largest market share in personal computing sales in the late 1990s. While innovation was the key to Dell's success, it would also be crucial to understanding its decline. In the late 2000s, the direct business model that was key to its growth strategy had run its course. By 2009, four years after the company topped *Fortune* magazine's list of "America's Most Admired Companies,"[6] Dell had lost 70 percent of its value. In an interview, former vice-president of marketing at Dell Tom Martin noted that the company's greatest strength, that of disrupting existing business practices through its direct business model, eventually led to an "anti-innovation culture" that ultimately resulted in a decline in their market position.[7] By focusing all their efforts on streamlining their direct business model, Dell's executives failed to see how competitors like Apple had started to change the market through their production of new tablets and smartphones. Although Dell tried to catch up, it eventually dropped out of the tablet and smartphone market in 2016.[8]

The story of the successes and failures of Dell serves as a powerful example of the forces that economists think fundamentally shape product markets. These forces have been described as "creative destruction" by the Austrian economist Joseph Schumpeter.[9] The central idea is that innovation creates new companies, while simultaneously destroying old ones that fail to adapt. In this view, economic change is fundamentally shaped by two forces: the innovation of entrepreneurs, who are doing new things or doing things that are already being done but in a new way, and the market power of dominant market players who are seeking to protect their market share. We argue that these same forces shape change in the markets for votes, seats, and political office. We develop here a theory of *political change* that evolves around innovation and dominance. *Dominance* refers to the market power of the dominant players, which they aim to protect. *Innovation* is brought about by challengers, and is the process through which these political entrepreneurs introduce a new or previously ignored issue and use it, along with antiestablishment rhetoric, to discredit rival parties. Political change is the outcome of the tug-of-war between these two forces. The interplay between dominance and innovation transforms the nature of political competition and shapes the fates of political parties.

Over the last few decades, we have witnessed a steady rise in electoral support for challenger parties, as we demonstrated in chapter 1. In that chapter we also demonstrated how both the *degree* and the *timing* of the challenges to market dominance of dominant parties differed not only within and but also across countries. We seek to explain this by focusing on how the forces of political innovation and market dominance interact. When it comes to the extent of change, clearly not all challenger parties are created equal. Some are much more successful than others. We argue that what sets successful challenger parties apart from less successful ones is a reliance on specific innovation strategies. Challenger parties are successful when they employ a dual innovation strategy that combines policy and rhetorical innovation. *Policy innovation* refers to the mobilization of new and divisive issues, while *rhetorical innovation* involves using rhetoric that is highly critical of mainstream elites. When it comes to the timing of change, we showed in chapter 1 that in some countries it took a very long time for challenger parties to break through, while in others challengers broke through early on. We have also suggested that the permissiveness of electoral rules matters; yet it is not the whole story, as countries with similar electoral rules still vary in the timing of change. This, we suggest, is because dominant parties have been able to successfully fight off or contain the initial electoral success of challengers by employing specific strategies to protect their market power. To be able to understand the timing and degree of political change in a party system, we need to understand how the forces of market dominance and political innovation interact. This is the core insight of our theory of political change.

Patterns of Party Competition in Western Europe

The fate of social democratic parties serves as a vivid illustration of the extent of political change in Europe in recent decades. It is well documented that the European mainstream left has been in decline for some time.[10] The social democrats in the Netherlands, for example, experienced their biggest loss in Dutch election history in 2017, losing 19 percent of their vote share by dropping from 25 to 6 percent. The socialists in France experienced a similar crisis in 2017, winning less than 6 percent of the votes in the second round of the National Assembly elections. In many European countries, social democracy has been in retreat.[11] While structural shifts, including deindustrialization and globalization, are important explanations for the steady loss of voter appetite for the mainstream left, this does not mean that social and economic policies normally associated with social democracy have lost their popular appeal.[12] Quite the contrary—many voters want social protection and are angry about precarious jobs and social inequality. One problem is that social democrats appear to have lost ownership of one of their signature policies: social protectionism. Far-right populist parties in Europe,[13] like Marine Le Pen's National Rally in France or Geert Wilders's Party for Freedom in the Netherlands, have steadily moved into what was traditionally left-wing territory on social policy and welfare protection. Interestingly, these parties defend the protection of the welfare state's generosity in a different way, bundling it with anti-immigration and welfare chauvinist positions.[14] At the same time, social democratic parties find themselves in a dilemma when dealing with national identity and protectionist rhetoric. They are trapped between trying to appeal to the center through more fiscally responsible, economically liberal, and cosmopolitan policies, and trying to appease their core constituencies, who are often skeptical of globalization, Europe, and immigration, by presenting themselves as both socially progressive and tough on immigration.

The question on the minds of many experts is whether these developments indicate a trend of wholesale political transformation, or merely represent a temporary shift away from the political equilibrium. The results of the 2019 elections in Denmark, Finland, Portugal, and Spain seem to run counter to this trend, as social democrats did well electorally. Indeed, the rate of mainstream decline and the rise of challenger parties are neither uniform across countries nor linear over time within a country, as we demonstrated in chapter 1. Many reasons have been put forward to explain cross-national and temporal differences in the rise and fall of challenger and dominant parties. They include changes in the composition of the labor market,[15] the impact of globalization,[16] the emergence of distinctive social identities that foster distrust of politicians,[17] a cultural backlash,[18] the development of new transnational political cleavages,[19] and a rise in anti-immigration sentiment.[20] The role played by political parties in translating these structural changes into policy programs that voters can choose from, or even in actively shaping demand for certain policies, has received far less scholarly attention.[21] Our theory of political change focuses explicitly on the role of political parties and the strategies they employ.

Generally, there are two approaches to explaining political change: a *sociological* one and a *strategic* one. The sociological approach stresses the *demand-driven* aspects of political change. It broadly uses the theory of cleavages, developed by Seymour Martin Lipset and Stein Rokkan and outlined in the previous chapter, which understands political parties as organizations rooted in historical social cleavages. Parties are seen as vehicles of social division, and thus responsive to ideologically driven activists and voters. As a result, they have limited flexibility in responding to new issues that arise on the political agenda. According to this view, new political parties are basically the result of a demand-driven process in which new issues emerge through citizens' responses to rapidly changing social and economic conditions. For example, changes in the class structure due to increased economic globalization have created new winners and losers. The development of these winners and losers is in turn closely tied to the rise and success of radical right parties and new left parties.[22]

In contrast, the strategic approach stresses the importance of *supply-driven* change. It suggests that although a change in demand might be a necessary condition for political change, it is not sufficient. Political parties themselves actively shape changes in demand,[23] for example, by generating, maintaining, or changing the importance that voters attach to programmatic appeals (this is something we will return to in chapter 7).[24] Political change within the strategic approach thus crucially depends on the activities and agency of political parties. The strategic approach starts from the assumption that politics is a competitive struggle among political parties about which issues come to dominate the political agenda.[25] Political parties are not understood, as they are in the sociological explanation, as vessels reflecting existing societal divisions, but as organizations that actively structure and determine the content of societal conflict. As a result, the content and nature of political competition varies from election to election as new policy issues are identified and mobilized by one party or another. Political parties politicize a previously ignored event, policy issue, or societal conflict and attempt to encourage public attention to generate controversy. Of course, they have to choose carefully which issues to mobilize and what position to stake out, in order to ensure that this resonates with voters. Nevertheless, from a strategic perspective, an issue is likely to structure the political debate only when a political party or candidate gives it political expression.[26]

Our theory of political change extends the strategic approach. It builds on the work by American political scientists Edward Carmines and James Stimson as well as that of William Riker.[27] Both Carmines and Stimson and Riker stress the importance of strategic politicians. Their work, however, has focused on the specific context of two-party American politics and on explaining vast political change leading to the realignment of a party system (e.g., race in American politics). We aim to develop a theory of political change that can apply more broadly, and that allows us to explain which actors initiate political change, the strategies they use, and when these strategies are likely to be successful. We do so by taking our cue from the large literature in the subfield of economics known as *industrial organization*, which aims to explain economic change through forces of innovation and protection of market power.

Political Change: Between Dominance and Innovation

Industrial organization is the study of markets in which no perfect competition exists—that is to say, in which only a limited number of players (firms) compete.[28] Models of industrial organization extend the theory of perfect competition to incorporate imperfect competition based on real-world complications, such as barriers to entry, research and development costs, consumer inertia, and first-mover advantages. Various approaches to the study of industrial organization exist. While macroeconomic models focus on measures of competition and the size concentration of firms in an industry, microeconomic models aim to explain internal firm organization and market strategy, which includes product innovation through research and development, for example.[29]

Building on notions of economic change within the study of industrial organization, our theory of political change conceives of the dynamics of party competition as the result of a tug-of-war between dominant market forces, which wish to uphold their market power, and disruptive political entrepreneurs, which want to unseat the dominant players through innovation. In the marketplace of goods and services, companies can deliver their products to consumers if there is a functioning supply chain and adequate consumer demand. The dominant players are those that have captured a larger share of the market, such as Apple or Dell in the market for personal computers, or Coca Cola and Pepsi in the market for soft drinks. However, in the political marketplace, the delivery of the product, here understood as a bundle of policies, is restricted to those parties that control the delivery of public policy—that is to say, those who are in office. Parties in opposition may have some influence over the shape of policies through the legislative process,[30] but ultimately the delivery of public policy is controlled by parties in government and the executive branch. As a consequence, the dominant players in the political market are not simply those who have a large market share (vote share), but those with a good chance of entering government and being able to implement their policies.

As discussed in chapter 1, our conceptualization of *dominant parties* is centered around government experience. Dominant parties are those that have controlled the delivery of policies in the past and are more likely to do so in the future. In contrast, *challenger parties* are those that have not been in government. There may be several reasons why parties have not been in office: they might be new, too small, seen as too extreme by competitors, or unwilling to make the necessary compromises to join a coalition government. Unlike their dominant counterparts, challenger parties are not the market leaders. Yet, they do have a growth potential. The way in which challenger parties can reach their growth potential is by challenging the dominance of existing players through political innovation.

The phenomenon of challenger banks in the United Kingdom in recent years serves as a nice illustration of the difference between dominant and challenger parties. Dominant banks are those that have traditionally had a large market share and branches on pretty much every high street in the United Kingdom: think Barclays, Lloyds, and the Royal Bank of Scotland. Yet, the environment for retail banking has evolved: barriers to entry have been lowered, with regulatory changes making it easier for customers to switch providers. Customers themselves are demanding more personalized services, and technological innovation is disrupting traditional business and delivery models. This has provided opportunities for a new set of challengers. Only a few of these challenger banks can be found on the high street; their main presence is on the Internet, serving their customers via mobile apps and online banking. These digitally led challenger banks have changed the nature of banking through digital innovation and differentiated services to meet customer demands. Successful challengers include Atom Bank, Monzo, and Starling Bank, which are perceived by experts as providing the innovation most closely aligned with consumer needs.[31] They have managed to reduce the market share of the dominant banks, and have also forced dominant players to shrink their branch networks and increase their online offering to remain competitive.[32]

Before applying core insights from business examples like these to an understanding of party competition, we first need to outline some *key assumptions* about the nature of the political marketplace as well as the main actors within it. We define the political market as a mechanism through which political parties (or candidates) can trade their products to voters in exchange for their votes. Parties, like firms, "produce" products, yet political products are often more intangible—a bundle of policies or political ideologies.[33] Political parties sell these "products" on the political market in exchange for votes. However, they do not sell the actual policies, but rather promises that they will deliver particular policies once they are in office. Winning elections gives parties access to the spoils of office. Voters, like consumers, "buy" these products by casting their ballot for a party. We define the products that parties sell and voters buy as a combination of two aspects: *policies* and *competence*. Parties advocate a specific set of policies and issue positions that they promise to implement in office, and parties promote their competence in terms of the skills or personnel that give them the ability to implement these policies.[34]

In line with the work of the Austrian and Norwegian political scientists Wolfgang Müller and Kaare Strøm, we assume that political parties seek to maximize votes, gain access to political office, and implement their preferred policies, albeit to varying degrees.[35] Parties care about the number of votes they receive because winning a substantial share of the vote increases the probability of gaining access to office, which allows them to implement their policies. By gaining parliamentary representation or acquiring cabinet posts, politicians can also reap certain benefits, like monetary compensation, power, or influence. Politicians may not have "partisan goals per se . . . rather they have more fundamental goals, and the party is only the instrument for achieving them."[36] Voters have many reasons to vote for a party, but we assume that the importance voters attach to particular policy issues and their ideological affinities are a crucial part of their decision making.[37] We also consider the importance of politicians' nonpolicy, or competence, attributes.[38] These nonpolicy characteristics, such as candidate competence or character traits, have been shown to matter to voters.[39] Voters' policy priorities and evaluations of competence are a combination of exogenously given identities—based on ethnicity, religion, or class, for example—and are endogenous to what political parties do. Parties respond to societal demands and are able to create a demand for their policy priorities and competence at least to some degree.[40]

Importantly, the political marketplace is characterized by imperfect competition. Electoral rules do not allow an infinite number of parties to represent all possible preferences in society. Due to the mechanical and psychological effects of electoral rules, party competition is most often a form of oligopoly, with a limited number of viable parties, high barriers to entry in the form of electoral thresholds, and tactical voting whereby voters support larger parties with a realistic chance of gaining office over smaller ones.[41] Moreover, the dominant parties enjoy more subtle forms of power, including voter attachments and the ability to keep certain issues on or off the agenda. The sources of market dominance are discussed in greater detail below.

Sources of Market Dominance

Since the political market is characterized by imperfect competition, some parties are able to dominate because of their greater market power. The concept of market power in the industrial organization literature refers to a situation in which a producer maximizes its profit by selling a product above marginal costs. The empirical measurement of market power is the intensity of competition and market concentration—for example, measured through a Herfindahl index (see chapter 7).[42] What is market power in politics? We argue that in the political realm, market power is fundamentally about government experience. It is about controlling office, since that allows parties to control the delivery of public policy. A party's seat share is the primary (although not only) factor that shapes a party's chances of office holding and the degree of influence it will have within a coalition government. We refer to political actors with market power as *dominant parties*.

Controlling office and thus having market power is not static but under constant threat. These threats relate to changes in both *demand* and *supply*, thus referring back to the two types of explanations, sociological and strategic, of political change that were discussed in the previous section. Demand threats can be either gradual or abrupt in nature. Gradual threats in demand refer to changes in voters' preferences based on generational replacement or long-term societal changes, such as technological shifts, for example. The seminal work of American political scientist Ronald Inglehart on the development of postmaterial policy preferences, such as environmental protection or equal rights for women, highlighted the importance of gradual changes in demand. He argued that the gradual replacement of older generations in a set of advanced industrial democracies in the mid-1970s and 1980s had far-reaching political implications. Because younger generations thought differently about a wide range of issues, from religiosity to marriage, homosexuality, and the environment, new parties mobilizing these differences began to emerge and existing parties were forced to change their platforms as a result.[43]

Drastic demand threats refer to changes in voter preferences based on external shocks, such as environmental disasters and economic crises. For example, evidence from the United States suggests that experience with terrorism, specifically the events of 9/11, increased right-wing authoritarian views and conservatism as well as support for President George W. Bush, a leader with a reputation among many citizens for protecting security.[44] Recent evidence from Europe shows that exposure to Chinese import shocks increased right-wing authoritarian and anti-immigration views among European voters.[45]

In addition to changes in demand, the entry or reemergence of competitors in the market also potentially threatens market power. These entry threats are the result of the activities of new, or previously unsuccessful, competitors in the marketplace. Demand and entry threats are of course linked, but we argue that changes in demand alone may be a necessary but not a sufficient condition for the decline in the market power of dominant parties. To pose a serious threat to market power, changes in demand need to be brought on to the political agenda by political entrepreneurs. The innovation by challenger parties is therefore key to understanding political change.

What are the sources of market power? The industrial organization literature discusses sources that are *exogenous* to firm strategies and those that are *endogenous* to them.[46] We will use the same terms here, although in political systems parties themselves have some influence over even the "exogenous" rules that govern them. Exogenous sources of market power are relatively stable features of the system that create structural benefits for dominant parties. One source of dominance is electoral rules. We know from a large literature on the origins of electoral systems that these rules are the outcomes of decisions made by ruling parties designed to maximize their vote share. Therefore, as long as the electoral arena does not change and the current electoral regime benefits the ruling parties, the electoral system is unlikely to be altered.[47] This means that most electoral systems that are in place tend to benefit the dominant parties in the system. As a result, dominant parties will attempt to block any changes to those systems, as changes may facilitate the successes of challengers. In other words, while electoral systems may be altered by parties themselves, they are rather stable and tend to operate to the advantage of the dominant parties. There are also numerous institutional benefits and resources associated with being in office. In their theory of "cartel parties," American and Irish political scientists Richard Katz and Peter Mair argued that dominant parties can effectively employ the resources of the state to limit political competition from newcomers.[48]

Another source of the market power of dominant parties stems from voters' behaviors. Voters' attachments to parties, and their loyalties to particular parties, are another important source of market power. Voters, like customers, are influenced by attachments to certain parties and habitual consumption patterns.[49] Research on firms suggests that buyers may stick for a considerable time with the first brand they encounter that performs the job satisfactorily, out of brand loyalty.[50] Marketers have coined the notion of "brand equity" to capture consumers' positive awareness of and loyalty to certain brands.[51] Companies naturally aspire to cultivate this form of consumer allegiance to their brand, as consumers who trust a brand are more likely to remain loyal and even adopt brand extensions. A similar, and often stronger, loyalty may develop to a political party owing to the intense psychological bonds to party brands that develop at an early age. Voters who identify with a specific party thus face considerable psychological barriers to switching. These psychological barriers to switching provide dominant parties with a more loyal following of partisan voters, and are an important source of market power.[52]

In addition to these "barriers to entry" in the form of electoral systems, incumbent resources, and party attachments, dominant parties can also adopt specific strategies to help solidify their dominance. These are the endogenous sources of market dominance. We identity three key strategies: *distinctive convergence, competence mobilization,* and *issue avoidance.* Distinctive convergence refers to a strategy by which political parties provide a bundle of policy issues that fits the tastes of as many voters as possible, while avoiding competition with other parties by offering a specialized product. Politically, this may involve dominant parties becoming large, broad-based parties that converge toward the center, with the aim of capturing a large proportion of voters. One can think of the big traditional party families in Europe, the social and Christian democrats, that sell their experience of government alongside the fact that as *Volksparteien* (people's parties) they represent the majority of voters in the system. Yet, at the same time they pitch themselves as being left or right of center respectively, to remain distinct.[53] Of course, a tension exists between appealing to "most tastes" and providing a "specialized offering." This tension comes partly from the fact that parties always aim to juggle their different goals—office, policy, and votes— simultaneously.[54] Parties that care about votes over policy may thus swing toward offering policy bundles in line with the majority of voters, while parties that care more about policies compared with votes may focus more on providing a specialized offering.

A second strategy to protect market dominance is *competence mobilization.* As dominant parties converge, they also tend to compete more on competence issues. In other words, they try to appeal to voters on the basis of their experience in government and ability to implement policies, rather than differences in ideological outlook.[55] This approach tends to benefit incumbents, but may also be a double-edged sword in cases of poor performance or shocks, such as economic downturns or corruption.

The final strategy, *issue avoidance*, refers to the ways in which parties aim to keep certain issues off the political agenda. They can do so through a strategy of ambiguity that blurs their positions or downplays their importance.[56] Dominant parties owe their advantageous position in the system to the mobilization of certain policies and competences. Hence, they have every incentive to keep issues that could hurt them off the political agenda. For example, experts on Dutch party politics suggest that this is exactly what the dominant parties, Labour and the Christian Democratic Party, did in the 1980s and 1990s with the issue of immigration, which they effectively ignored as a salient political issue.[57] Issue avoidance is an important strategy for dominant parties to try to deter political innovation. Ultimately, however, it can be seen as a form of tacit collusion, in which dominant parties without any formal agreement or coordination nonetheless keep policy bundles off the political market because it serves their strategic interests to do so.

Innovation of Political Entrepreneurs

Disruptive political entrepreneurs are constantly challenging the market power of dominant parties through a process of *innovation*. We label these entrepreneurs *challenger parties*. Analogous to the role of innovation within the study of industrial organization, we think of innovation within party competition as the introduction of a "product." It is the process through which political parties introduce a new or previously ignored issue and aim to discredit dominant parties by employing antiestablishment rhetoric. Innovation requires a good understanding of customers' needs and wants, of the competitive environment, and of the nature of the market. The scope for political innovation is likely to be more limited in politics compared with product innovation in the economic realm. While firms can try to satisfy the needs and wants of customers by introducing products of varying qualities through different brand extensions at different price levels, political parties are much more constrained. For example, a party cannot credibly be simultaneously pro- and anti-abortion or introduce redistribution from the rich to the poor and tax breaks for the rich. Nor can it introduce a "cheap" and a more "expensive" version of the same product. Despite these differences, we expect the dynamics between market players when it comes to political innovation to be similar to those guiding product innovation.

Innovation normally requires a sunk costs investment. A sunk cost is a cost that has already been incurred and cannot be recovered.[58] Think, for example, of a firm that spends a large amount of money to buy new software to streamline its online sales and train its employees to use it. No matter how effective the software turns out to be, the money spent to acquire it and train employees is a sunk cost. In the context of party competition, this is the investment every party needs to make to engage in innovation. In order for parties to be able to compete in the electoral arena, they will need to pass a certain threshold of funding and organizational capability. One can, for example, think of the resources invested in understanding voter concerns and rival strategies, developing a media and information campaign, funding additional personnel, and investing in advertisement. Innovation may, however, have financial, organizational, and electoral benefits. We expect parties to engage in innovation when the potential benefits outweigh the costs. Because challenger parties are often newcomers to the system or hold marginal positions, the potential gains of innovation are considerable, as even a small increase in votes will be an improvement to their current situation.

Dominant parties owe their advantageous position in the system to the mobilization of existing issues. This previous commitment to specific issues is important, because many voters will associate them with these issues and many activists will self-select into the party because of them. Because of these previous investments, dominant parties will experience sunk costs if they reorient themselves to new issues. Behavioral economists have shown that sunk costs strongly influence actors' decisions, because people display a tendency to prefer avoiding losses to acquiring equivalent gains.[59] Dominant parties that engage in innovation will also face considerable risks, such as uncertainty about how their voters or coalition partners will respond. Moving away from existing issues could drive a wedge within the membership or voter base and lead to internal rifts or even defections, because the allegiance of activists and voters to the party stems from the old issues it used to mobilize. Innovation is risky for dominant parties and may cost them more votes than it attracts. Furthermore, dominant parties might be constrained by not wanting to upset rivals with whom they have previously governed or are likely to do so in the future.[60] While innovation could turn out to be a big gamble for dominant parties, challenger parties might be more willing to innovate. The likelihood of parties adopting innovative strategies is also going to be affected by the barriers to market entry. Specifically, we expect innovation to be more frequent in permissive electoral systems. This is because small electoral gains translate more directly into seats. In these contexts, the electoral return on an innovation is likely to be greater.

The policy aspect of innovation is what we call *issue entrepreneurship*. It hinges on the question of which political issues parties should pick to mobilize. The literature on product innovation suggests that innovation is most likely to occur when products allow for a high degree of *appropriability*—that is to say, when a firm has the ability to protect some of the gains that result from its innovation.[61] Firms can do this through patenting, for example. Translating this to party competition, we expect challenger parties to mobilize issues that allow for a high degree of appropriability. We define issues with high appropriability as those that are not easily subsumed within the dominant dimension (the left–right dimension in West European party competition) and may thus have the potential to internally split dominant parties. Since these issues may drive a wedge between party members or within their constituencies, dominant parties are likely to steer clear of them, and this allows challenger parties to carve out a unique appeal to voters around these issues. Policy issues relating to European integration, immigration, and the environment can be seen as having high appropriability in the European context. All three issues have the potential to cut across the dominant dimension of political conflict in Western Europe, and to not be easily aligned with the left–right dimension on which dominant-party success is built.[62]

While firms have legal means, such as copyrights and patents, to appropriate their products, political parties have to rely on other means, like a first-mover advantage or strategies to prevent imitation, to stay ahead of competitors. A first-mover advantage refers to the situation in which the first entrant on the product market gains a competitive advantage through the control of resources.[63] In the initial stages, a party that engages in successful political innovation can enjoy an effective monopoly on the issue and reap the electoral benefits accordingly. Although rival parties may try to imitate a party's innovation, doing so is likely to take time and will be costly. In her seminal work on party competition, Bonnie Meguid has argued that one way in which dominant parties can react to competitors is by accommodating their issues. While it is possible for dominant parties to attempt to copy the innovation of challenger parties, it will involve a major redirection of the party and its program.[64] If it takes too long for competitors to respond, challenger parties may already "own" the issue and voters may have already developed a loyalty to their brand.[65] Thus first movers can initially be rewarded with huge profits and a monopoly-like status.

We expect parties with market power to have little incentive to innovate, as it can be costly, most importantly because of the costs associated with previous investments and uncertainty about how the rank and file and their existing voter base will respond to the innovation. Yet, when the innovation of challenger parties looks successful, dominant parties might just respond by copying their efforts. Yet, this is risky for dominant parties as challenger parties are likely to try to protect their first-mover advantage by discrediting the dominant parties and branding them as copycats.

This strategy to prevent imitation and devalue the brand equity of competitors refers to the competence part of innovation described earlier as antiestablishment rhetoric. We define antiestablishment rhetoric as a discursive style or form of communication that condemns the ruling classes as an elite and the political system as something that predominantly serves the interests of that elite.[66] It is employed with the aim of devaluing the "brand equity" of dominant parties. Whereas issue entrepreneurship is targeted at disrupting the dominance of mainstream parties by mobilizing new issues, the antiestablishment strategy seeks to attack the value of the dominant party "brand" as a whole, rather than its specific policy offering. This strategy is well known from the study of populist parties, which seek to gain electoral support by mobilizing anti-elitist attitudes and nurturing antiestablishment sentiments, among other things.[67] Anti-elitist or antiestablishment political discourse focuses on challenging the integrity of dominant parties and their competence to serve the interests of the people they are meant to serve. Challenger parties will seek to disrupt the linkages between voters and dominant parties by emphasizing the distance between "the people" and the "the elite," and by claiming that only they side with "the interests of the people." Such a strategy is obviously more likely to succeed if voters already harbor doubts about the ability of dominant parties to deliver on their promises, and if voter attachments to such parties have weakened. Antiestablishment rhetoric is generally not an add-on to the policy aspect of innovation, but an important strategy in its own right for challenger parties to appropriate their positional innovation and to ensure that dominant parties find it difficult to respond. This in turn increases the chances of challenger parties achieving their potential for growth.

The Potential for Political Transformation

The potential for political change (or *transformation*, as we label it) is the interaction between the strategies dominant parties employ to protect their market power and the innovative strategies employed by challenger parties to take some share of that market. A primary source of dominant parties' market power are electoral rules and voters' attachments (see chapter 3), but the parties themselves can also try to protect their dominance (see chapter 4). The strategies that dominant parties employ to do so are threefold. First, they aim to control the political agenda by adopting broad-based, centrist policy positions. Second, they avoid issues that may harm them. Third, they aim to showcase their competence in delivering policy in office. As long as the market power of dominant parties remains relatively intact, there is unlikely to be significant political change. Electoral outcomes and governments are likely to remain stable and predictable. In other words, mainstream party families will continue to get a large share of the parliamentary seats, dominate government, and shape the political agenda.

However, if the market power of dominant parties becomes more fragile—for example, through structural changes that reduce their institutional benefits or weaken their ties to voters—then innovation by challenger parties has the potential to cause real damage to the market power of the dominant parties and thus lead to a transformation of the political system. The extent to which it does depends on how successful dominant parties' strategies to protect their market power are, as well as the strategies of challenger parties to innovate. The innovation strategies of challengers are twofold. First, through issue entrepreneurship, challenger parties mobilize new issues that may drive a wedge within the membership and voter base of dominant parties and encourage voters to switch. Second, challenger parties can also take advantage of any underlying discontent with the political and economic status quo by attacking the "brand" of mainstream parties through antiestablishment rhetoric. If challenger parties are successful in their efforts to disrupt the market power of dominant parties, this may unlock greater political transformation. Challenger parties may change existing patterns of electoral behavior, representation, government formation, and government stability.

Conclusion

Our theory of political change conceives of party competition as a constant struggle between dominant parties, the key players on the political market trying to defend their market power, and challenger parties, acting as disruptive political entrepreneurs trying to challenge this dominance through innovation. Innovation is the process through which political parties introduce a new or previously ignored policy issue and aim to discredit dominant parties by employing antiestablishment rhetoric. Political parties will only engage in innovation when the potential benefits of doing so outweigh the costs. Challenger parties, especially those within permissive electoral systems, are most likely to engage in innovation, because of the costs and potential electoral risks to dominant parties associated with mobilizing issues different than the ones they traditionally do. Parties that wish to innovate are likely to choose issues that allow for a high degree of appropriability, issues that are not easily subsumed within the dominant dimension and that may internally split dominant parties. Parties can rely on a first-mover advantage as a means of securing appropriability. If innovation is successful, innovators can enjoy an effective monopoly on the issue, at least in the short term, and reap considerable electoral benefits because rival parties react more slowly and have to incur switching costs. Innovators attempt to extend their advantage by preventing imitation through discrediting the activities and reputations of rivals.

As with Dell having to come to terms with the changing market for personal computers discussed at the beginning of this chapter, we expect political change to be the result of the interplay of two forces, the protection of market power and innovation. While Dell's disruptive innovation based on the direct business model was the source of its initial success, it ultimately became a source of its stagnation. Because the focus of the company became so closely linked to improving the execution of its direct business model, it devoted too little time to forward thinking and product development. As a one former Dell operations director appropriately put it: "We were so good at execution, we didn't have time for innovation."[68] After its direct business model lost traction, Dell recovered ground by competitive pricing, growing its e-commerce activities, and the return of its founder Michael Dell. Despite all this, Dell's market share in personal computing lags behind some of its main competitors.[69] More importantly perhaps, Dell has not been able to keep up with fast-paced technological innovation and has failed to penetrate growth markets, such as smartphones, as other competitors have.[70] Again, we see important parallels to the changes in European party competition in past decades, although political change has been more gradual. In the remainder of the book, we examine these mechanisms of dominance, innovation, and transformation empirically.

PART II

Dominance

3

Voter Loyalty

A large majority of the electorate identify themselves with greater or less intensity as Republicans or Democrats and this identification is impressively resistant to change. To the extent that they so identify, their political perceptions, attitudes, and acts are influenced in a partisan direction and tend to remain consistently partisan over time. Those members of the electorate without party attachment are free of this influence and are consequently less stable in their partisan positions from year to year.

—ANGUS CAMPBELL, AMERICAN SOCIAL PSYCHOLOGIST[1]

Amazon is a convenience brand. You're not loyal to Amazon, you're loyal to the convenience it provides and if someone can do that convenience better or cheaper, I think people would switch quite quickly, which is different to a genuine brand where you have an emotional relationship.

—ZOE HARRIS, MARKETING DIRECTOR OF TRINITY MIRROR GROUP[2]

iSheep is the derogatory term sometimes used to describe devoted Apple consumers, willing to stand in long lines outside Apple stores just so they can be the first to get their hands on the latest version of the iPhone. Over two-thirds of Apple consumers admit to such a strong loyalty to the brand that they would never even consider buying alternative products.[3] Most companies, however, can only dream of such levels of consumer loyalty. When companies have a "brand" rather than merely a range of products, consumers can more easily distinguish them from rival organizations and products. The notion of "brand equity" is well established in the marketing literature as a value that encompasses brand awareness, brand associations, and perceived brand quality as well as consumer brand loyalty.[4] This is a form of consumer allegiance that all companies seek, where consumers develop an emotional connection to a brand that goes beyond a simple appreciation of its quality and value for money. Consumers may also be more attracted to a brand if they think that people "like them," or the people they would like to be, are more likely to consume it—hence the use of brand ambassadors, carefully targeted advertising, and brand placement in popular entertainment. If being an Apple consumer is associated with being hip and cool, it might attract customers who aspire to such values, while Android users may view themselves as purists who value cutting-edge technology over sleek design. By consuming certain products, people send signals about which groups they belong to and the people they want to be like.[5] Moreover, brand loyalty acts as an informational shortcut for consumers: they do not need to read up on the latest developments in mobile technology if they know that Apple provides them with the "right" product. From a company's point of view, this is attractive as it increases demand for both current and future products from customers who believe in the value of the brand and who are less likely to switch and to be attracted to lower-priced alternatives. If dominant brands, such as Apple and Google, have a high brand equity, it also makes it more difficult for new challengers to enter the marketplace.

There are obvious similarities between the loyalty that consumers may feel for a brand and the attachments of voters to a particular political party.[6] But consumer brand loyalty often pales into insignificance when compared to the deep-seated allegiances that many people have to political parties. One very obvious reason is that, unlike companies, parties do not offer individual products that allow consumers to pick and choose on the basis of quality, price, and convenience, but instead they offer policy bundles tied together by an overarching political ideology. The value of such products only becomes fully realized if the party is elected to office.[7] Also, consumer products have built-in obsolescence—phones, cars, and washing machines are not intended to last a lifetime—whereas party political choice relates to more fundamental choices about who we are and the kind of society we want to live in, and partisan loyalties often have deeper structural roots.[8] Voters who feel attached to a party are often deeply loyal to that party and reluctant to switch between parties, regardless of the specifics of policy positions and performance. Dominant parties thus tend to benefit from a very loyal customer base of *partisans*—that is, voters who identify with their party.

In systems where dominant parties enjoy a loyal following of partisans, it is very difficult for challenger parties to break through. Partisanship thus represents a significant "barrier to entry" for challengers. If voters identify with certain parties, they are also less likely to switch to another party, even if that party is appealing on policy grounds. In contrast, a political system with many unattached, or floating, voters offers more fertile ground for challenger parties. Voters who are not attached to a dominant party will start to assess its performance more critically and consider alternatives more seriously. The loosening of ties between parties and voters does not necessarily lead to the emergence of challenger parties, but it is an important precondition for their success.

Scholars have suggested that we are witnessing a decline of the strong partisan allegiances of the past. Many argue that parties have become increasingly disconnected from voters,[9] that voters identify less with parties overall,[10] and that increasing voter volatility has resulted in the decline of mainstream parties.[11] In his work on Latin America, the American political scientist Noam Lupu has shown that the decline of mainstream parties in the region during the late 1990s was due to a steady erosion of voters' attachments to the main parties that had occurred over the preceding decades.[12] Lupu showed that, without the stable support of a partisan base, the mainstream parties became more susceptible to the short-term retrospective evaluations of voters, who were more likely to abandon them in favor of new parties. We argue that a similar process of erosion of voter loyalty has taken place in Europe. However, there is a lack of systematic and comparative evidence of the extent and development of party loyalties in the European context. As we saw in chapter 1, mainstream parties have largely remained the dominant players in the party system across most of Western Europe (with some variation between countries), but this does not tell us whether there is a potential for greater change in the electoral landscape because of a lowering of barriers to entry where voters have become more willing to switch between parties.

In this chapter, we examine the barriers to entry that challenger parties face, most notably the strength of party attachments to dominant parties. First, we explore the development of party membership, which is the most formal expression of an attachment to a party, and where we have witnessed a stark (but far from uniform) decline across Western Europe. Second, we look at subjective measures of party attachment, which show cross-national volatility, but also clear signs of loosening ties. Third, we focus on actual behavior—namely, voter volatility, which captures individual-level party switching between elections. Here we see that voters in the countries we look at have become much more willing to switch parties. Finally, we highlight the importance of different barriers to entry by comparing British and Danish case studies. Overall, the evidence presented in this chapter suggests that voters are becoming more like consumers and more willing to switch if there is something more appealing on offer.

Barriers to Entry for Challenger Parties

Why is it seemingly so difficult for challenger parties to enter party systems? Similar to imperfect markets, party systems are generally characterized by an oligopoly and high barriers to entry. There are many formal and informal institutional barriers to entry. Dominant parties will have better access to resources and important networks. American and Irish political scientists Richard Katz and Peter Mair have argued that dominant parties act as "cartels" and employ the resources of the state to limit political competition from challengers and ensure their own electoral success.[13] In many European countries, the state provides public financing for parties, and dominant parties influence how such subsidies are apportioned, making it more difficult for newcomers outside the "cartel" to compete. Electoral rules also act as barriers that do not allow for an infinite number of parties to represent all possible preferences in society. The best-known expression of this is idea is Duverger's law, put forward by French sociologist and jurist Maurice Duverger. This "law" states that elections under plurality rule structured within single-member districts tend to favor a two-party system, whereas proportional representation tends to favor multiparty systems.[14] This relationship between the electoral system and the fragmentation of the party system is due to both mechanical and psychological effects. The mechanical effect is the process by which a distribution of votes is transformed into a distribution of seats, which tends to favor the dominant parties in first-past-the-post systems, while the psychological effect is the anticipation by voters and parties of the punishment of smaller parties, which leads them to adapt their behavior, or act strategically, in order not to waste their vote.[15] Taken together, the mechanical and psychological effects of electoral rules mean that a finite number of parties will compete for votes and that the electoral market is characterized by imperfect competition.

Plurality systems in particular make it difficult for challenger parties to enter the electoral arena, unless their support is very geographically concentrated.[16] The one example of this electoral system in Western Europe is the United Kingdom, where challenger parties such as the Greens and the United Kingdom Independence Party (UKIP) have so far never achieved more than a single seat in Parliament. Chapter 1 showed the vote share of dominant and challenger parties across Western Europe and clearly illustrated that challenger parties perform worse in the United Kingdom than elsewhere (see figure 1.4). Even in systems with proportional representation, electoral rules such as a high threshold for entering parliament can represent a significant barrier to entry for challenger parties. Research on new party entry has shown that less permissive electoral systems make it more difficult for new parties to enter parliament.[17] There are several aspects of electoral rules that can make it harder or easier for challenger parties to enter and be successful: proportional representation voting systems, low electoral thresholds, and large district magnitudes all incentivize voting for small parties and have been shown to benefit challenger parties, such as radical right-wing parties.[18] One example of high barriers to entry in a proportional system is Germany, where the 5 percent threshold for entering parliament has caused problems for challenger parties—such as the Party of Democratic Socialism and Alternative for Germany—in the past. Another example is the emergence of the populist Five Star Movement in Italy. Recent research demonstrates that it was easier for the Five Star Movement to emerge locally where mayoral elections were held under the more permissive runoff system—which encourages more candidates on the ballot and more sincere voting—than under the more restrictive single-round plurality elections.[19] Hence, institutional barriers to entry matter to the entry opportunities and success of challenger parties.

Yet, such formal institutions are not the only, or even the most important, source of market power for dominant parties. Informal barriers also exist. We argue that partisanship is a crucial, albeit less tangible, barrier to entry for challenger parties, and to understand when and why challenger parties become successful it is crucially important to look at the underlying attachment of voters to dominant parties. Partisanship, or party identification, is a core concept in the study of electoral behavior. Early studies of elections demonstrated how important an attachment to a party was in determining voters' electoral choices and political outlook.[20] According to the so-called Michigan School, pioneered by the American social psychologist Angus Campbell and colleagues, party identification is characterized as a simple loyalty, acquired early and largely unimpaired by subsequent learning: "only an event of extraordinary intensity can arouse any significant part of the electorate to the point that its established political loyalties are shaken."[21] Partisanship, according to Campbell and colleagues, is thus an "unmoved mover" that is intrinsically sticky and creates a bond between parties and their supporters that is difficult for newcomers to break.

The scholarship on partisanship that originates in this Michigan model of voting sees partisan attachment as a stable emotional loyalty developed early in life in socialization with family members and others in a person's social network. To the extent that partisanship is established early, particularly within the family during childhood and early adulthood, this suggests a link to socioeconomic groups, such as that highlighted in the pioneering work by Lipset and Rokkan on cleavage structures that we discussed in chapters 1 and 2.[22] Lipset and Rokkan's theory sets out how macro developments, such as national revolutions, the Reformation, and the Industrial Revolution, have produced enduring structures of conflict that continue to shape political structure, political organization, and the substantive character of conflict. According to this theory, cleavages arise out of social structures—chiefly, class, religion, and spatial location—that determine political preferences and partisan allegiances. These cleavages have produced the major party families that have dominated West European politics for decades: the conservative, liberal, Christian democratic, and socialist party families.

However, the social structures that gave rise to the West European party systems have been gradually eroding through processes such as secularization, the decline in manufacturing, women's entry to the labor force, and migration. The underlying societal foundations of European party systems have changed. This gradual erosion of the cleavage structure had already been highlighted by Lipset and Rokkan, who noted that "decades of structural change and economic growth have made the old, established alternatives increasingly irrelevant."[23] But such changes have accelerated in recent decades. Swiss political scientist Hanspeter Kriesi and his colleagues have

argued that structural changes brought about by intensified globalization over the past three decades have created a division between
the so-called "winners" and "losers" of globalization, and given rise
to a new "cultural" dimension of competition, with an emphasis on
opposition to immigration and European integration.[24] These structural changes, in turn, have led to a transformation of party systems
into a tripolar configuration of the left, the moderate right, and the
new populist right, driven by a voter realignment around the new
cultural dimension. Another prominent account of the changing
electoral dynamics in Europe has been put forward by the British
and Belgian political scientists Gary Marks and Liesbet Hooghe,
who have proposed a "neocleavage theory." They argue that Europe
is undergoing not only a process of dealignment of attachments along
the lines of traditional cleavages, but also a realignment as a new
"transnational divide" becomes solidified among voters while old
divides lose their significance.[25]

These structural explanations tell an important part of the story
of how societal changes and shocks can disrupt the foundations of
party systems, and provide opportunities for new configurations
and party-system divides to emerge. The question addressed in this
book is how political entrepreneurs can exploit changing demand
structures to mobilize voters around new issues and antiestablishment sentiments. Importantly, we also examine the strategies available to mainstream parties, even in times of structural change, to
explain why party systems have nonetheless remained relatively
stable, as shown in chapter 1, and how the mainstream party families
have managed to hold on to much of their vote.

Some of the stickiness in the electoral support for mainstream
parties is due to people's psychological attachments to parties. When
voters are attached to parties, they are much less likely to abandon
them at the ballot box and are more forgiving of fluctuations in party
performance and unclear policy messages. Yet, some evidence suggests that attachments are also waning. Indeed, political scientists
have challenged the classic notion of partisanship as an "unmoved
mover" and argued that younger voters in particular have much more

malleable attachments to parties.[26] Critics claim that the Michigan model exaggerates the assumption that party identification is very stable, and argue that party identification can change in light of a party's performance or other circumstances. A prominent "revisionist" take on partisanship by American political scientist Morris Fiorina describes party identification as "a running tally of retrospective evaluations of party promises and performance."[27] According to this perspective, partisanship is not simply a socialized, stable attachment, but a rational calculation by voters of the future benefit they can derive from a particular party in office based on past political experience of the platforms and policies of that party. Such an approach suggests that voters may be more willing to update their evaluations of parties and even defect from their preferred party in light of experiences and performance. In the work on the decline of dominant parties in Latin America mentioned earlier, Noam Lupu showed that when a party's "brand" becomes diluted and the major parties become indistinguishable from one another, voters detach and start looking more critically at their performance when deciding how to vote.[28]

In a European context, there is some evidence of a decline in party membership and in party identification,[29] as well as changes in voter volatility and a general disconnect between voters and parties.[30] Yet, we lack sufficient systematic cross-national and cross-temporal evidence on the individual-level ties between voters and parties to be able to draw any clear conclusions, so we will now focus on the question: Have European voters really become disconnected from parties?

Shrinking Party Membership

To measure the stability and strength of the connection between voters and parties, we focus on three aspects: formal membership of political parties, attachment to parties, and electoral loyalty (and volatility). We start by looking at membership of political parties, as it is one of the clearest measures of a strong tie between voters and the parties they support. Being a party member is a costly signal of belonging and attachment, and party members are more likely to be actively engaged in political campaigning for, to donate to, and to vote for the party than nonmembers are. Any consistent decline in party membership across dominant parties is thus very tangible evidence of a weakening of the linkages between voters and parties. Figure 3.1 plots the development in party membership in Western European countries since the Second World War.

The party membership data reported in figure 3.1 is based on a data set maintained by the Members and Activists of Political Parties working group,[31] and represents the most comprehensive data-collection effort on party membership figures to date. It relies on country experts providing data on party membership for all parties that have been or are currently represented in national parliaments, as well as major regional parties, going all the way back to 1945.

The Members and Activists of Political Parties data set thus allows us to look at the trends over time in party membership figures across most Western European countries. Figure 3.1 clearly shows a steep and consistent decline in the absolute numbers of party members, in line with other research.[32] In most countries, this decline occurs from the 1980s and 1990s onwards, but in others it starts much earlier. The figure also shows that dominant parties in particular have been struggling to hold on to their existing membership organizations and failing to recruit new members in significant numbers. While dominant parties have a higher membership base than challenger parties, they are also the parties that have experienced the steepest decline in membership.

The general trend in falling party membership is clear, but we also find considerable cross-national variation. In terms of absolute numbers, we can see that Austria, Italy, Sweden, and the United Kingdom were historically countries where a very high number of people were members of political parties, but this number has been declining, although at different rates. The decline in the Netherlands, Sweden, and the United Kingdom started in the 1960s and 1970s, whereas membership rates remained high in Austria and Italy until the 1990s. In a few countries, such as Belgium and France, there is

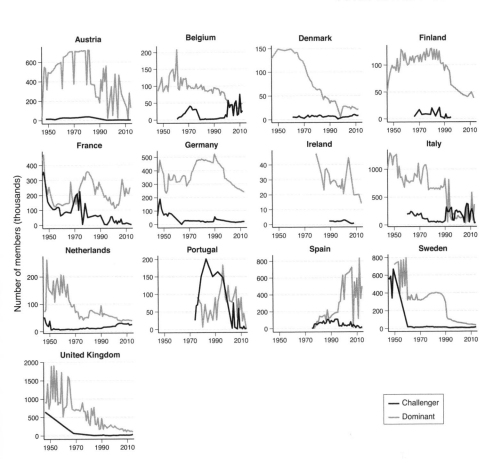

FIGURE 3.1 Party membership in Western Europe, 1945–2014
Source: Members and Activists of Political Parties data set

no clear trend in membership figures, while Spain appears to be unique in having seen a sharp increase in party membership since the 1990s.[33] A review of the main trends in party membership in 20 European democracies between 1980 and 2000 noted that "the only countries which have bucked this trend [of decline] are drawn from the group of relatively recently democratized polities, including Greece, Hungary, Slovakia and Spain."[34]

Declining membership of political parties, however, does not necessarily imply that people no longer feel any attachment to particular parties. Rather, there has been a steep decline in the membership of many of the organizations associated with the classic cleavage structure in Western Europe, such as trade unions and churches, and the decline in party membership may be just one part of this broader trend. While most party members are fiercely loyal to their party, it is possible to be attached to a party without being a member. That is why in the next stage of our examination of the loosening ties between voters and parties, we focus on subjective party identification.

The Decline of Party Identification

As discussed above, party identification is central to the study of electoral research and party competition, and has been shown to shape electoral behavior and political attitudes more broadly. To study the development of party identification, we use two cross-national and cross-temporal data sets on individual attitudes: Eurobarometer data (1975–96) and European Social Survey data (2002–16).[35] The distinct advantage of these two data sets is that they use the exact same question to measure partisanship: "Generally speaking, do you feel close to a party?" (very close, fairly close, sympathizer, not close), thus allowing us to compare over time and across countries. Moreover, the explicit reference to "closeness" captures the emotional attachment to a party that is central to the concept of party identification.[36] As long as the vast majority of the electorate feels "close" to one of the dominant parties, it is a significant hurdle for new challenger parties to enter to political market.

To capture the trends in party identification over time we measured the proportion of citizens who say that they are "very close" or "fairly close" to a party. Figure 3.2 shows the average trend across Western Europe since 1975. It shows a decline from two-thirds of people feeling close to a party in the mid-1970s to around 55 percent four decades later. The decline is not as steep as that in party membership figures, however. But it does suggest that more people today are willing to be more critical of the dominant parties and look at "alternatives" to their preferred party.

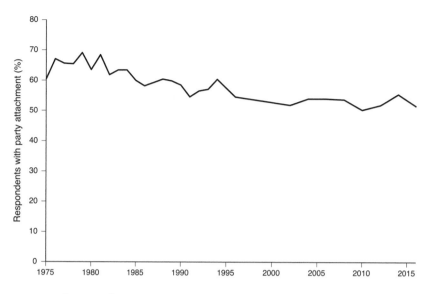

FIGURE 3.2 Party attachment in Western Europe, 1975–2016
Source: Eurobarometer surveys and European Social Surveys

The next step is to look at these trends in each of the Western European countries, as shown in figure 3.3. The first thing to notice is that some countries, notably the Scandinavian countries and the Netherlands, generally have higher levels of party attachment, reaching as high as over 70 percent of the electorate feeling attached to a party, whereas identification with a party is much lower in other countries, such as Ireland and Spain. In most countries, we observe a steady decline in party identification. Declining party attachments are the norm in Italy, Germany, France, Greece, Luxembourg, and the Netherlands. In contrast, in Spain, where we have observed an increase in party membership (figure 3.1), we also find a small increase in the number of people who state they feel close to a party. In Belgium, Denmark, and Norway, party identification rates appear fairly stable over time.

The dramatic fall in party membership and the slow but steady decline in the proportion of the electorate who identifies with a single party suggests that the dominant parties may be losing some of their hold over their voters. If voters strongly identify with one of

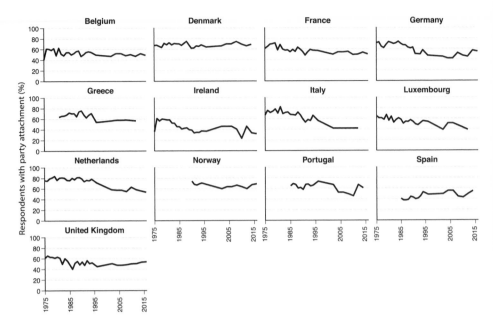

FIGURE 3.3 Party attachment in Western European countries, 1975–2016
Source: Eurobarometer surveys and European Social Surveys

the dominant parties, they are unlikely to lend their electoral support to a challenger party. But in a world where between 30 and 50 percent of the electorate is happy to switch party affiliation, there are ample opportunities for challenger parties to come in and shake up the party system. So, the most important question is perhaps how loyal voters are when they are at the ballot box. Do they tend to vote for the same familiar party over and over again, or are they willing to consider new parties?

The Rise of Electoral Volatility

Attachment to parties matters in so far as it shapes behavior. If the links between dominant parties and their supporters have weakened, we would expect more voters to be willing to defect from the parties they usually support and perhaps even vote for challenger parties. When voters strongly identify with a party it will be difficult for them to defect, regardless of what else is on offer. This is a source of market power for dominant parties. The crucial test of whether informal barriers to entry for challenger parties have been lowered is therefore to the extent to which voters are willing to switch between parties on election day itself.

We therefore need a measure of *electoral volatility*. Most of the literature on electoral systems uses the well-known Pedersen index, which measures the net change within the electoral party system resulting from individual vote transfers.[37] The advantage of this measure is that it is easy to quantify using simply data on the outcome of elections. The problem with the Pedersen index, however, is that since it measures only *net* electoral volatility it cannot capture when voters switch their votes between existing parties, but only the volatility caused by the entry and exit of parties from the political system.[38] If we want to understand the barriers to entry for challenger parties that are caused by the ties between voters and dominant parties, we need to be able to measure not only voters' willingness to switch to a new party, but also the extent to which they switch between existing parties.[39] This matters, because voters who are generally more likely to switch between parties are also going to be more open to considering new alternatives.

Consider this example from the market for smartphones. In the third quarter of 2017, Samsung's and Apple's sales shares were virtually tied at 35 percent each. They were clearly the dominant players in the smartphone marketplace. The same year, Google launched its first serious bid to challenge these dominant players with the introduction of a new smartphone, the Pixel 2 XL. If you were CEO of Google, making the calculation of whether you could break the dominance of Samsung and Apple in the smartphone market, it would matter whether this was a market where iPhone consumers loyally stick to buying iPhones and Samsung customers remain loyal to Samsung's version of the smartphone, or, alternatively, where consumers happily switch between the two brands. As it turned out, the Pixel phones were not the success that Google had hoped for, and few iPhone or Samsung users switched to Pixel. Presumably, as the leader of a challenger company or party, you would enter such an oligopoly only if you believed that consumers sometimes switched between brands and that you had something different to offer. However, a net volatility measure, such as the Pedersen index, does not allow us to distinguish between these two scenarios.

To more adequately capture the true level of volatility in an electorate, we cannot use aggregate measures of net volatility; instead, we are interested in examining the individual propensity to switch between parties. We therefore measure electoral volatility as the percentage of individuals switching votes from the previous to the current election. We operationalize this as a binary variable, which takes the value 0 when the individual voted for the same party in the current election and the previous election, and takes the value 1 if the individual voted for different parties in the two consecutive elections. The electoral volatility variable ranges from 0 to 100, with higher values indicating higher rates of party switching.[40] In other words, if electoral volatility is at 60 that means that 60 percent of voters opted for a different party compared with the last election, while just 40 percent stayed with the same party. Since we rely on individual-level survey data, we can only capture over-time trends in volatility in countries that have a long tradition of election studies. For data availability reasons, we therefore focus on Denmark, Germany, the Netherlands, Sweden, and the United Kingdom. The results are shown in figure 3.4.[41]

Figure 3.4 clearly shows an increase in party switching, or electoral volatility, across the West European countries. In other words, voters have become more willing to switch between parties. Levels of party switching have remained the most stable in the United Kingdom,[42] perhaps not surprisingly given that the first-past-the-post electoral system makes it most difficult for challengers to enter the system. But even here, we observe an increase in volatility from around 20 percent of the electorate switching between parties in the 1970s to around 30 percent in the 2010 and 2015 elections, although with a slight dip in the latest (2017) election.

In Germany levels of electoral volatility are generally low, but we nonetheless observe a clear rise in volatility in the 1990s, up from around 10–15 percent in the 1980s to around 20 percent of the electorate defecting from their previous party of choice.[43] In the Neth-

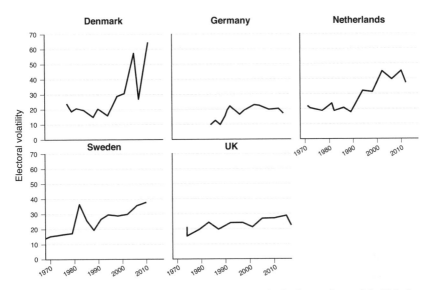

FIGURE 3.4 Party switching in Denmark, Germany, the Netherlands, Sweden, and the United Kingdom (UK)
Source: Danish National Election Studies, German National Election Studies, Dutch National Election Studies, Swedish National Election Studies, and British National Election Studies. See note to main text.

erlands, we observe the rise in electoral volatility much more dramatically, as volatility increases from around 20 percent in the 1970s and 1980s to over 40 percent in the 1990s and beyond. A similar trend is evident in Denmark, where we have some of the highest levels of individual-level electoral volatility to date, with over 50 percent of the electorate switching between parties.[44] This may not seem surprising given the highly fragmented party system. But it is worth noting that whereas the party system in Denmark was fragmented already in 1973 in the infamous "earthquake election"—where the vote for the four established parties fell by more than 30 percentage points—electoral volatility remained relatively low and stable throughout the 1980s and early 1990s at around 20 percent, and only started increasing at a rapid rate in the late 1990s. In contrast, in Sweden we can see that the increase in volatility had already started in the 1980s, where levels rose from a low 10–15 percent in the 1970s to over 30 percent in the 1980s and increased steadily in the 1990s and early 2000s.

Taken together, these graphs show that electoral volatility is not simply a function of changes in demand, but varies greatly across countries, even those where there are similar institutional characteristics. It is worth noting that, with the exception of Denmark, the majority of voters stick with the party that they have previously voted for. However, the willingness to switch is clearly on the rise and this is an important precondition for challenger-party success. To understand this better, let us delve into the issue of barriers to entry for challenger parties in greater depth by comparing elections in Denmark and the United Kingdom over the last half a century.

The Barriers to Entry in Denmark and the United Kingdom

General elections were held in both Denmark and the United Kingdom in 1950. In each country, the dominant center-left party emerged as the largest party, yet struggled to form a stable government. The Danish Social Democrats had won a plurality with 40 percent of both votes and seats. Yet, the two mainstream center-right parties, the liberal Venstre and the Conservatives, formed a minority government. In the United Kingdom, the Labour Party had won 46 percent of the votes, and a slim majority of just five seats. Despite winning a majority, this was seen as a disappointing result compared with 1945, when Labour had achieved a comfortable 146-seat majority. As a consequence, the Labour government called a snap election in 1951 hoping to increase its parliamentary majority. However, despite winning the popular vote, Labour was defeated by the Conservative Party, who won the most seats. This election marked the beginning of the Labour Party's thirteen-year spell in opposition.

There were clear similarities between party competition in Denmark and that in the United Kingdom at the time. Both countries were dominated by the competition between a social democratic party on the left and conservative/liberal parties on the right. In the United Kingdom, these three parties took just shy of 100 percent of the vote and controlled all but three seats in parliament; in Denmark they attracted about 80 percent of the vote and a similar seat share. In both countries, electoral competition was largely one-dimensional, centered on the left–right class divide.[45] In Denmark the urban/rural divide, which had given rise to Venstre, had diminished in significance and given way to the dominance of occupation/class as the primary divide. Similarly, in the United Kingdom class was the main political divide, especially after the introduction of universal franchise, where the Labour Party came to represent the working class and the Conservatives represented the interests of land and business owners. Hence, both party systems in the early 1950s were characterized by one-dimensional left–right competition between the dominant social democrats and conservative/liberal parties.

Fast-forward more than six decades, and these two party systems have evolved very differently. In the 2017 general election in the United Kingdom, a very similar picture emerges to that of 1950, on the surface at least. Again, it was a close election. The governing Conservatives, which had called the election, lost their majority, and had to form a minority government with the support of the small, right-wing Northern Irish party, the Democratic Unionist Party. As in 1950, the two major parties dominated the vote: roughly 82 percent voted for either a Conservative or a Labour candidate, and as many as 87 percent in England. In contrast, the challenger parties performed badly outside their regional strongholds in Scotland, Wales, and Northern Ireland. The vote share of the main challenger party, the populist, Euroskeptic UKIP, had collapsed to below 2 percent, and the party won no seats. The Green Party won a single seat and about 2 percent of the national vote. In contrast, in Denmark in 2015, the three large mainstream parties of the 1950s—the Social Democrats, Liberals and Conservatives—now controlled just shy of half the votes. Challenger parties have grown increasingly powerful in Danish politics, in particular the right-wing, populist Danish People's Party, which emerged as the largest party on the right in the Danish parliament with 21 percent of the vote.

So, while Danish party competition has become highly fragmented and multidimensional, with the emergence of immigration as a salient issue, party competition in England has remained centered on the unidimensional competition between two dominant parties. Why have the two party systems evolved so differently? The simple answer is that the institutional barriers to entry are much higher in the plurality electoral system of the United Kingdom than in the proportional representation system (with a 2 percent threshold) in Denmark. As discussed above, the first-past-the post system makes it very hard for a challenger that does not have regionally concentrated support to break through. In contrast, the proportional representation system, especially with low electoral thresholds and high district magnitudes, is very permissive to political entrepreneurs.

The permissiveness of the Danish electoral system was most clearly illustrated in the election in 1973, dubbed the "earthquake" or "landslide" election. This election led to a permanent fracturing of the Danish party system. Five new parties entered parliament, and more than half the members of the parliament were replaced. The Social Democratic Party, which had led a minority government until this election, lost a third of its seats. The most memorable of the challengers was the populist Progress Party, whose leader Mogens Glistrup campaigned on a platform of radical cuts to income tax and the proposal of replacing the entire Ministry of Defense with a voicemail message saying "we surrender" in Russian. The party became the second largest in parliament, with 28 out of 179 seats. After the election, the leader of the liberal Venstre formed the smallest minority government in Denmark's history, with only 22 seats out of 179. Since 1973, the Danish party system has been characterized by high levels of fragmentation, which has resulted in an uninterrupted series of relatively weak minority governments (with a single exception of a majority coalition) and shifting (formal and informal) coalitions across the political spectrum.

Challengers have also attempted to break through in British politics. Notably in 1981, when four prominent Labour politicians formed the new Social Democratic Party, which threatened to change the nature of British politics from the center. Forming an electoral "Alliance" with the old Liberal Party, it became a powerful electoral force in the 1980s. In 1983, the Alliance garnered about 25 percent of the vote, but less than 4 percent of the seats in the House of Commons. In the same election, the Labour party won only about 2 percent more votes than the Alliance, but gained about 37 percent of the seats. After an attempted breakthrough in 1987 failed when the Alliance mustered only about 23 percent of the vote, it merged instead with the Liberals to become the Liberal Democrats, a party that has continued to be squeezed between the dominant Labour and Conservative parties. The two-party dominance in the United Kingdom cannot be attributed simply to the relative salience of economic left–right issues and class-based politics to British voters, or indeed to the extraordinary strength of partisanship in the United Kingdom. While levels of partisanship are high, they have also been declining for some time.[46] Notably, the electoral landscape is much more fragmented when UK voters elect their representatives under proportional representation in European Parliament elections. In the 2014 European Parliament elections, the populist anti–European Union, anti-immigration UKIP topped the polls with almost 27 percent of the votes and 16 percent of the seats. In contrast, UKIP has never been able to make a real breakthrough into the House of Commons, where candidates are elected using the first-past-the post system. In the next British European Parliament elections in 2019, the newly established Brexit Party—another anti-EU challenger party, led by Nigel Farage—stormed into first place with 30.5 percent of the votes. These second-order European Parliament elections with permissive electoral rules and little at stake for voters thus provide a good platform for challenger parties to increase their visibility nationally and potentially reap electoral success also at the national level.[47]

The British-Danish comparison illustrates the importance of barriers to entry in protecting dominant parties from the rise of challenger parties. Although the "informal" barriers of party attachment are slightly higher in Denmark than in the United Kingdom, the institutional barriers to entry are clearly significant in terms of stifling challenger parties. But the United Kingdom remains a rather exceptional case in the degree to which institutional barriers to entry, notably its electoral system, have protected the position of dominant parties, despite shifting voter demands and innovation by challengers. Even in the face of exceptional political events such as Brexit, the British decision by referendum in 2016 to leave the European Union, challenger parties still face an uphill battle in the United Kingdom, given the forbidding electoral rules.

Conclusion

Are Western European voters devoted partisans who loyally follow their party without seriously considering the alternatives? Or are they increasingly fickle, critical of the dominant party brands and willing to consider other options? Are they dedicated *iSheep* or Amazon customers of convenience? The answers to these questions matter if we want to understand when and why challenger parties are able to break the market dominance of mainstream parties. Voters' attachments to parties remain a significant barrier to entry for newcomers, as significant as formal barriers, such as electoral rules. When voters are attached to a party it can become part of their social identity and inform how they evaluate politics, how they perceive the performance and messages of parties and ultimately how they vote in elections. Partisan voters are generally far more uncritical of their party and less likely to consider alternative options with an open mind. On election day, they are also more likely to turn out and vote for their party.

Traditionally, voters in Western Europe have had strong bonds to their parties, as party members, partisan identifiers, and loyal voters. These bonds remain strong for a majority of voters, as we have seen in this chapter. Over half of voters feel close to a particular party, and an even larger proportion of voters opt to vote for the same party in successive elections. However, there is also evidence that these ties between voters and parties are loosening. Most significant is the steep decline in party membership, although it is important to remember here that only a small proportion of the electorate were ever formal party members. We have also observed a decline in subjective attachments to parties, and an increase in the willingness to switch to another party at election time.

The weakening of party loyalties creates a strategic opportunity for challenger parties who want to break the stable oligopoly of the dominant parties. When voters are less attached to a single party, they can assess the performance of the dominant parties more critically and may be more receptive to the messages of challenger parties, who introduce new and salient issues and challenge the competence and integrity of the dominant parties. However, there are also strategies that parties can employ to remain dominant, as we already discussed in chapter 2. In the next chapter, we will look at some of these strategies by dominant parties, focusing on ideological convergence, issue avoidance, and competence.

4

Strategies of Dominance

The integration potential of the catch-all party rests on a combination of factors whose visible end result is attraction of the maximum number of voters on election day. For that result the catch-all party must have entered into millions of minds as a familiar object fulfilling in politics a role analogous to that of a major brand in the marketing of a universally needed and highly standardized article of mass consumption.

—OTTO KIRCHHEIMER, GERMAN POLITICAL SCIENTIST[1]

At its heart, Coca-Cola is a brand business, and our brands are nothing more than promises. If a good brand is a promise, then a great brand is a promise kept.

—MUHTAR KENT, FORMER CHAIRMAN AND CEO OF COCA-COLA[2]

One of the most recognizable brands in the world is Coca-Cola. For over a century, Coke has been one of the best-known products globally. The essence of Coca-Cola's success is not a specific product, but a brand associated with an experience or a feeling that appeals to everyone. Its incredibly effective branding strategy has focused on getting people to associate its product with ideas of pleasure, relaxation, friends, love, and so on. Coke is about "Tasting that feeling," "Have a Coke and a smile," "Open Happiness," "Enjoy," and "Life tastes good." To develop these marketing strategies, the company uses a customer-based approach to market research—an approach that focuses on consumers' brand knowledge, associations, and attachments, more than the product as such. Coca-Cola has remained dominant in the market partly because of this emphasis on brand over product, and the clear and consistent marketing of a positive and distinctive brand image that has wide appeal.

In the political marketplace, can dominant parties employ similar strategies to secure their long-term electoral success and control of office? Analogous to the Coca-Cola Company, dominant parties can benefit from voters' long-standing attachments to their "brand." But, as we saw in the previous chapter, voters' identification with parties is on the decline. Dominant parties have other tools at their disposal, however. They can employ strategies to make them more appealing to a larger segment of the electorate, and seek to prevent challengers from gaining ground. Dominant parties make use of three main strategies: (1) they seek to appeal to a broad segment of voters while retaining their distinct brand, (2) they ensure that political competition is played on their home turf, and, finally, (3) they highlight their competence and experience in contrast with the newcomers.

The first of the dominant-party strategies is that of *distinctive convergence*, whereby dominant parties take positions closer to the center ground in order to appeal to the tastes of a larger share of the electorate. As early as the 1960s, the German political scientist and jurist Otto Kirchheimer described how parties developed *catchall* strategies to analogous to those of "a major brand in the marketing of a universally needed and highly standardized article of mass consumption."[3] As a consequence of voters feeling less attached to a party by virtue of their social class, geographical location, or religion, parties have needed to appeal more broadly to retain their dominance. They strive to be the Coca-Cola of the political world: an immediately recognizable brand with a broad-based and innocuous appeal to consumers. Yet, they also need to retain a distinct brand that sets them apart from competitors, as Coca-Cola needs to remain distinct from Pepsi Cola. Even as dominant parties converge in a fight for the center ground, each one needs to retain some core element of distinct identity that defines its brand and satisfies core partisan voters.

Secondly, dominant parties seek to keep challengers at bay by controlling the political agenda and *avoiding issues* that may be disadvantageous to them. Dominant parties have risen to power in political systems structured along a left–right dimension, with political programs that focus on the role of state intervention in the economy. Each party's distinctive brand is thus closely associated with the distinct positions that it adopts on left–right issues, and its partisan voters uniting behind that core message. In contrast, challengers will seek to avoid issues associated with the brand of dominant parties. They aim to seek other distinctive issues that may drive a wedge within the membership and voter bases of their dominant competitors. Issue avoidance is an important strategy for dominant parties to try to deter political innovation, as they seek to keep certain policy options off the political market because it serves their strategic interests to do so.

The final strategy concerns the emphasis of dominant parties on their *competence*. To secure the middle ground in competition with very similar parties, they end up offering "valence" policies that emphasize their competence in implementing policies that are widely agreed on by a broader electorate. When competing with challenger parties, dominant parties also highlight their experience in office. They benefit from the "incumbency advantage" of having government experience and the brand value attached to that. The focus is on the well-established brand over the distinctive product.

These strategies and their associated risks are summarized in table 4.1. In combination, the strategies of distinctive convergence, issue avoidance, and competence have kept the old center-right and center-left parties in a dominant position in most of Western Europe for decades. Yet, these strategies are not without risk. As dominant parties converge to the center, there is a real risk that voters perceive them as too similar and feel they lack a genuine alternative. This is

TABLE 4.1 Dominance and Risks

Strategies of Dominance	Strategic Behavior	Risks
Distinctive convergence	Convergence to the center of the left–right dimension, while retaining "left"/"right" profile (no leapfrogging) Grand coalitions between major center-left and center-right parties	Lack of choice between mainstream parties could lead to lower turnout or even defection among voters Lack of "distinctiveness" may lead to a decline in partisan identification
Issue avoidance	Focus on economic left–right issues Avoidance of issues that do not align with the left–right dimension as they can divide supporters and coalition partners	Some issues may be difficult to keep off the agenda, due to demand effects and mobilizing efforts by challengers Dominant parties will lose "first-mover advantage" on such issues
Competence mobilization	Emphasize competence and government experience Campaign on competence	Parties in government are vulnerable to the "cost of governing" Major competence shocks can lead to short- and long-term damage to voters' trust in parties

a particular problem when the mainstream center-left and center-right parties form "grand coalitions," thus leaving dissatisfied voters with little choice but to vote for challengers. Countries where grand coalitions become the norm are a fertile breeding ground for the rise of challenger parties. Similarly, the emphasis on "competence" and "experience" is also a double-edged sword. Mobilizing competence is an asset when times are good, but it will lack credibility when performance is poor and voters want to "throw the rascals out."[4] An even greater threat to the longevity of dominant parties is serious "competence shocks," such as corruption scandals, that undermine any credible claims they might have to being a safe pair of hands. The strategy of issue avoidance also contains inherent risks. By ignoring issues that are salient to many voters, such as immigration, European integration, and environmental issues, dominant parties allow challengers to become "first movers" on these issues. As a result, challengers are often seen as offering more credible positions on these issues, even when dominant parties adapt and begin to engage with these debates.

In the rest of this chapter, we look at how dominant parties have used each of the three strategies outlined above to retain their leading position within party politics, and when and why they have come up short.

Distinctive Convergence

Most dominant parties in Europe today began as mass parties, representing a specific group in society, often a social class. According to the cleavage theory of Lipset and Rokkan that we have discussed in previous chapters,[5] patterns of party competition in postwar Europe are rooted in historical developments that produced enduring lines of conflict that continue to shape political structure, political organization, and the content of political conflict. These cleavages arose out of social structural characteristics, chiefly class, religion, and geographical location, and define European party competition among the major party families (conservative, liberal, Christian democratic, social democratic) to this day. While the urban-rural, center-periphery, and state-church cleavages are important in some party systems, the most salient cleavage is rooted in the classic class struggle between owners and workers, the bourgeoisie and the proletariat. The dominant dimension of competition that has structured party competition has thus been that of left–right ideology, centered on the role of the state in the economy, and stemming from the dominance of class politics in Europe.[6] Historically, voters in Europe have been tied to specific political parties through their social class: working-class voters have traditionally identified with parties on the left, and the business owners and managers with parties on the right.

Over the decades, as the composition of the electorate has changed in nature owing to the expansion of suffrage and the changing nature of the underlying societal cleavages, dominant parties have had to adapt. Simply being a mass party with the support of a single group is rarely sufficient for a party to remain dominant on its own, so parties have had to appeal across group boundaries. The concept of catchall parties developed by Otto Kirchheimer in the mid-1960s describes how dominant parties have adapted to changing social conditions by becoming more centrist in an effort to appeal to ever-wider audiences. Kirchheimer also observed that this a strategy driven by the professional party elite, rather than party members, and that the party organization becomes increasingly professionalized with the clear aim of retaining a broad electoral appeal and competing for office. As Kirchheimer noted, "abandoning attempts at the intellectual and moral encadrement of the masses, [the modern party] is turning more fully to the electoral scene, trying to exchange effectiveness in depth for a wider audience and more immediate electoral success."[7] In other words, the mass parties have toned down their advocacy for specific groups in favor of pursuing wider electoral support. Two decades later, the Italian political scientist Angelo Panebianco coined the phrase "electoral-professional party" to describe how mainstream parties had turned to professionals, such as pollsters and public-relations managers, to help adjust their image to make it appeal to more voters.[8]

Examples of this strategy of distinctive convergence adopted by the dominant parties are provided by the big traditional party families in Europe. The social and the Christian democrats both seek to appeal to the electorate on the basis of their experience in government and the fact that as *Volksparteien* (people's parties) they represent the "median voter," yet at the same time they seek to pitch themselves as left or right of center, respectively, to maintain their distinct constituencies. Dominant parties are like the McDonald's and Burger King of the political world: accessible and appealing to a broad range of consumers. McDonald's serves 70 million people per day and holds 80 percent of the market in the fast-food burger category. Burger King is its nearest rival, with around 11 million customers per day. Both fast-food restaurants sell burgers, but they also have distinct brands. Loyal customers of Burger King will insist that its burgers are better than those McDonald's serves. What they have in common is that both companies are clearly catering to broad-based tastes and are aiming to attract a sizeable share of the market, rather than offering the niche appeal of, say, a strictly Kosher restaurant or a vegan burger chain. In their product development, they seek to appeal to the tastes of the average consumer at a price accessible to the vast majority of people, and they deliver a consistent and reliable product. It is therefore not surprising that McDonald's is the largest restaurant chain in the world, measured by market capitalization, with Burger King also featuring in the top 10.[9]

Just as fast-food restaurants seek to capture the largest possible market share by appealing to a wide range of consumers, dominant parties try to design a policy bundle that is attractive to a majority of citizens. Assuming for a moment that political competition takes place on a single left–right dimension, this means that it is in the interest of political parties to place themselves as close to the center as possible to attract as many voters as possible. Parties with extremist positions are very unlikely to gain a large vote share. As the American economist Anthony Downs has argued, we expect parties to converge on the median voter, at least in two-party systems, as parties tries to attract voters in the center: "in the middle of the scale where most voters are massed, each party scatters its policies on both sides of the mid-point. It attempts to make each voter in this area feel that it is centered right at this position. Naturally, this causes an enormous overlapping of moderate policies."[10]

Building on this classical notion, we also anticipate such convergence among dominant parties on the left–right dimension in our model of party competition. Importantly, however, parties must also ensure they retain some distinctiveness; or, as Kirchheimer put it, "there is a need for enough brand differentiation to make the article plainly recognizable, but the degree of differentiation must never be so great as to make the potential customer fear he will be out on a limb."[11] Loyal party members need to be able to recognize their party as distinct from its main competitor. Hence, we would rarely see "leapfrogging" on the left–right dimension, where for example, a social democratic party adopts a position more right wing than its conservative rivals', or vice versa, as that would muddle the party brands. We thus expect that the dominant parties of the center right and the dominant parties of the center left will converge on the center of the left–right political space to protect their dominant positions, yet each will remain on its "side of the aisle" on the left or the right to retain some distinctiveness.

We can examine this proposition empirically by plotting the left–right positions of parties in their election manifestos. Party manifestos provide an invaluable source for comparing the policy positions of parties over time and across countries, as all parties produce manifestos ahead of parliamentary elections. The Comparative Manifesto Project, MARPOR,[12] has produced widely used measures of party positions by hand coding policy estimations of party manifestos, including left–right-position estimates of the main political parties in a wide range of democracies going back to the Second World War.[13] The left–right position is calculated by taking the difference between the sums (percentages) of the references of the issues associated with the right (e.g. free enterprise, pro-military, social services limitation, law and order) and those associated with the left (e.g. regulating markets, antimilitarism, expansion of social services, nationalization).[14] The resulting left–right scale runs from extreme left (−100) to extreme right (+100). In figure 4.1 we plot the left–right positions of the dominant parties of the center left and the center right in 11 Western European countries in the postwar period.

Figure 4.1 demonstrates that, as a rule of thumb, the dominant parties of the left and the right are clustered around the center ground of the left–right spectrum, as expected. There are exceptions with periods of greater polarization, such as Denmark in the 1980s and 1990s, Greece until the mid-1990s, Britain in the 1980s and early 1990s, and the Netherlands in the 1970s. However, the more common pattern is one where the dominant parties of the left and the right both adopt positions very close to the center. Indeed, sometimes the parties are so close that they are barely indistinguishable. Yet, interestingly, we observe almost no "leapfrogging." This is again in line with our expectation of the distinctive convergence strategy adopted by the dominant parties: they seek to appeal to the center ground, while retaining their distinct "left" and "right" brands.

This strategy of distinctive convergence should ensure that dominant parties are able to capture the vast majority of voters, as long

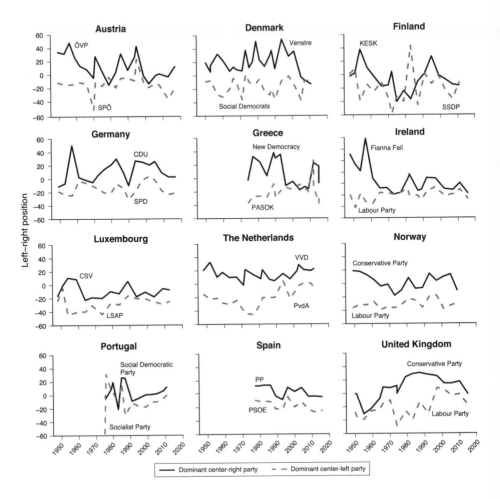

FIGURE 4.1 Convergence among the dominant left and right parties
Source: Authors' own calculations based on MARPOR data (Volkens et al., Manifesto Data Collection)

as we assume that most voters are not located on the ideological extremes. We thus expect voters to perceive the dominant parties as "moderate" in the policy bundles that they offer. To examine whether this is the case, we can take advantage of national election studies that ask voters to place parties on an ideological left–right scale, ranging from 0 on the extreme left to 10 on the extreme right, with 5 as the most centrist position. Unfortunately, not all national election studies include such questions consistently over time, so figure 4.2 plots voter perceptions of party positions in four countries

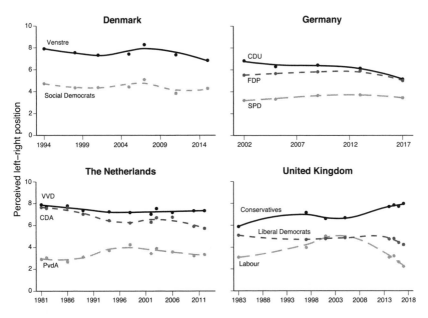

FIGURE 4.2 Voter perceptions of party positions
Source: Authors' own calculations based on national election study data capturing voters'
placement of parties on a left–right scale (see national election study sources cited in note
relating to figure 3.4)

where the data are available: Denmark, Germany, the Netherlands,
and the United Kingdom.

The first thing one notices looking at figure 4.2 is that voters'
perceptions of parties are very stable over time. Even when parties
seek to moderate their policy offers, as shown in figure 4.1, voters
are relatively slow to update their perceptions.[15] The United Kingdom
is an interesting case, since voters clearly perceived the parties converging in the early 1990s, after Labour Party leaders John Smith
and then Tony Blair deliberately moved the party in a more centrist
direction. This convergence is most pronounced around the 1997
general election, when Labour came to power after 18 years in opposition. At this point voters perceived only a 1-point difference
between the two major parties on the 11-point scale. This perception
changes again after Tony Blair stepped down in 2007, where voters
begin to see the dominant parties as polarizing. The convergence in
the 1990s is clearly mirrored in the manifesto data in figure 4.1. It is

also noteworthy that voters generally perceive the dominant parties as quite centrist, located between 3 and 8, rather than on the extremes, yet also clearly distinct from one another. While Dutch and German voters tend to locate the liberal and conservative/Christian democratic parties closely together, they clearly perceive them as distinct from the social democratic parties on the left. Both the manifesto and the voter data indicate that dominant parties have adopted a strategy of distinctive convergence—appealing to the center ground while remaining consistently on the "left" or on the "right."

Another clear indication that dominant parties are willing to converge ideologically in order to appeal to voters and, importantly, to hold on to power is the high frequency of so-called "grand coalitions" in European politics. Grand coalitions occur when the dominant party of the left and the dominant party of the right form a government together, sometimes with other coalition partners.[16] Grand coalitions demonstrate that dominant parties are prepared to have overlapping moderate policies, and suggest to voters they are willing to compromise on core positions to stay in power. In figure 4.3, we plot the percentage of grand coalitions in any year in Western Europe in the postwar period. The figure shows that grand coalitions account for between 5 and 40 percent of all West European governments in any given year, with more grand coalitions in the last decade. In Austria, Belgium, Finland, Germany, the Netherlands, and Switzerland grand coalitions are particularly common, while some countries have never been ruled by a grand coalition.

While the strategy of distinct convergence appears to have been successful, judging by the dominance of the mainstream center-left and center-right parties in postwar West European politics, there are inherent risks associated with this strategy. If convergence among dominant parties leads voters to see elections as a choice between Tweedledum and Tweedledee, they may have little incentive to vote at all, since there is little to choose between the parties. Indeed, average turnout for national parliamentary and European parliamentary elections in Western Europe has declined since the early to mid-1990s,[17] including in countries with converging parties and grand coalitions, such as Austria, Germany, the Netherlands, Por-

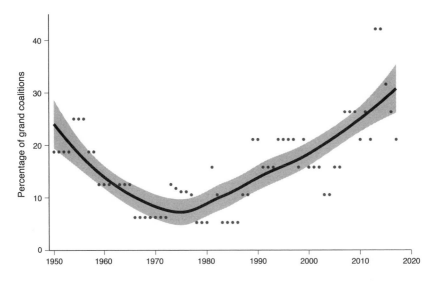

FIGURE 4.3 Grand coalitions in Western Europe, 1950–2017
Source: Authors' own calculations based on ParlGov data

tugal, and Switzerland. Moreover, such "indistinct" convergence of dominant parties may also lead voters to consider alternative options on the political extremes. Studies have shown that grand coalitions tend to facilitate electoral support for far-right parties, because voters feel there is a lack of political alternatives. Moreover, supporters of the mainstream right may become alienated if they do not see their preferred policies being enacted and do not enjoy seeing their party play the role of principled opposition.[18] Also, the strategic advantage of distinctive convergence rests on the assumption that most voters hold moderate preferences on the left–right dimension, rather than more extreme views. As we discuss at greater length in chapter 5, challenger parties can be effective at mobilizing new issue dimensions and appealing to voters on these issues.

Issue Avoidance

As we have established, dominant parties seek to appeal to a wide variety of voter tastes at the same time as trying to give their loyal support base a distinctive "brand" on the right or left in politics.

When issues emerge that do not fit this neat dichotomy, dominant parties may seek to avoid or obscure them. As the dominant axis of competition the left–right dimension acts as the focal point for parties and coalition formation, and it is an important heuristic for voters and party activists when they decide which party best serves their interests.[19] Left-wing parties' "distinctiveness" lies in their appeal to state intervention in the free market, a strong welfare state, and redistribution. Such policy bundles will unite their supporters, ranging from the low-skilled working class, benefitting from labor market protection and redistribution, to highly skilled public sector professionals, who are dependent on a well-funded public sector. Similarly, the right-wing brand of the unregulated market and low taxes will appeal to both small business owners and wealthy private sector professionals. Hence, while dominant parties offer moderate positions appealing to the center ground, their distinctive appeal often lies in policies that align with their left- or right-wing brand, and thus satisfy their partisan followers. As Anthony Downs noted, "each party will sprinkle these moderate policies with a few extreme strands in order to please its far-out voters. Obviously, each party is trying to please an extreme opposite to that being pleased by the other party."[20]

However, some issues cannot easily be integrated into a left–right party brand. Such issues will tend to irk some supporters while appealing to others. In such cases, converging on the center ground is no longer the optimal strategy, because politics has ceased to be unidimensional and there is no one position that will appeal to a majority of voters. For challenger parties, such issues are "high appropriability" issues that can be mobilized to enhance their electoral appeal, as we discuss in the next chapter. Dominant parties instead adopt the strategy of *issue avoidance*, aiming to keep such issues off the agenda. They can do so through a strategy of ambiguity that blurs their position or downplays the issues' importance.[21]

One example of an issue that dominant parties have largely tried to avoid or downplay is that of European integration. As the power of the European Union's supranational institutions has increased and the scope of EU jurisdictional authority has widened, European integration has become ever more contested within domestic politics, and this has led to tensions within parties on both the left and the right. Conservative and right-wing liberal parties, such as the British Conservatives and Dutch People's Party for Freedom and Democracy, tend to favor market integration in Europe, but oppose the transfer of authority to supranational actors in other policy areas. For the Dutch Liberals, these internal divisions prompted Geert Wilders's successful split from the People's Party for Freedom and Democracy to create a challenger party, the Party for Freedom. The issue of European integration has been equally divisive for parties of the left. For socialist parties, economic integration in Europe is often seen to jeopardize national socialist achievements by facilitating international free trade. At the same time, however, further political integration in Europe offers an opportunity to regulate labor markets and advance social equality and to introduce what Margaret Thatcher once called "socialism creeping through the back door."[22] The lack of fit has resulted in unusual patterns of party competition in a number of countries, where parties on both the left and right extremes advocate an anti-Europe position, while centrist parties are predominantly pro-European.[23]

Another increasingly salient issue that cannot easily be subsumed by the dominant left–right dimension is immigration. Parties on the left are frequently torn between the preferences of their traditional working-class base, which are often wary of immigration, and the better educated middle-class partisans who favor liberal immigration policies.[24] An example of this can be found in Denmark, where the Social Liberals are on the right of the Social Democrats on the left–right dimension, but advocate less restrictive immigration policies.[25] In other party systems, this "lack of fit" may be less obvious in party competition since mainstream parties will seek to avoid mobilizing issues that have the potential to drive a wedge between factions in their party or between parties in a coalition. This does not alter the fact, however, that the immigration issue cannot easily be subsumed into the left–right dimension. This is further reflected by a recent trend that West European radical right parties like the Danish People's Party, the Dutch Freedom Party, or the French National Rally

have started to combine right-wing immigration positions with welfare chauvinism, advocating that welfare-state benefits should be
restricted to certain groups.[26]

In contrast, dominant parties have an incentive to keep such issues off the political agenda, to avoid creating divisions within their
membership and voter base. Issue avoidance is an important strategy
for deterring political innovation. One way in which dominant parties seek to control the political agenda is by emphasizing the issues
where they have a competitive advantage—namely, left–right economic issues. We can look at this empirically, by using data from the
Chapel Hill Expert Survey (CHES). CHES asks local party experts
to estimate party positioning on European integration, ideology,
and policy issues for national parties in a variety of European countries. The first survey was conducted in 1999, with subsequent waves
in 2002, 2006, 2010, 2014, and 2017 in 14 Western European countries. In the 2014 survey, experts were asked to rate the "relative
salience of economic issues in the party's public stance" on a scale
from 0 to 10, where 10 was "great importance." Figure 4.4 shows that
while all types of parties attach considerable importance to economic

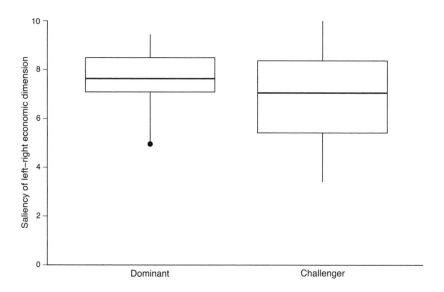

FIGURE 4.4 Emphasis on the left–right economic dimension
Source: Authors' own calculations based on CHES 2014

issues, this is significantly higher for dominant parties (7.6 compared with 6.9 for challengers). The figure also shows much lower variance among dominant parties—in other words, almost all dominant parties attached considerable importance to economic issues, while some challenger parties emphasize them far less.

Controlling the political marketplace is not always easy, and particularly not when there is a demand for policies on new issues and when challenger parties seek to mobilize such issues, as we will show in chapters 5 and 7.

Competence

So far, we have focused on the policy strategies that dominant parties can adopt. But dominant parties also have a strategic advantage that is not directly linked to their policy offering, but rather to their experience in office and the benefits that brings to their "brand." As Otto Kirchheimer noted, "the catch-all party that has resided over the fortunes of a country for some time, and whose leaders the voter has therefore come to know on his television set and in his newspaper columns, enjoys a great advantage."[27] Like Coca-Cola or McDonald's, dominant parties are well-known brands and voters feel they can count on them for reliable and consistent product delivery whilst in government. When a person is feeling hungry and goes to McDonald's, she knows that she will get a burger quickly that will fill her up and taste similar to other McDonald's burgers she has tasted in the past. On the other hand, if she chooses her local deli instead, she is much less certain about what she will get and how fast it will be delivered.

Dominant parties thus often have a *competence advantage* that they can use to their benefit. Also, to secure this middle ground, the parties end up offering valence politics to the electorate, wherein they all agree on the ends, such as the need to improve public services, and differ only on the means of achieving them. Competence is about voters' evaluation of policy management, trust, delivery, and competence, and hence much less about the product itself, and more about trusting the brand to deliver. Political scientists often contrast "valence issues" with "positional issues." Whereas positional issues involve ideological competition—for example, between a left-wing view and a right-wing view—valence issues are those about which a broad consensus exists and where the question thus becomes "which party is best to deliver?" American political scientist Donald Stokes defined valence issues as "those that merely involve the linking of the parties with some condition that is positively or negatively valued by the electorate," whilst position issues are those on which a set of alternatives exist "over which a distribution of voter preferences is defined."[28]

When parties have converged ideologically, we would expect that valence issues matter more.[29] In other words, voters will care more about who is the most competent manager of the economy, of social welfare provision, education, and so on when there is little difference between parties' policy positions on these issues. As social democratic parties have abandoned their radically different visions of how to manage the capitalist economy, they focus instead on their ability to "improve public services" and their commitment to "reduce unemployment." Similarly, the center-right parties have softened their laissez-faire economic stance in favor of arguments about more-prudent management of the economy. In their theory of "cartel parties," the American and Irish political scientists Richard Katz and Peter Mair anticipated that the reduced ideological distinctiveness of parties would cause a shift from policy-based competition to competition on valence factors such as leader personality and party image.[30] According to these authors, dominant parties have a common interest in colluding as a cartel and focusing mainly on efficient and effective management, rather than ideological competition. An optimal strategy by dominant parties is thus to focus on their *competence*.

Competence is about the degree to which parties are trusted to govern and deliver policies. It thus makes sense that dominant parties have incentives to prime competence, as this should benefit them electorally. Dominant parties are the best-known brands in the political marketplace. They have a high profile with voters and a track record of serving in government and delivering policies. As a consequence, voters should be more likely to associate the dominant-party brands with competence and trust them to govern in the future, rather than the maverick challenger parties without a record.

Indeed, there is evidence to suggest that voters generally favor the incumbent party or candidate over the challenger. This so-called "incumbency advantage" refers to the extent to which incumbent candidates perform better in elections *because* they are incumbents. The incumbency advantage is well established in both US and West European elections, and a substantial body of research has developed to help explain why it exists.[31] Some explanations focus on the institutional benefits of incumbency—for example, arguing that it is easier for incumbents to raise funds or that the electoral institutions work in their favor. Others have focused on the familiarity of incumbents: both parties and politicians in office are better known than those in opposition.[32] Finally, incumbents may also perform better because of their superior quality. That is, incumbents may perform well in elections partly because they are good and trustworthy candidates who match the preferences of the electorate. Certainly, the crucial aspect of the incumbency advantage is that voters generally *perceive* parties and candidates in office as more competent. When a party enters office, voters have the chance to observe its politicians' qualities as policy makers and this will generally strengthen a dominant party's brand.

We can look at perceived party competence by using survey data about which party citizens think is best at "handling" the most important issue facing the nation. Unfortunately, such issue competence questions are not asked regularly in most cross-national surveys. However, British and German election studies both contain these questions, and figure 4.5 plots party competence since 2000.[33] The vertical axis shows the share of respondents who think that dominant or challenger parties are best at handling the most important issue facing the nation. The question is the same across both countries and the party groupings are kept constant over time. Hence, only Labour and the Conservatives are classified as the main dominant parties in the United Kingdom, and the Christian Democrats and Social Democrats in Germany.

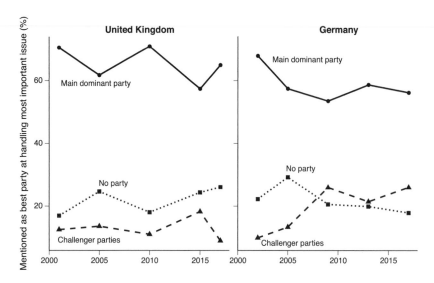

FIGURE 4.5 Voter perception of party competence
Source: Authors' own calculations based on British Election Studies and German Election Studies (sources listed in note relating to figure in main text)

Figure 4.5 clearly shows that the dominant parties are generally perceived as far more competent than challenger parties. This is not surprising given that more voters are also partisans of those parties. However, it does indicate a clear competence advantage. There is also no sign of a massive downward shift during the last decade. But in Germany, in particular, we see that around a quarter of voters now perceive challenger parties as the most competent in handling the issue that they see as the most important, compared to only 10 percent in 2002.

Emphasizing competence is thus one of the strategies that dominant parties can employ to retain their electoral appeal. However, it is not without risk. While incumbents generally outperform challengers in elections, there can also be a "cost of governing" when a party remains in office for a long time.[34] After a honeymoon period when a party takes over, there is usually a decline in popularity. Some of this may simply be a return to normal after a strong election performance as weak supporters abandon the party, but another reason is that the governing party is held to account for any adverse economic and political events during its time in office. It has further been suggested that there is a certain "grievance asymmetry" as governments are more likely to be punished for adverse events than they are to be rewarded for positive ones. When a party first enters office, it is possible to pin the blame on the outgoing party. However, after a second or third term in office it becomes much more difficult to blame others for any poor performance or downturns.

The cost of governing may not, however, benefit challenger parties directly, but rather the rival dominant party currently in opposition. In periods where dominant parties are able to successfully retain their control over the party system (using the strategies discussed here) we are likely to observe cyclical alternations of power between them, as the governing party experiences a gradual decline in popularity over its time in office and is beaten at the ballot box by another dominant party, and so on. But sometimes we can observe more dramatic "competence shocks," either to a party or to the system as a whole, which can transform the party competition more permanently. British political scientists Jane Green and Will Jennings argue that parties' issue competence can be altered in a more lasting manner either because of a major performance shock or a major symbolic policy change. Examples include the British Conservatives' loss of perceived competence on the economy around the time of the oil price crisis and the three-day week in 1973, while the British Labour Party lost its competence advantage on labor and employment during a period of industrial disputes and miners' strikes in the 1980s. These competence shocks meant that the issue ownership previously associated with one dominant party was negatively affected— the Conservatives on the economy/Labour on unemployment—giving the other dominant party an advantage on that issue.

Some competence shocks lead to even more radical and long-lasting changes to the party system as a whole. An example of this is the nationwide judicial investigation into endemic political corruption in Italy held in the 1990s, which led to the demise of the so-called "First Republic." During Italy's First Republic, from 1946 to 1994, politics had been characterized by frequent government turnover—61 governments in total—yet also the dominance of the center-right Christian Democratic Party, which was in government for most of the time, keeping the main opposition, the Italian Communist Party, out of power. However, this equilibrium of stable yet polarized politics ended in the early 1990s when a judicial investigation revealed the widespread nature of political and administrative corruption in Italy. The "Clean Hands" (*mani pulite*) judicial inquiry began in Milan in February 1992 with the arrest of Mario Chiesa, an Italian socialist politician. The investigations subsequently expanded to the entire country, and over the next couple of years, six former prime ministers, more than five hundred members of parliament, and several thousand local and public administrators were caught up in the investigations. The scandal led to a dramatic crisis of faith in the political system: in a few months, most leading political figures had been forced to resign or go into exile, and the major parties disappeared or underwent radical transformation. The previously dominant parties never regained their strength in Italy, and since then Italian party politics has been characterized by a high degree of volatility and the rise (and fall) of challenger parties.

While the Italian case is extreme, we have witnessed other competence shocks in recent European history, such as the Bárcenas scandal in Spain, involving corruption in the then-incumbent party, the Popular Party. The scandal uncovered widespread corruption, mainly the misappropriation of funds by many high-ranking politicians in the Popular Party, including the previous prime ministers Mariano Rajoy and José María Aznar. On January 31, 2013, internal party documents handwritten by the party treasurer, Luis Bárcenas, were leaked to the most widely circulated Spanish newspaper, *El País*. The documents, referred to as the Bárcenas papers (*los papeles de Bárcenas*), revealed a parallel bookkeeping system involving undeclared and illegal cash donations to Swiss bank accounts that was operated by the party for 18 years (1980–2009). The revelations involved many high-ranking Popular Party officials and sparked off a series of court cases.[35] The former treasurer Luis Bárcenas was sentenced to jail time, several other high-ranking party officials admitted to wrongdoing, and the Popular Party was condemned for using misappropriated funds to renovate its party headquarters.[36] The scandal also left its mark on Spanish politics. The second government of Mariano Rajoy, comprising Popular Party members, was forced out of office by a motion of no confidence initiated by the leader of the Socialist Party Pedro Sánchez on June 7, 2018. This was the first successful motion of no confidence against a sitting government since the Spanish transition to democracy in 1978.[37] Moreover, the scandal galvanized the electoral support for two new challenger parties, the left-wing Podemos (We can) and right-wing Ciudadanos (Citizens), and helped transform Spain from a two- to a four-party system.[38] Since then Spain has also witnessed the electoral breakthrough of a far-right challenger party, VOX, in the 2018 regional elections in Andalucía and subsequent national elections.[39]

Major competence shocks, even when they are not on the scale of those we witnessed in Italy and Spain, also provide an opportunity for challenger parties to contest the "competence advantage" of dominant parties and their brand equity more generally. It is therefore not surprising that we have an upward surge in the popularity of challenger parties in the aftermath of the financial crisis and the Great Recession in Europe, as shown in chapter 1. This included the emergence of successful new parties, such as the Alternative for Germany, the Five Star Movement (Italy) and Podemos (Spain), the surge in support for the established radical right parties across northern Europe, and, notably, the formation of a coalition government in Greece in 2015 comprising two challenger parties—the left-wing Syriza and right-wing Independent Greeks. The crisis not only caused economic hardship, but also cast doubt on the competence of the dominant political parties. Many voters have reacted to this by turning their backs on the traditional parties and opting instead for new, or reinvigorated, challenger parties that reject the mainstream consensus of austerity and European integration.[40]

One of the common denominators of the challenger parties that increased their electoral appeal during the economic crisis was their antiestablishment rhetoric. In other words, challenger parties confront dominant parties not only by introducing new issues, but by questioning their brand value more generally. By employing antiestablishment rhetoric, challenger parties seek to attack the value of the dominant party "brand" as a whole, rather than its specific policy offering (see also chapter 6). The competence advantage of incumbents gives challenger parties the incentive to seek to close the competence gap, as they have more to gain from focusing on valence in their rhetoric. Also, parties that have been in office can more readily be blamed for the problems and grievances of ordinary voters, and it is easier to paint them as dishonest or corrupt than parties that have never held office. Antiestablishment political rhetoric is thus an effective way for challenger parties to chip away at the market power of dominant parties and damage the public perception of their integrity and competence to serve the interests of the people they are meant to serve. Such a strategy is obviously more likely to succeed if voters already harbor doubts about the ability of dominant parties to deliver on their promises, and if voter attachments to such parties have already weakened, as we have seen in the previous chapter. Indeed, recent evidence from Italy suggests that voters who were eligible to vote for the first time in the 1994 parliamentary elections, held after the "Clean Hands" scandal, when widespread political corruption was uncovered, are much more receptive to the antiestablishment message of the Five Star Movement and the League and more likely to vote for them.[41]

In chapter 6, we will analyze the differences between the antiestablishment rhetoric of challengers and that of dominant parties more systematically using advanced quantitative text analysis. To illustrate the stark differences here, figure 4.6 plots the answers from the CHES expert survey on the "salience of anti-elite rhetoric" by party type on a 0 to 10 scale. The figure clearly shows that such rhetoric is far more important for challenger parties than for dominant parties.

Conclusion

Market power is not static; it is under constant threat. Not all political parties can match Coca-Cola's feat and remain the industry leader for over a century. Dominant parties have several tools at their disposal, however, to remain popular with voters: they can seek to appeal to the middle ground while retaining their distinct brand,

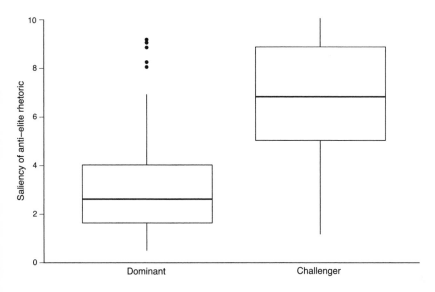

FIGURE 4.6 Antiestablishment rhetoric by dominant and challenger parties
Source: Authors' own calculations based on CHES 2014 (Polk et al., "Explaining the Salience of Anti-elitism.")

they can try to control the scope of political debate, and, finally, they can highlight their competence and experience. In this chapter, we have shown that dominant parties are likely to employ all of these strategies: they have converged ideologically, yet remained distinctly "left" or "right"; they continue to emphasize economic left–right issues more than other parties and more than other issues; and they are perceived to be more competent than challengers on key issues that voters care about.

Given these strategic powers available to dominant parties, how does their market power wane? As we showed in chapter 1, the major party families have remained surprisingly stable in their electoral success despite the radical changes to their underlying electoral base. Yet, there are now fundamental threats to their continued dominance. These threats are in part due to the weaknesses of the strategies of dominance discussed here. Ideological convergence may allow parties to capture the center ground, yet it is also risky if the major alternatives become so similar that voters become apathetic and feel there is no real choice. Similarly, it is difficult to continue to avoid emphasizing issues that voters start to care greatly about because of real-world changes or shocks. And challenger parties can gain a first-mover advantage by mobilizing such issues first (see next chapter). But these challenges may not lead to the death of dominant parties—unless they are accompanied by major competence shocks that lead voters to lose faith in the ability of the dominant parties to govern and deliver policies. When such shocks are severe, as we saw in Italy, there may be no coming back for dominant parties, and the party system will go through a process of reestablishing itself, often after a period of turmoil, and the erstwhile challengers may become the new dominant parties. In the next chapter, we discuss the strategies employed by challenger parties to exploit the weaknesses of dominant parties and gain market share.

PART III

Innovation

5

Issue Entrepreneurship

For all parties will of course, at any given time, provide themselves with a stock of principles or planks and these principles or planks may be as characteristic of the party that adopts them and as important for its success as the brands of goods a department store sells are characteristic of it and important for its success.

—JOSEPH A. SCHUMPETER, AUSTRIAN ECONOMIST[1]

Whatever you do, be different. I can't think of better advice for an entrepreneur. If you are different, you will stand out.

—ANITA RODDICK, FOUNDER AND CEO OF THE BODY SHOP[2]

In the late 1950s, Leonard Lord, the head of the British Motor Corporation, developed an idea that would revolutionize the automobile market: the design of a small, high-performing yet relatively spacious car. After the sales of large cars slumped and petrol was rationed because of fuel shortages hitting the United Kingdom at the time of the 1956 Suez Crisis, Lord laid down some basic design requirements for a very small car. A team working around designer Alec Issigonis took up the challenge, and designed a miniature car called the Mini.

The Mini would become one of the most iconic and popular cars in history. Its space-saving transverse engine combined with front-wheel drive not only allowed 80 percent of the car's volume to be used for passengers and baggage, it also allowed for a top speed of 75 miles per hour (120 kph), which was much faster than other economy cars at the time.[3] Virtually all cars developed since then have used a similar engine configuration. Since the late 1950s millions of Minis have been sold, and the car remains popular to this day. In 2017 alone almost 400,000 vehicles were sold worldwide.[4] The innovation of the Mini would inspire a generation of carmakers.

The technical and design innovation of the Mini is an example of what Joseph Schumpeter called "creative destruction."[5] The term refers to product and process innovation by which new products challenge and eventually replace existing ones. Schumpeter identifies innovation as the key dimension of economic change. It is the driving force of product markets. In order to compete, the players in the market need to differentiate themselves from their competitors by producing ever more innovative products. Innovation comes in different shapes and sizes. Consumers can be swayed to buy a completely new product (a tablet versus a laptop) or a better version of an existing product (a Mini versus a traditional car). The degree to which the market will change depends on the interplay between the innovation introduced by disruptive entrepreneurs and the strategies of dominant market players aiming to protect their market dominance. In this book we have translated these Schumpeterian insights and adapted them to the political market place. Innovation and dominance are also the crucial building blocks for understanding change in the political market. They determine the changing electoral fates of political parties.

As we highlighted in chapter 2, innovation in the political market involves two aspects: a *policy* and a *rhetorical* aspect. While the policy aspect of innovation refers to the mobilization of high appropriability issues, the rhetorical aspect refers to the devaluation of dominant rivals through antiestablishment rhetoric. In this chapter, our focus is on the policy aspect of innovation, which we label *issue entrepreneurship.*[6]

Issue Entrepreneurship

Complex societies produce a multitude of diverse conflicts over public policy. American political scientist Elmer E. Schattschneider has suggested that "the game of politics depends on which of these conflicts gains the dominant position."[7] Political parties play a pivotal role in shaping political conflict. An important way in which they do so is by highlighting certain issues while downplaying others. Experts on European politics suggest that competition over specific issues has become more important in Western Europe in recent decades because party competition is less structured along societal cleavages, such as religion or class, than it once was.[8] Also, in chapter 3 we demonstrated that traditional voter ties to dominant parties have weakened in Western Europe over the past decades. All this raises the question of why certain parties choose to emphasize particular issues while ignoring others.

The prevailing consensus among political scientists has been that parties mobilize policy issues that might benefit them while ignoring issues that may benefit their competitors, and selectively emphasize those issues on which they hold a competency advantage, while ignoring issues on which they do not.[9] The question then becomes: Which types of parties raise which types of issues? Danish political scientists Christoffer Green-Pedersen and Peter Bjerre Mortensen argue that it is important to distinguish between government and opposition parties in this respect. They suggest that government parties are unable to emphasize only those issues that benefit them, but also have to respond to issues that are important within the larger political debate—the so-called "party system agenda," which refers to a hierarchy of issues to which political parties must pay attention even as they compete about the future content of this hierarchy.[10] This begs the question of how issues become part of the party system agenda in the first place. Green-Pedersen and Mortensen argue that opposition parties are less responsive to the party system agenda because they are able to focus more on issues that are beneficial to themselves.[11] Work by American political scientist Bonnie Meguid suggests that important differences also exist between niche and mainstream parties when it comes to issue mobilization.[12] Niche parties—like green or regional parties— promote a single, or niche, issue or narrow range of issues, and are largely unresponsive to the issue agendas of other parties. She goes on to suggest that the responses by mainstream parties to the issue mobilization of niche parties has important implications for their electoral success. Mainstream parties are more likely to respond—that is, engage with issues of niche parties—when niche parties are perceived to be an electoral threat.[13]

These contributions help us to understand why certain parties choose to mobilize certain issues. They also suggest that specific party attributes matter: being in government or not, or being a niche or mainstream party. Yet, they provide far less guidance on the criteria we might use to determine *ex ante* which issues will be mobilized by which parties and to what strategic end. We attempt to shed light on these questions by building on insights from the literature on industrial organization from the study of economics.

The strategy used by political parties to mobilize new or previously ignored issues is what we coin *issue entrepreneurship*.[14] Political parties, like firms, have strong incentives to differentiate themselves from their rivals. One way of doing so is through mobilizing policy issues that other parties ignore because these issues would expose them to risk, such as possible rifts within the party or government coalition. While we conceive issue entrepreneurship to be similar to product innovation, there is a notable difference in scope. The overall scope for policy innovation may be somewhat more limited in the political marketplace, compared with the economic market. This is because firms can innovate in order to try to satisfy the needs and wants of customers through diversifying their product in specific ways that political parties cannot. For example, firms can introduce products of varying qualities through different brand extensions at different price levels. Think about a car company that introduces a cheaper yet smaller car, or a lower quality brand of cars under a different name. Political parties are much more limited in this respect. They cannot introduce a cheaper version of the same policy. Nor can they credibly commit to being both in favor of and against a policy at the same time. They can perhaps only aim to blur their position, although that is a strategy that may not always pay off electorally.[15]

Despite these differences, we expect the underlying logic of political innovation to mimic that of product innovation: it needs to be cost-effective. Market players will only engage in innovation when the potential benefits of doing so outweigh the costs. The costs of innovation on the product market relate primarily to research and development. Research and development involves the research efforts undertaken by a company to find solutions to problems with existing products or processes, or to create new products and services.[16] The technological and design efforts involved in the development of the Mini car mentioned earlier are an example of the importance of research and development, and allowed the British Motor Corporation to find new areas of opportunistic growth. More current examples of research and development include the continuing investments made by technology companies like Facebook or Google in the areas of artificial intelligence and virtual reality. Innovation is not only about investing resources; it is also about creating new ideas and technologies, which can be difficult for many established companies to compete with. Established companies have an existing brand to protect, so may be less flexible, and sometimes find the most effective approach for them is to buy up an innovative start-up company either so they can adopt an innovative technology to serve as their own or to remove a competitor in the market, or both. An example of innovation through mergers and acquisitions is Facebook deciding to buy the virtual-reality start-up Oculus in 2014. According to Hussam Hamadeh, the founder of the private-company market analyst PrivCo, "as soon as buyers like Facebook and Twitter see any traction from a new app or piece of software, they buy it and then kill it. It has become easier than trying to compete with something totally new."[17]

Far-reaching innovation is not a strategy that can easily be pursued by dominant players on the political market and is predominantly the domain of disruptive entrepreneurs, not dominant parties. This is because, beside potential electoral gains, issue entrepreneurship also carries potential risks.[18] The mobilization of a new or previously ignored policy issue could destabilize parties internally, put off some voters, and even jeopardize future coalition negotiations. Think of the mobilization of the immigration issue by right-wing challenger parties, and the difficulties it posed for many social democratic and conservative parties, for example.[19] Shifting the issue agenda is a risky decision, potentially endangering a party's brand and identity,[20] which may explain why political agendas often remain stable for a very long time. There is little incentive for the dominant players in the market to change the political agenda. The tendency toward sticking to the mobilization of the same policy issues is strong because parties want to protect their brand and appear reliable in the eyes of voters,[21] or because activists demand it.[22]

The risks associated with issue entrepreneurship are particularly pronounced for dominant parties, who have government experience. Because of their overall advantageous market position, dominant parties have an incentive to reinforce existing patterns of political competition and the policy issues underlying them. Dominant parties who engage in innovation will incur uncertainty costs. Mobilizing new or previously ignored policy issues could split both their members and their constituencies. They also face considerable uncertainty about how voters and members will respond. If issue entrepreneurship causes a rift in the support base of a dominant party, it may lead to defections among members in parliament. These defections could in turn threaten the electoral fortunes of the party and reduce its ability to make good on its electoral promises whilst in office. The mobilization of a new or previously ignored policy issue may also jeopardize the relationships that dominant parties have with current or previous coalition parties, thus reducing their chances to enter future government coalitions.[23] Consequently, dominant parties will be reluctant to act as issue entrepreneurs.

For challenger parties, with no government experience, the potential gains associated with the introduction of a new or previously ignored policy issue will nearly always outweigh the potential costs. Challenger parties are newcomers in the system or hold marginal positions. As a result, any potential vote gain will constitute an improvement on their current electoral position. Given that they have never formed a government or been part of a government coalition, they have no government record to defend or relationship with coalition partners to protect. Therefore, they are much less constrained in the policy issues they can mobilize compared with dominant parties. Not only is issue entrepreneurship less risky for challenger parties, the potential benefits, both in the short and in the long term, are likely to far outweigh those for dominant parties. Challenger parties have thus every incentive to mobilize issues that could disturb the political equilibrium in order to potentially reap electoral benefits. William Riker highlights this point using the issue of slavery in the United States as an example of such conscious manipulation of the political agenda to generate disequilibrium in the political system.[24] He argues that the slavery issue was introduced by Abraham Lincoln and his supporters in the 1860 presidential election specifically to put a strain on and potentially split the persistent, winning Jeffersonian-Jacksonian coalition, thereby creating a disequilibrium that allowed him to win.[25] Similarly, we expect challenger parties to engage in a strategy of issue entrepreneurship by mobilizing a new or previously ignored policy issue to change the basis on which voters make political choices, and thereby potentially improving their own electoral fortunes.

The Importance of Appropriability

The question now becomes: Which issues are challenger parties likely to mobilize? The selection of an issue is of key importance as it is clearly pointless for a party to mobilize an issue on which it cannot win. The literature on product innovation in industrial organization suggests that firms will innovate when products allow for a high degree of *appropriability*. Appropriability here refers to the extent to which a firm can protect and capture the profits generated by an innovation.[26] High appropriability can be ensured through legal means, patents for example, but also through other means, such as a first-mover advantage. Only when the ability to protect gains from an innovation is high will the costs of innovation for firms outweigh the costs. When we translate the notion of appropriability to the political marketplace, where political parties cannot patent their product (or policy) innovations, it becomes about things such as the first-mover advantage. A first-mover advantage refers to the situation in which the first entrant on the product market gains a competitive advantage through the control of resources.[27] In a political context, a first-mover advantage is when a party that first mobilizes a high appropriability issue can enjoy an effective monopoly, at least for some time, and reap electoral benefits from it. Rival parties may attempt to copy a party's innovation, but doing so is likely to take time, be costly, and could even backfire and split their voter and activist base. Parties may be willing to incur switching costs—commonly defined as the additional resources that late entrants must spend in order to attract customers away from the first-mover firm—[28] but if it takes too long for competitors to react, consumers may have already developed a loyalty to the brand of the innovators.[29] A similar loyalty to a political party may develop when a party mobilizes the key policy issues that voters care about.[30]

Which policy issues allow for a high degree of appropriability? We suggest that these are issues that are not easily subsumed in the dominant dimension, and thus may internally split dominant parties. In Western Europe, the dominant dimension of political conflict is the left–right dimension, which bundles a large array of specific policy issues, such as taxes, social welfare, and education policy.[31] While policy issues relating to the left–right dimension have a low degree of appropriability, issues such as European integration, immigration, and the environment can be seen as high appropriability issues in the European context.[32] These are issues that are not easily aligned with the dominant left–right dimension.[33] We suggest that while dominant parties will most likely steer clear of them, challenger parties will have every incentive to mobilize them.[34] So let us now turn to the empirical test of these expectations.

Examining Issue Entrepreneurship

We test our expectations by examining the process of policy innovation for four issues: three high appropriability issues—the environment, immigration, and European integration—and one low appropriability issue relating to the role of state intervention in the economy. We have chosen state intervention in the economy as an example of a low appropriability issue as it lies at the core of the economic left–right dimension. As mentioned earlier, the environment, immigration, and European integration issues are generally viewed as not easily subsumed in the dominant left–right dimension. By focusing on these issues, we can utilize a rich data source on party positioning and salience on issues of the environment, immigration, and European integration that we introduced in the previous chapter: the Comparative Manifesto Project, now known as MARPOR. Unlike other measures of party policies, MARPOR data are based on the coding of election manifestos and provide data over time on the importance parties attach to issues in a wide range of democracies, going back the Second World War. Here we present evidence from 1950 to 2018.[35] Given that party manifestos are created in the context of elections, our data cover election years only. Our analysis includes data on over 200 political parties from 19 West European countries.[36]

In order to test our expectations about who will act as issue entrepreneurs and which policy issues they will choose to mobilize, our first task is to operationalize and measure the dependent variable; namely, issue entrepreneurship of parties. A party mobilizes an issue by attaching more importance to it than to other issues. Consequently, we need measures of the emphasis that parties place on the environment, immigration, European integration, and state intervention in the economy.[37]

MARPOR data are particularly well suited to examining the importance that parties attach to a range of issues. The coding scheme is rooted in "salience theory," which argues that political parties do not seek direct confrontation on issues, but rather engage in selective emphasis of issues.[38] As a consequence, the coding scheme is based on importance (salience) measures of issues that are mentioned in the manifestos, and "position" measures that are created only by grouping issue categories into "right" and "left" categories and subtracting one from the other to generate a position on the left–right dimension. For the purpose of investigating issue entrepreneurship comparatively and over time, MARPOR data are ideal as we can simply calculate the proportion of the manifestos devoted to a specific issue.

For the environment, we use one MARPOR category that represents the overall positive support for environmental protection and preservation.[39] The measure varies from a minimum level of emphasis on the environment of −7.86 to a maximum level of 0.40. For immigration, we adopt a similar approach to capture emphasis on multiculturalism, national identity, and minorities by using the following MARPOR categories: positive and negative mentions of multiculturalism and of minority groups, and positive references to a national way of life and law and order.[40] This measure varies between a minimum level of emphasis on immigration of −8.48 to a maximum level of 0.83.[41] For the importance of the European integration issue, we use two MARPOR categories that capture favorable and unfavorable mentions of the European Union (European Community), including references to the desirability of joining/remaining in the European Union, the desirability of further enlargement and further European integration, and evaluations of specific EU policies and institutions.[42] The measure varies from a minimum level of emphasis on European integration of −8.04 to a maximum level of −0.60. Finally, in order to capture the emphasis parties place on the market economy and government regulation of the economy we rely on five MARPOR categories, capturing the classic issues related to economic left–right politics, including favorable mentions of the free market economy, positive mentions of economic incentives, support for market regulation, and support for economic planning and controlled economies, as well as references to sound economic policy making.[43] The measure varies from a minimum level of emphasis on the economy of −7.27 to a maximum level of 0.47.

To understand whether challenger parties are more likely to act as issue entrepreneurs, we rely on the challenger party operationalization presented in previous chapters, based on government experience. We employ two variables, a dichotomous and a continuous measure. Our dichotomous measure, *Challenger Party*, takes a value of 1 when a party has never been in government in the period of analysis, and a value of 0 when a party has been in government.[44] In order to allow for a more dynamic operationalization of government experience, we also employ a continuous measure, *Government Experience*, which captures the number of years a party has been in government during the time period under investigation, 1950 to 2018. It ranges from a minimum of 0 to a maximum of 68 years. Because of the particularities of the Swiss political system and the way governments are formed, most Swiss parties have been in government throughout the entire period of investigation.[45]

Our models also include control variables. First, we control for party family. We classify parties based on the party family membership indicated in the MARPOR database, but we have also cross-validated this against other sources.[46] We differentiate between parties belonging to the radical right, conservative, liberal, Christian democratic, socialist, radical left, green, regionalist, confessional (religious), and agrarian party families. Adding party family dummies allows us to deal with a plausible alternative explanation for the importance that parties attach to issues that stresses the importance of social divisions and cleavage structures.[47] This also serves to make our test a more cautious one, since challenger parties tend to cluster within party families on the fringes, as we showed in chapter 1. Second, we control for changes in vote share between the previous election and the current election. Specifically, we subtract the vote share in the previous election from that in the current election so that positive values indicate electoral gains while negative values correspond to losses. Controlling for changes in vote shares is important because previous studies suggest that electoral defeat provides a strong incentive for political parties to adjust the importance they attach to policy issues.[48] Parties that have lost elections may therefore try to shift the political agenda toward issues that favor them.[49] Third, we include a measure tapping into the extremity of a party's left–right position by including a squared term as a control. This is to rule out the possibility that our explanation of challenger parties is simply a function of ideological extremity on the left–right dimension. We use the market economy/government regulation of the economy item from the MARPOR data in order to capture parties' economic left–right positions.

We now turn to the statistical estimation of our models. Our unit of observation is the party. Due to the natural hierarchies in the data, where parties are nested in countries and time, we need to deal with both temporal and nested data. To do so we employ a panel data generalized least squares (GLS) regression.[50] We include country dummies to control for any possible omitted factors that may differ between countries. In order to deal with the fact that issue entrepreneurship in an election is likely influenced by issue entrepreneurship in the previous election, we include a lagged dependent variable to the analysis.[51] Finally, to address the fact that we are dealing with repeated observations for the same party across time, we estimate random effects varying across parties.

The Issue Entrepreneurship of Challenger Parties

Are challenger parties more likely to engage in issue entrepreneurship based on issues with high appropriability? The results presented in models 1 through 6 in table 5.1 suggest that they do when it comes to the three issues of the environment, immigration, and European integration. The coefficient for challenger parties is positive and statistically significant, suggesting that they are more likely to act as issue entrepreneurs and to mobilize high appropriability issues such as these compared with dominant parties. Moreover, these results are robust when we include party family dummies to account for the sociological and cleavage-based explanation of issue emphasis, and also when we control for the extent to which the party gained or did not gain votes compared with the previous election, or for its left–right extremity. Parties that take more extreme positions on the left–right dimension are also more likely to act as issue entrepreneurs on the environment, immigration, and European integration compared with parties closer to the political center. Yet, the results in models 5 and 6 show that electoral success of parties only affects issue entrepreneurship on the European integration issue. When parties do better electorally, they are less likely to act as issue entrepreneurs on this issue.

In order to get a sense of the size of these effects, figure 5.1 presents the predicted levels of issue emphasis based on the environment,

LE 5.1 The Mobilization of High Appropriability Issues by Challenger Parties

	Environment		Immigration		European integration	
	Model 1	Model 2	Model 3	Model 4	Model 5	Model 6
rcept	−2.820***	−2.857***	−2.345***	−2.857***	−3.133***	−3.202***
	(0.194)	(0.195)	(0.217)	(0.195)	(0.218)	(0.213)
ged dependent	0.461***	0.463***	0.368***	0.367***	0.439***	0.447***
ariable	(0.022)	(0.022)	(0.022)	(0.022)	(0.022)	(0.022)
llenger party	0.215***	0.210***	0.150**	0.157**	0.160**	0.144***
	(0.065)	(0.066)	(0.074)	(0.074)	(0.072)	(0.070)
toral gain		−0.006		−0.004		−0.011*
		(0.005)		(0.005)		(0.005)
−right		−0.0001**		−0.0001**		−0.0002**
xtremity		(0.000)		(0.000)		(0.000)
y family ummies	✓	✓	✓	✓	✓	✓
ntry dummies	✓	✓	✓	✓	✓	✓
	0.50	0.50	0.42	0.43	0.45	0.46
bservations, roups)	1679, 211	1679, 211	1689, 223	1689, 223	1679, 211	1679, 211

ce: Authors' calculations based on MARPOR data.

s: Table entries are regression coefficients with standard errors in parentheses based on a panel GLS estimation with om effects varying across parties and country dummies (not shown).

gnificant at $p \leq 0.05$.

ignificant at $p \leq 0.01$.

immigration, and European integration issues respectively (shown by the dots), as well the uncertainty around these estimates (the confidence intervals, shown as horizontal lines), for challenger parties versus dominant parties. These predicted levels are calculated based on the results presented in models 2, 4, and 6 in table 5.1. Recall that the degree of issue entrepreneurship for each issue is based on the emphasis parties put on the environment, immigration, or European integration in their manifestos. The environment measure varies from a minimum level of emphasis of −7.86 to a maximum level of 0.40, the immigration measure from a minimum level of −8.48 to a maximum of 0.83, and the European integration measure from a minimum level of −8.04 to a maximum of −0.60.

Figure 5.1 shows that the predicted level of issue emphasis on the environment of dominant parties is about −4.5 on average; it is about

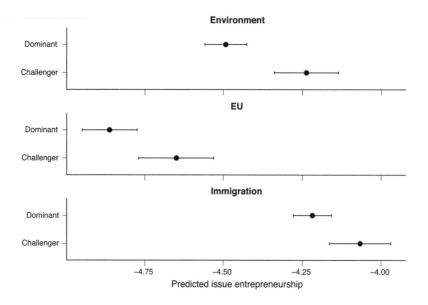

FIGURE 5.1 Predicted level of issue entrepreneurship by party type
Source: Authors' own calculations based on MARPOR data
Note: The figure shows predicted levels of the dependent variable (log of emphasis on issue; *dots*) accompanied by 90% confidence intervals (*lines*). These postestimation results are based on the results presented in table 5.1.

a quarter of a point higher for challenger parties at −4.28. This 0.22-point increase on an overall approximately 8-point scale constitutes a roughly three-percentage-point increase in issue emphasis on the environment for challenger parties compared to dominant parties. We find a similar pattern for the immigration issue. The predicted level of issue emphasis on immigration by dominant parties is about −4.05 on average, and −4.2 for challenger parties. This 0.15-point increase on an approximately 9-point scale constitutes a roughly two-percentage-point increase in issue emphasis on immigration for challenger parties compared with dominant parties. Finally, figure 5.1 shows that the predicted level of issue emphasis on European integration for dominant parties is about −4.9 on average, and is a fifth of a point higher for challenger parties at −4.7. This 0.20-point increase on an approximately 8.5-point scale constitutes a roughly three-percentage-point increase in issue emphasis on the environment for challenger parties compared with dominant parties. The results presented in figure 5.1, especially given the fact that our models control for levels of issue emphasis in the previous election, suggest that the effect of being a challenger party on the emphasis placed on the environment, immigration, and European integration issues is both statically and substantively significant.

The results presented in table 5.2 probe the robustness of our findings thus far. It predicts issue importance of the environment, immigration, and European integration issues using the same model specifications as before, but employs a different measure to capture the distinction between challenger and dominant parties. In table 5.1 our distinction between the two types of parties is based on their government experience: while dominant parties hold advantageous positions in the system and have considerable experience in government, challengers have never been part of the government. For the analysis presented in table 5.2 we use a continuous measure of government experience that captures the number of years a party has been in government between 1950 and 2018. We expect to find a negative coefficient for the government experience variable, as parties that have a greater dominance in the party system as demonstrated by their longer tenure in government should be less likely to mobilize high appropriability issues like the environment, immigration, or European integration. This is indeed what we find.

The results in models 1 and 2 suggest that as a party is in government for a longer period of time, it is less likely to mobilize the environment. The coefficient for government experience is negative and remains statistically significant even when we control for changes in parties' electoral standing or the extremity of their left–right positions. One additional year in government makes parties emphasize the environment 0.005 less on an approximately 8-point scale. Parties with more extreme left–right positions in turn are more likely to mobilize the environment compared with parties with more centrist positions. The evidence presented in models 3 and 6 shows a similar pattern for the immigration and European integration issues. Parties with more government experience are less likely to emphasize the immigration or European integration issue, even after we control for their issue emphasis in the previous election, which party family they belong to, left–right extremity, and the fact that they won or

TABLE 5.2 The Mobilization of High Appropriability Issues by Government Experience

	Environment		Immigration		European integratio.	
	Model 1	Model 2	Model 3	Model 4	Model 5	Model
Intercept	−2.638***	−2.862***	−2.201***	−2.345***	−2.980***	−3.055*
	(0.187)	(0.187)	(0.206)	(0.204)	(0.210)	(0.204)
Lagged dependent	0.461***	0.463***	0.371***	0.371***	0.442***	0.452*
variable	(0.022)	(0.022)	(0.022)	(0.002)	(0.022)	(0.022)
Government	−0.005***	−0.005***	−0.005***	−0.005***	−0.004**	−0.004*
experience	(0.002)	(0.002)	(0.002)	(0.002)	(0.002)	(0.002)
Electoral gain		−0.005		−0.003		−0.011*
		(0.005)		(0.005)		(0.005)
Left–right		−0.0001**		0.0001**		−0.0002
extremity		(0.000)		(0.000)		(0.000)
Party family	✓	✓	✓	✓	✓	✓
dummies						
Country dummies	✓	✓	✓	✓	✓	✓
R^2	0.50	0.50	0.43	0.43	0.45	0.46
N (observations,	1679, 211	1679, 211	1687, 222	1687, 222	1679, 211	1679, 211
groups)						

Source: Authors' calculations based on MARPOR data.
Notes: Table entries are regression coefficients with standard errors in parentheses based on a panel GLS estimation with random effects varying across parties and country dummies (not shown).
**Significant at $p \leq 0.05$.
***Significant at $p \leq 0.01$.

lost votes compared with the previous election. These effects are of a similar magnitude to the effects for the environment issue.

So far, we have theoretically argued and empirically substantiated that challenger parties are more likely to mobilize high appropriability issues compared with dominant parties in the system. This finding remains robust against different model specifications and different ways of measuring the distinction between challenger and dominant parties. While this evidence provides important empirical support for our idea of innovation through issue entrepreneurship, we would equally expect challenger parties to be no more likely to mobilize low appropriability issues. We examine the degree to which challenger and dominant parties mobilize a low appropriability issue by focusing on their emphasis on the market economy. We repeat

TABLE 5.3 The Mobilization of a Low Appropriability Issue

	Market Economy			
	Model 1	Model 2	Model 3	Model 4
Intercept	−2.677***	−3.017***	−2.546***	−2.926***
	(0.289)	(0.271)	(0.277)	(0.259)
Lagged dependent variable	0.427***	0.418***	0.432***	0.423***
	(0.023)	(0.022)	(0.023)	(0.022)
Challenger party	0.155	0.095		
	(0.099)	(0.093)		
Government experience			−0.002	−0.002
			(0.003)	(0.002)
Electoral gain		−0.004		−0.003
		(0.006)		(0.006)
Left–right extremity		0.0004***		0.0004***
		(0.000)		(0.000)
Party family dummies	✓	✓	✓	✓
Country dummies	✓	✓	✓	✓
R^2	0.53	0.56	0.53	0.56
N (observations, groups)	1553, 204	1553, 204	1553, 204	1553, 204

Source: Authors' own calculations based on MARPOR data.
Notes: Table entries are regression coefficients with standard errors in parentheses based on a panel GLS estimation with random effects varying across parties and country dummies (not shown).
**Significant at $p \leq 0.05$.
***Significant at $p \leq 0.01$.

the analyses presented in tables 5.1 and 5.2 with parties' emphasis on issues relating to the market economy as the dependent variable. These results are presented in table 5.3. They indicate that, in line with our expectation, challenger parties are no more likely to mobilize issues relating to the market economy compared with dominant parties. Interestingly, we do not find evidence for the idea that dominant parties mobilize issues relating to the market economy more than challenger parties. When we compare means, dominant parties on average mobilize issues relating to the market economy more than challenger parties, −3.65 versus −4.25, yet this difference is not statistically significant in our panel data analysis that also controls for issue emphasis in the previous election or party family membership. The results presented in table 5.3 do suggest that more extreme parties on the left–right dimension emphasize the market economy more than centrist parties.

All in all, the statistical results presented support our concept of issue entrepreneurship as a means for challenger parties to differentiate themselves from dominant parties on policy issues that are not easily subsumed in the left–right dimension. This is because the benefits of introducing high appropriability issues will almost always outweigh the costs for challenger parties, since they are either new parties or hold disadvantageous positions in the party system. Dominant parties are less likely to act as issue entrepreneurs because of the risks involved, such as splitting the rank and file and weakening their party brand.

Case Studies of Issue Entrepreneurship

Having empirically established the relevance of issue entrepreneurship to understanding how challenger parties bring about innovation based on the mobilization of policy issues, we explore how this works in practice through single-country case studies. Specifically, we discuss the mobilization of the immigration issue in Denmark, the European integration issue in the Netherlands, and the environment issue in Germany.

MOBILIZING THE IMMIGRATION ISSUE: THE DANISH CASE

The immigration issue is one of the most salient issues in European politics today, and one that has been a major contributor to the electoral successes of radical right parties in Europe in the last decade.[52] The Danish case illustrates the fact that the mobilization of this issue is by no means a recent phenomenon. Indeed, challenger parties were already effective issue entrepreneurs in Denmark in the early 1970s, beginning with the so-called "earthquake" election of 1973. This election caused a major upset to Danish politics as five new parties won seats in parliament, replacing more than half of the members. The governing Social Democratic Party lost a third of its seats, and the center-right Liberal Party formed the smallest minority government in Denmark's history with only 22 seats. The biggest surprise in the election was the success of a populist radical right-wing party, the Progress Party, which gained 28 of 179 parliamentary seats, making it the second largest party in parliament. As a quintessential challenger party, the Progress Party was fiercely antiestablishment and antitax. It was led by the charismatic Mogens Glistrup, who wanted to get rid of income taxes and bureaucracy. The Progress Party began as an anti-elite protest movement against taxes and state bureaucracy and did not make much of the immigration issue until the 1980s, when it became central to its political program.[53]

While the immigration issue was not salient in the public debate in the 1980s,[54] it would gain in prominence soon after. The anti-immigration position became the central policy platform of the Progress Party and its successor, the Danish People's Party, which was founded as a breakaway faction of the Progress Party in 1995. The Danish People's party focused heavily on anti-immigration themes, with an emphasis on the cultural threat to Danish values and norms.[55] In its 1997 manifesto, the party wrote:

> Denmark is not, and has never been, an immigrant country, and the Danish People's Party is opposed to Denmark evolving into a multi-ethnic society. . . . The current mass immigration is a serious threat to Denmark's continued existence as a peaceful welfare state.[56]

This nativist rhetoric turned out to be a recipe for success, as the Danish People's Party has consistently been one of the most popular radical right-wing parties in Europe, with a large electoral appeal and considerable policy influence. Part of the reason for the party's electoral success is that its anti-immigration rhetoric tapped into widespread public concerns. A poll from 1998 showed that over 70 percent of Danish People's Party voters agreed with the statement that immigrants pose a threat to Danish culture. This was also a view shared by around half of voters of center-right and center-left parties.[57] Yet, these parties found it more difficult to address the issue as the party elites tended to favor more open immigration laws and their electorates were split between the two positions. Moreover, voters of the social democratic parties were more opposed to immigration than voters of the center-right liberal and social liberal parties. In other words, immigration was not an issue that naturally aligned with the left–right debates on the government's role in the economy, making it an ideal high appropriability issue for a challenger to pick. The Danish People's Party not only tapped into demand for ethnonationalist rhetoric in Denmark, it mobilized the issue to its own advantage. The importance of immigration in public debate rose sharply in Denmark between 1990 and the mid-2000s.[58] In his systematic analysis of how European party system agendas have evolved, Danish political scientist Christoffer Green-Pedersen shows that attention to immigration has risen in all Western European countries since 1980, but nowhere has this increase been as pronounced as in Denmark.[59]

While the immigration issue was initially mobilized by the "new kid on the block," the Progress Party, and subsequently the Danish People's Party, the other center-right and center-left parties, with the exception of the Social Liberals, also shifted their position toward a more anti-immigrant stance as they felt threatened by the success of the populist right and had little to gain from siding with the Social Liberals.[60] While other parties have adopted similar positions, the Danish People's Party has retained its first-mover advantage on the issue, and is still the party that is seen as most credible on the issue of stricter immigration and integration policies. Moreover, the Danish People's Party has managed to remain a "challenger" to the dominant parties by staying out of government. But it acted as a parliamentary support party of a center-right minority government between 2001 and 2011 and again from 2015 to 2019. From this position, it has been able to exert considerable policy influence, especially on issues related to asylum and immigration, playing an active part in the tightening of Danish immigration, asylum, and integration policies.

Challenger parties have thus disrupted Danish politics in many ways: by changing the nature of issue competition, increasing the importance of ethnonationalist concerns, influencing Danish immigration policy from opposition, and making it more difficult to form stable governments.

MOBILIZING THE EUROPEAN INTEGRATION ISSUE: THE DUTCH CASE

Another example of a challenger party mobilizing a high appropriability issue at the expense of the mainstream is the politicization of the European integration issue in Dutch politics by Geert Wilders and his Party for Freedom. The issue of European integration was largely ignored in Dutch politics, even by "Euroskeptic" political newcomers such as Pim Fortuyn in the early 2000s. Fortuyn mobilized immigration as his key policy issue, and at that point European integration was merely a sideshow.[61] For Wilders and the Party for Freedom this would be very different. Wilders was a member of the Dutch parliament representing the liberals, but left the party on September 3, 2004, over its stance on the accession of Turkey to the European Union. The liberals supported the policy of the European Union concerning Turkish accession, according to which Turkey would become a member if and when the country would meet specific criteria, such as a strict separation between church and state. Wilders was, however, fiercely opposed to Turkish membership. The Dutch would take on the rotating presidency of the European Council that autumn and Wilders wanted to be able to freely oppose the decision to start the accession process with Turkey from parliament.[62] He first served as an independent member of parliament when he broke away from the liberals, but ultimately he founded his own party, the Party for Freedom, on February 22, 2006, prior to the election that year.[63]

Wilders's success in the opinion polls was already evident in 2005.[64] In that year, he launched his big campaign *tourNEE* (a tour for no) against the European Constitutional Treaty. A referendum on the treaty was scheduled to be held on June 1, 2005, and on May 16 Wilders started his campaign against it in his hometown of Venlo, in a bus that would visit cities in every province. His tour received a lot of media attention. The Young Democrats, the youth organization of the liberal pro-European party Democrats66, followed the bus in a blue caravan, seeking to counter Wilders's arguments wherever he went. Wilders distributed leaflets entitled "Protect the Netherlands." His main objections to the European constitution were the loss of Dutch sovereignty and the possibility that Turkey might become a member. If Turkey joined, he argued, it would subsequently exercise considerable influence through the constitution as a populous member state.[65]

The first day of June 2005 will go down as an exceptional one in Dutch political history. The first referendum on European Union matters in Dutch politics, contrary to prior expectations, resulted in a clear and resounding "No": 61.5 percent of Dutch voters voted against the treaty. The result was disastrous for both the Dutch governing coalition—consisting of the Christian Democrats, the liberals, and D66—as well as the largest party in opposition, the Labour Party, all of whom were in favor of the treaty. In the aftermath, journalists and scholars alike were left wondering what had happened to the pro-European consensus in the Low Countries. Citizens of one of Europe's founding members, the Dutch, had given a clear signal: this far and no further.[66] The outcome of the first European Union referendum in the Netherlands was a clear defeat for the biggest mainstream parties both in government and in opposition.

What followed was an intense debate in parliament and the media about the exact reasons for the "no vote." Politicians and commentators were keen to suggest that Dutch citizens had voted down the treaty simply because they could not understand the elaborate and technical reforms laid down in the Constitution. Viewed in this light, they argued, the outcome did not constitute a vote of no confidence, but rather reflected a lack of understanding of European affairs. Analyses of the voting behavior show that this was not necessarily the case. Although the Constitutional Treaty was clearly a difficult document to grasp, by the end of the campaign Dutch voters were fairly well informed about it. They were even better informed about party stances on the issue.[67] The reasons for the no vote were also not necessarily only domestic issues like government approval.

Rather, voters' decisions were largely driven by their broad percep-tions of European integration.[68] Interestingly, however, the aspects of European integration that most affected voters' choices were Dutch sovereignty and national identity, the cost of membership, and Turkish accession to the European Union, which last was not part of the Constitutional Treaty.[69] These issues were, however, at the heart of the campaigns of the Euroskeptic politician Geert Wilders.[70] Another important issue was the expanding European Monetary Union and the Euro, mobilized by another challenger, the Socialist Party on the left of the political spectrum.[71] This issue gained more traction in the wake of Wilders's strong mobilization efforts.[72]

In the 2006 parliamentary election, Geert Wilders and his Party for Freedom would go on to win 9 out of 150 parliamentary seats. The Party for Freedom manifesto included many Euroskeptic refer-ences and policy positions, for example:

[The Netherlands is] a country that is proud of its own identity, that dares to protect that identity and dares to stand up for its preservation within the ever-expanding Europe. . . . Therefore we want:

- No new countries can access the European Union
- Turkey in the EU, means the Netherlands out
- Abolish Schengen visas, the Netherlands is entirely in charge of its own admission policy for foreign nationals
- No new European Constitution or transfer of national powers to Brussels
- Cooperation within the European Union especially economically, bringing political control back to national parliaments
- Abolish the European Parliament, strongly restrict the European Commission and stop paying Dutch billions of Euros annually to Brussels.[73]

In the decades that followed, this Euroskeptic sentiment reso-nated with significant parts of the Dutch population. Traditionally, public opinion in the Netherlands had been very much in favor of further integration, yet polls from 2016 suggested that only 32 percent of the Dutch public now wished to see more political and economic integration in Europe.[74] Wilders's successful anti-European campaign combined with his anti-Islam and anti-immigration rhetoric would ultimately make the Party for Freedom the second largest force in Dutch parliament by 2017. Moreover, his Euroskeptic mobilization has driven rifts in the two largest mainstream parties, the liberal and social democratic parties, who tried to downplay the issue.[75] Challenger parties like the Party for Freedom and the Socialist Party have changed Dutch politics by mainstreaming Euroskeptic sentiment and increasing the importance of European integration concerns in Dutch party politics and among Dutch voters.[76]

Challenger parties have disrupted Dutch politics in many ways: by changing the nature of the political agenda and emphasizing the importance of European integration, and by influencing the popular debate about the European Union from the opposition ranks.

MOBILIZING THE ENVIRONMENT ISSUE: THE GERMAN CASE

Following the Danish and Dutch examples, one might think that issue entrepreneurship is a feature of the far right. Yet, this is not the case. As already discussed in chapter 1, parties on the left of the political spectrum are also prominent issue entrepreneurs. The mobilization of the environment issue in German politics illustrates this perhaps most clearly. Looking at the role the Green Party has played in Germany shows that after the successful mobilization of a new issue, challenger parties themselves can cease to remain challengers.

In the 1983 elections in West Germany, the Green Party was the first new party since 1953 to successfully pass the 5 percent electoral threshold to enter the German parliament. By winning over two million German voters, the Greens had "intruded into what had seemed an impenetrable two-and-a-half party system."[77] Up until that time the two major parties, the Christian Democrats and Social Democrats, and the much smaller liberal party had dominated German politics. The Greens became electorally successful very quickly. They first participated in the federal elections in 1980 and won 1.5 percent of the vote, in 1983 they won 5.6 percent of the vote and 27 seats, in 1987 8.3 percent of the vote and 42 seats, and since then have stabilized their vote share at around 8 to 10 percent in German federal elections, and have even gained more recently.[78] Since the 1980s the Green Party has also performed well in several state-level elections, but only in the western part of Germany.[79]

Its rapid rise made the German Green Party a popular object of journalistic and academic writing. It was seen as the first successful "postmaterialist" party in Europe. Indeed, the emergence and success of the German Greens has its roots in the changing social structure and the emergence of the materialist–postmaterialist conflict dimension.[80] Against the backdrop of the economic prosperity of the late 1960s and early 1970s in West Germany, a breeding ground was created for the mobilization of postmaterial issues, especially the environment. In their 1980 manifesto, the German Greens highlighted their strong commitment to the environment and how existing parties failed to deal with it:

> We the Greens want to challenge the current one-dimensional growth politics with a program that is aimed at the re-establishment and preservation of the well-being of the people. . . . Our policy is ecological, to give priority to the preservation of the natural livelihoods of the current and future generation and to the needs of people and foster their creative abilities.[81]

The German Greens were able to tap into this potential and represent a significant part of the German population, especially the young and urban.[82] While some initially suggested that Green Party support constituted a protest vote,[83] this view was later contested and revised based on survey evidence.[84] The Green Party had in a very short time been able to establish a loyal voter base. While in 1980 about two-thirds of green voters had previously voted for the Social Democrats, by the time of the party's electoral breakthrough of 1984, over half of these voters had previously voted for the Greens at either the national or regional level.[85]

The Greens have not only been instrumental in keeping the issue of the environment on the political agenda, they have also modified the traditional party system, opening up a new dimension of politics to the old left–right cleavage structure in the German party system.[86] As the German political scientist Ferdinand Müller-Rommel argues, "in doing so the green party initiated a gradual political realignment in Germany."[87] This realignment process has also significantly affected the established parties, especially the Social Democrats. It has created splits in the German left between the more traditionally left and postmaterial factions. While these two factions have some common concerns, such as social justice and equality, they are also split on questions of economic growth and environmental protection. This division within the left cuts across the core constituency of the Social Democratic Party, but has also made the Greens themselves vulnerable. Especially at the time of German unification, much less attention was being paid in German politics to green issues, especially in the poorer eastern regions of Germany, and the party merged with its counterpart the East German Alliance 90 in May 1993.[88] In the eastern region another challenger party, the Left Party, was gaining more electoral traction.[89]

The Greens also affected the fortunes of the Liberal Party, not least because they unseated it as the natural junior coalition party. Indeed, from 1998 until 2005, under the charismatic leadership of Joschka Fischer, the Green Party entered into a coalition with the Social Democrats under Chancellor Gerhard Schröder. In coalition, it was able to implement a lot of its environmental policy agenda. Yet, even before it entered government and ceased to be a challenger party, the green party had already left a mark on Germany policy by preventing the construction of new high-speed roads and nuclear power plants, and in the redesign of waste disposal plans.[90] Indeed, in his 1993 book on the Greens, German political scientist Thomas Poguntke suggests that the issue of the environment was firmly established in German politics by the early 1990s, and that the impact of the party on policy reached far beyond its share of seats in parliament.

As a challenger party, the Greens have disrupted German politics in many ways, increasing the importance of environment and other postmaterial issues and gaining considerable electoral success from doing so, a success which ultimately led them to office in the late 1990s to mid-2000s. To this day a progressive environmental policy remains part and parcel of German political discourse.

Conclusion

This chapter has examined issue entrepreneurship, an innovation strategy through which political parties mobilize a new or previously ignored issue. We have argued that political parties will engage in issue entrepreneurship when the electoral gains of doing so outweigh the costs. Challenger parties are more likely to act as issue entrepreneurs than dominant parties because the potential costs relating to possible bad reactions of the voter base or coalition partners are likely to be lower for the former. At the same time, the potential electoral gains are more uncertain for dominant parties than for challenger parties. Parties that wish to politically innovate by mobilizing new or previously ignored policy issues are likely to choose issues with a high degree of appropriability—that is to say, issues that are not easily subsumed in the dominant left–right dimension. These issues may drive a wedge in the constituencies of dominant parties and lead to internal rifts.

In this chapter, we have presented empirical tests of some of the core insights of our theory of political change—namely, that challenger parties are more likely to engage in issue entrepreneurship. Our analysis of the environment, immigration, and European integration issues, three high appropriability issues, shows that challenger parties are far more likely to emphasize such issues than their dominant counterparts. Yet, challenger parties are not more likely to mobilize low appropriability issues relating to the market economy. In addition, we have provided a more in-depth look into the mobilization of high appropriability issues by presenting qualitative evidence from three case studies, the mobilization of the immigration issue in Denmark, the European integration issue in the Netherlands, and the environment in Germany.

We have shown that challenger parties have successfully mobilized these three issues. This has important implications for our understanding of how political change comes about. Existing work explaining the mobilization of the environment, immigration, and European integration in European party systems has focused very much on the importance of structural changes in society that led to the expansion of vote shares of particular party families, most notably the greens, radical right, and radical left. Although we do not dispute that these factors are important, we suggest that they are not the entire story. The decline of dominant parties has not been uniform across and within the countries in Europe. We suggest that an important factor that has been somewhat overlooked is the strategic activities of parties. By redirecting our focus from demand-led to supply-led factors, we are able to explain which parties are more likely to mobilize issues such as the environment, immigration, and European integration, issues that challenge the mainstream status quo. This chapter has demonstrated that the issue basis of party competition is never a stable equilibrium; rather, it is constantly under siege from parties that want to find an alternative that undercuts the advantages that dominant parties have from mobilizing the currently most popular issue.[91]

6

Antiestablishment Rhetoric

Nothing attracts a crowd as quickly as a fight. Nothing is so contagious. Parliamentary debates, jury trails, town meetings, political campaigns, strikes, hearings, all have about them some of the exciting qualities of a fight; all produce dramatic spectacles that are almost irresistibly fascinating to people. At the root of all politics is the universal language of conflict.
—ELMER E. SCHNATTSCHNEIDER[1]

Our true competition is not the small trickle of non-Tesla electric cars being produced, but rather the enormous flood of gasoline cars pouring out of the world's factories every day.
—ELON MUSK, FOUNDER OF SPACEX AND COFOUNDER OF TESLA[2]

Like many other tech entrepreneurs, Elon Musk is highly educated, holding university degrees in both economics and physics, but he eventually dropped out of Stanford University's PhD program in applied physics and material sciences to try his luck as an entrepreneur. In 1995, at age 24, Musk and his brother started a web software company called Zip2. The company developed an Internet city guide, which it marketed to the newspaper publishing industry and quickly secured deals with many of the dominant players, including the *New York Times*. Musk's rapid rise to success made him something of a Silicon Valley poster child. In February 1999, the computer company Compaq acquired Zip2 for 307 million US dollars. Musk made his first million from the sale. Since then, he has gone on to found many more companies that have disrupted a variety of sectors, from financial services and electric automobiles to space travel. In December 2016, he was ranked twenty-first on the *Forbes* list "The World's Most Powerful People," and has a net worth estimated at over 22 billion US dollars.[3]

Elon Musk is known for thinking big and often praised for turning big ideas into innovative and ambitious products.[4] Tesla Inc., for example, is a company he cofounded with the aim of proving that people need not compromise when driving electric cars. "Electric vehicles can be better, quicker and more fun to drive than gasoline cars."[5] Musk not only is a celebrity businessman known for his engineering skills and business savvy, but has also gained a certain notoriety for his abrasive language toward critics, competitors, and authorities. For example, in 2017 the tech magazine *Wired* reported that Musk had criticized public transport at a tech conference. He reportedly said: "I think public transport is painful. It sucks. Why do you want to get on something with a lot of other people, that doesn't leave where you want it to leave, doesn't start where you want it to start, doesn't end where you want it to end?"[6] A public transit planning and policy consultant, Jarrett Walker, responded to the article via Twitter, tweeting that "in cities, @elonmusk's hatred of sharing space with strangers is a luxury (or pathology) that only the rich can afford. Letting him design cities is the essence of elite projection." Musk responded using only a few words: "You're an idiot."[7] Musk also uses this type of rhetoric to attack his competitors, mainly gasoline car manufacturers. In an interview with the *Wall Street Journal* in June 2018, at a time when doubts surfaced about whether Tesla would be able to meet the approaching deadline for mass-producing its Model 3 car, Musk attacked Ford Motor Company by suggesting that it was lagging behind. Musk said in the interview that "there's a good vibe [at Tesla] . . . the energy is good . . . [but]

go to Ford, it looks like a morgue."[8] Musk's rhetorical style is seen by some as a by-product of his "extraordinary ability to think big and challenge the status quo."[9] Others view his rhetorical interventions as counterproductive and a liability to his companies' brands.[10]

As with Elon Musk, the actions and rhetoric of disruptive entrepreneurs in politics are often controversial. European party systems have been shaken up in recent years by the rise of political entrepreneurs who defy traditional mainstream politics in both style and rhetoric. Think of Emmanuel Macron, for example. He led a new centrist political movement, La République En Marche!, to victory in the French presidential and parliamentary elections in 2017. During the campaign, Macron spoke of "changing the face" of France, and smashing "the system that [has been] incapable of dealing with the problems of our country for more than 30 years."[11] Leaders of many populist right parties in Europe are also renowned for their strong antiestablishment rhetoric. The leader of the Austrian Freedom Party in the 1990s, one of the most electorally successful populist right parties in Europe, Jörg Haider was notoriously antiestablishment in his rhetoric. His focus on "the little guy," who had been ignored by "those on top" proved an enormously successful rhetorical tool.[12] In the 1994 parliamentary election, the campaign poster of the Austrian Freedom Party even featured a picture of Haider accompanied by the slogan: "They are against him. Because he supports you."[13] This type of rhetoric attacking the Austrian mainstream political elite was considered a sharp break from the more consensual style that had previously characterized politics in Austria.

In the United Kingdom, Nigel Farage has ruffled the feathers of the political establishment as the leader of two parties, first UKIP and subsequently the Brexit Party. While the policies of both parties have focused on leaving the European Union, the rhetoric is more broadly antiestablishment. Farage, who prefers being photographed in a pub with a pint in his hand, rails against the "coalition of the politicians against the people."[14]

Antiestablishment rhetoric is not only used by many political entrepreneurs to paint themselves as outsiders, but is also a core feature of populism.[15] Populist parties aim to distinguish themselves from the political mainstream not only by advocating anti-immigration or anti-EU stances, but also by attacking the mainstream political parties. Yet in this chapter we show that antiestablishment rhetoric is a strategy used not only by populist parties, but by other political parties as well. We also situate the use of antiestablishment rhetoric in our more general argument about party strategy and our theory of political change. Antiestablishment rhetoric by political parties, we argue, is predominantly aimed at attacking the competence of competitors,[16] and is especially used by challenger parties.

Antiestablishment rhetoric is crucial for innovation, firstly because it protects innovators against copycats. Building on the previous chapter, where we demonstrated that challenger parties are more likely to engage in policy innovation through a strategy of issue entrepreneurship, we suggest that parties engaging in issue entrepreneurship need to make sure that they can protect the competitive advantage associated with their policy innovation. In order to prevent competitors (or possible new entrants) imitating them, parties engaging in issue entrepreneurship rely on antiestablishment rhetoric.

Despite his aversion to patents, Elon Musk pointed out in a Tesla blog post from 2014 that his company had built a patent portfolio after all, owing to the fear that "big car companies would copy our technology and then use their massive manufacturing, sales and marketing power to overwhelm Tesla."[17] Although policy innovations on the political market of course cannot be patented, issue entrepreneurs are not powerless when it comes to preventing imitation. One way to protect the appropriability of the policy issue they introduce is to attack the competence of competitors through antiestablishment rhetoric.

Second, antiestablishment rhetoric is crucial for innovation because it helps challenger parties to overcome their own competence disadvantage. They can attack dominant parties for being corrupt or not having the interests of the people at heart, but as incumbents the dominant parties still have a distinct advantage over challengers because they have many more opportunities to demonstrate their competence. So antiestablishment rhetoric may allow challenger parties to defy this advantage and to turn experience in office from being an advantage to a liability. For challenger parties that have never been in government, it is easier to paint a picture of "dishonest" and "incompetent" political elites and target dominant parties than it is for dominant parties to attack challengers that have never been in office.

The Nature of Antiestablishment Rhetoric

While antiestablishment rhetoric (or the phenomenon of antiestablishment parties) is by no means new,[18] it has gained renewed attention in recent years because of the electoral success of populist parties.[19] A growing body of scholarly work suggests that populist parties differ from other party families by their strong focus on rhetoric and communication styles.[20] Following the seminal work of the British political theorist Margaret Canovan, who has conceptualized populism as a thin-centered ideology that does not exhibit the theoretical complexity of ideologies such as socialism or liberalism,[21] Dutch political scientist and populism expert Cas Mudde defines populism as a "thin centered ideology that considers society to be ultimately separated into two homogeneous and antagonistic groups, 'the pure people' and 'the corrupt elite', and that holds that politics should be an expression of the *volonté générale* (general will) of the people."[22] From this perspective, whereas broad ideologies are generally understood to focus on a "set of basic assumptions about the world" (should it be fair, free, or equal, for example), populism, because of its thin ideological focus, can be best understood as a "language that unwittingly expresses" certain specific ideas (to save the "true and pure people" from a "corrupt and self-serving elite").[23]

It is important to note that antiestablishment rhetoric is just one of the defining features of populist rhetoric, and studies of the latter have identified three key components.[24] The first component consists of references to "the people" (the in-group). The second component is negative references to the political establishment (the elite). The third and final component focuses on statements that assign blame to particular out-groups (for example, immigrants). The growing focus on rhetoric in the study of populism fits with recent advances in the study of party competition more generally that use quantitative analysis of text to distil the positions that parties take, as well as to measure their rhetorical and communicative styles.[25] The conceptual starting point here is that "political ideas must be communicated discursively to achieve the communicator's goals and the intended effects on the audience."[26] Seminal work on populist parties suggests that rhetoric or communication style may even be more important for understanding the widespread appeal of these parties than the content of their policies.[27] This attention to rhetoric and communicative style also fits popular discourse on how political leaders have changed their styles by directly communicating to voters via social platforms such as Twitter and Facebook. Perhaps the most famous example of this is the tweets of US president Donald J. Trump. Technological changes have allowed political outsiders to bypass powerful gatekeepers in the traditional party and media organizations, and this is a key element of their success.[28]

A related literature within political science highlights the importance of antiestablishment sentiment in politics, but focuses on voters rather than on political parties. This literature uses the term "antipolitics" rather than antiestablishment. Antipolitics is a term that has been used over the last few decades in a variety of ways to describe disengagement from politics or overall distrust of political leaders and the political system.[29] One of the most comprehensive analyses of antipolitics to date focuses on public opinion in the United Kingdom. A team of social scientists at the University of Southampton has examined responses to public opinion surveys alongside diaries and letters about politics that have been collected by Mass Observation, a British social research organization, since the 1940s. The group's research findings show that antipolitics, defined as "negative sentiment towards the activities and institutions of formal politics," has grown in scope and intensity over the years.[30] Moreover, the researchers suggest that changing preferences about the desired traits of politicians and changing beliefs about what constitutes a good politician can go a long way in explaining the increase in antipolitics sentiment in recent years. By the end of the time frame under investigation, 2017, over 85 percent of British respondents thought that the most important traits a politician should have were "honesty," "trustworthiness," and "meaning what one says." These characteristics are now valued more by citizens than a politician being "clever" or "wise" (44 and 57 percent, respectively, thought those traits were important).[31] These conclusions fit with other work from political science that suggests judgments about the character of politicians are becoming crucially important to voters.[32]

While the populism literature and that on antipolitics differ in many respects, they share a common focus on understanding and describing critiques of the political system and the ruling political elites. By building on this literature, we distil a conceptualization of antiestablishment rhetoric that focuses on discontent with or attacks on mainstream politics. Mainstream politics includes the political elites as well as the political system more broadly. Specifically, we define antiestablishment rhetoric as a discursive style or form of communication aimed at condemning the ruling elite and the political system for predominantly serving the interests of this elite.[33] This type of rhetoric allows actors to define themselves as political outsiders who can mend or transform the existing, malfunctioning system. Specifically, we differentiate between four key aspects of antiestablishment rhetoric:

> **Antisystem:** Communication suggesting that the political system as it currently stands not only needs reform but is broken, or even rigged. It is a political system that serves only the interest of the ruling political class. An implication of this, or even the stated idea, might also be that the political system as it stands is unresponsive, exploitative, and prone to patronage or even corruption.
>
> **Anti–political elite:** Communication portraying the existing political elite as self-serving insiders who are part of a cartel aimed at trying to keep outsiders out. These political elites are accused of being irresponsible, dishonest, and prone to cronyism.

Antitechnocratic: Communication portraying the political system and/or elite as part of a broader technocratic system or part of a larger form of international governance. These technocratic forms of government are condemned as undemocratic, unresponsive, and serving their own interests. This would include references to the European Union, International Monetary Fund, World Trade Organization, and other international organizations or (bureaucratic) agencies.

Generic anti-elite: Communication that defines a self-serving elite more broadly to include economic and intellectual elites, for example. These could include references to the capitalist (elite), big money, big business, the 1 percent, (greedy) bankers, the superrich, millionaires, the powerful, the mainstream media, and so on.

The rhetoric used by a political actor can thus be more or less antiestablishment and refer to one, two, three, or all four of the elements outlined above. This conceptualization allows us both to establish the degree of antiestablishment rhetoric employed by an actor and to delineate it from other types of rhetoric, such as populist rhetoric. Whereas there is clearly some overlap between antiestablishment and populist rhetoric, the former is more encompassing. While all populist parties are antiestablishment, not all that employ antiestablishment rhetoric are populist.

A brief discussion of the rhetorical styles of the candidates in the final round of the 2017 presidential election in France illustrates this. The two presidential contenders, Emmanuel Macron and Marine Le Pen, both challenged the traditional French party system and condemned the French mainstream political elites. Macron, who had been virtually unknown only a few years before the election, led his campaign to victory without the support of any established political party, and instead created his own political movement, La République En Marche! Ideologically, he may have been a centrist, but he also embodied the idea of political renewal and a challenge to the political mainstream. His campaign was based on portraying himself as a political outsider. Le Pen, in contrast, represented a more conventional challenge to the political mainstream—namely, the far-right National Front (now National Rally). Similar to other radical right-wing politicians across Europe, her campaign focused on issues of immigration and Euroskepticism, as well as appeals to antisystem and anti-elite sentiments. Le Pen's campaign, like Macron's, was antiestablishment, but unlike Macron's it was also populist: it framed immigrants and the European Union as "bad influences" that were to blame for the problems and deprivations of the real French people ("the good people"). The victory of Macron in the elections was hailed as a "defeat of populism" by many commentators, but he achieved it by framing himself as a political outsider, employing antiestablishment rhetoric to challenge the competence of existing political elites. Indeed, as we will argue in the next section, antiestablishment rhetoric is frequently used as a communicative device through which candidates or political parties can signal that they are political outsiders, and not part of the political establishment. Moreover, we suggest that challenger parties are more likely to employ antiestablishment rhetoric compared with dominant parties.

Who Employs Antiestablishment Rhetoric?

As demonstrated in the example above, antiestablishment rhetoric is a strategy used by those actors who wish to disrupt the political market in order to reap electoral gains. First, challenger parties have strong incentives to challenge the dominance of existing parties through innovation and antiestablishment rhetoric, which allows them to protect their innovation from possible imitation. Second, because dominant parties as incumbents can showcase their competence in office, challenger parties who are not in office have an incentive to use antiestablishment rhetoric to challenge the record of the incumbents and the established parties. Let us consider both of these arguments in more depth.

In chapter 2, we defined innovation as the process through which political parties introduce a new or previously ignored issue and then aim to discredit dominant parties by employing antiestablishment rhetoric, so innovation has policy and rhetorical aspects. With regard to policy, we have demonstrated that challenger parties are more likely to engage in issue entrepreneurship compared with dominant parties (see chapter 5). Specifically, challenger parties mobilize high appropriability issues like the environment, European integration, and immigration, with the aim of breaking the agenda-setting power of dominant parties. As in the economic market, appropriability matters a great deal for innovation incentives in the political marketplace.[34] A higher degree of appropriability allows a political party to protect the gains that result from its policy innovation, and its incentive to innovate depends on the difference between preinnovation and postinnovation vote shares. Only when a party expects to electorally gain from a policy innovation will it decide to mobilize an issue and exert the effort needed to do so.

Even though it is difficult for dominant parties to respond to the policy innovation of challengers because they have policy reputations and relationships with past and present coalition partners to protect, they may choose to imitate the challenger party's strategy if they think that the heightened importance of the high appropriability issue among the electorate leaves them electorally vulnerable if they do not address it. Moreover, new entrants may decide to enter the political market in order to imitate the policy innovation of challenger parties. These actions reduce the level of appropriability, thus lowering the chances of electoral success for the challenger party engaging in issue entrepreneurship. Imitation squeezes its margins for victory—which are slim anyway. But like a firm with a new product, a policy innovator on the political market is not entirely powerless when it comes to protecting its intellectual property. While a firm can protect its innovation through patents, copyrights, and court cases, a political party can choose to mobilize issues that do not fit neatly into the existing dimension of political conflict. This lowers the risk of imitation by dominant parties. A party can even go one step further and employ antiestablishment rhetoric to scare off its rivals. Antiestablishment rhetoric is aimed at devaluing the "brand equity" of dominant parties. Much like Elon Musk lashes out at other automobile manufactures, such as the Ford Motor Company, to protect his innovation, so challenger parties are likely to discredit their dominant competitors in order to prevent them from imitating their issue entrepreneurship.

Viewed in this light, antiestablishment rhetoric is a crucial part of the innovation strategies of challenger parties. It is not just an add-on to the policy aspect of innovation. Through antiestablishment rhetoric, challenger parties aim to attack the value of the dominant party "brand" as a whole, rather than its specific policy offering.[35] By trying to discredit rivals, challenger parties aim to keep imitators at bay and fulfil the growth potential associated with their policy innovation. Antiestablishment rhetoric is not so much aimed at the policy positions of competitors, but rather it is targeted at their integrity and competence to deliver on policies. It is not surprising, therefore, that parties compete as much on the basis of competence, or perceived competence, as they do on policy positions.[36]

While antiestablishment rhetoric is a well-known discursive tool used by populist parties in order to reap the electoral gains of anti-elitist attitudes and nurture anti-elitist feelings,[37] we have suggested that they are by no means the only ones to use it in this way. Given that challenger parties are more likely to employ issue entrepreneurship compared with dominant parties, we expect challenger parties, whether they are populist or not, to also engage strongly in anti-establishment rhetoric.

In addition to protecting the policy innovation of challengers, antiestablishment rhetoric may be beneficial to challenger parties in its own right. Political scientists suggest that incumbents have a distinct competence advantage over challengers.[38]This advantage arises in part from the fact that voters are expected to systematically elect candidates of higher quality into office.[39] Incumbents also have many more opportunities to showcase their effectiveness and competence in office. Incumbency status is often used as a cue for competence by voters.[40] Such an advantage of incumbents gives challenger parties an incentive to seek to close the competence gap, as they would stand to gain more from discrediting the competence of incumbents through their rhetoric. Antiestablishment rhetoric is an effective tool for challenger parties to chip away at the power of dominant parties. Challenger parties also have more ammunition to do so, because dominant parties are or have been in office recently and thus can more easily be blamed for problems and grievances. It is far easier to paint dominant parties as "dishonest" or even "corrupt" than challenger parties that have never held office.[41] These reasons simply underline our overall expectation that challenger parties are more likely to engage in antiestablishment rhetoric compared with dominant parties. Before we move on to the empirical test of this expectation, the next section introduces our novel measurement of antiestablishment rhetoric.

Measuring Antiestablishment Rhetoric

Scholars of party competition in Europe have paid much more attention to the policy component of innovation, by studying which parties put novel issues on the political agenda, than the rhetorical aspect of innovation.[42] This is surprising, given that we know parties devote a significant portion of their campaigns to establishing their competence and attacking competitors through negative campaigning,[43] and that evaluations of competence play an important part in voter's choices at the ballot box.[44] As a result of this scant scholarly attention, we lack empirical measures of the degree of antiestablishment rhetoric employed by political parties across countries and over time. Although CHES includes a useful measure tapping into the "salience of anti-elite rhetoric" by parties, it is not ideal for our purposes. First, the measure only exists for two time points: the 2014 and 2017 rounds of the survey. This limited time frame does not allow us to judge whether earlier waves of challenger parties in Europe that acted as issue entrepreneurs, such as the green parties in the 1980s and 1990s, used antiestablishment rhetoric to protect their policy innovation. Second, CHES taps into the salience of anti-elite rhetoric, but not the content of the antiestablishment rhetoric itself. Hence, we cannot be sure exactly how experts interpreted the term "antiestablishment," nor do we know if perceiving that antiestablishment rhetoric is more important for a party in fact coincides with the party employing more of this type of rhetoric in its communication. That said, our measure of antiestablishment rhetoric is highly correlated with the CHES measure; but it has the clear advantage that it allows us to capture changes in antiestablishment rhetoric over time.[45]

We have argued that antiestablishment rhetoric is a distinct discursive style, and thus needs to be measured as such. In order to do so, we have developed a novel measure in collaboration with the Dutch political communication expert Mariken van der Velden.[46] To determine whether a party employs antiestablishment rhetoric, we rely on party manifestos from MARPOR.[47] While we used the MARPOR coding of the importance parties attach to issues in their election manifestos in chapter 5 on issue entrepreneurship, here we rely on the party manifestos collected and made available through MARPOR, but devise our own coding based on a supervised machine learning approach. Party manifestos have a clear advantage for us as they are available for a long period and for many parties, as well as being relatively comparable over countries and time. They also allow us to examine the rhetoric of the same parties across elections using the same unique source, their own electoral manifesto. In order to be able to code using a machine learning approach, our case selection is constrained by the language skills of coders as well as our own, and the ability to use the manifestos in digitized form to enable the computerized coding. Specifically, we examine political parties in six countries—Austria, Germany, France, Ireland, the Netherlands, and the United Kingdom—between the 1970s and 2017. This country selection provides us with ample variation in antiestablishment rhetoric. Some of these countries are known to have parties that are fiercely antiestablishment—the Freedom Party in Austria, the National Rally in France, and the Party for Freedom in the Netherlands, for example—while other countries less so (Ireland) or only recently (Germany and the United Kingdom).

While we explain the technical procedure in detail elsewhere,[48] it is worthwhile explaining the process we used for coding the antiestablishment rhetoric using the supervised machine learning approach. Generally, machine learning approaches involve three steps.

In the first step, human coders code all sentences in a randomly selected set of manifestos for each party in each country into categories based on rules using a detailed coding scheme (also referred to as a holistic grading scheme).[49] This in our case amounted to 10 percent of all manifestos being coded by hand. The hand coding was checked by us as researchers to make sure that it indeed fitted with our conceptualization of antiestablishment rhetoric as outlined earlier. Based on the hand coding, a computer model is trained to sort or classify the training documents into different categories. In the third step, this model is then applied to the remaining manifestos in order to arrive at an antiestablishment-rhetoric score for each party in each country in a given election year.

In order to develop our coding scheme, we started by analyzing the electoral manifestos of the parties participating in the 2015 British elections and 2016 Irish elections. We selected the sentences that contained antiestablishment rhetoric, according to the conceptual categories outlined above. This procedure yielded a high overlap between the coding of different coders (an intercoder reliability Cohen's Kappa of 0.82), indicating that there was a high level of agreement about which sentences included antiestablishment references. Examples of antiestablishment sentences in the United Kingdom are: "People across the British state are looking for an alternative to the broken Westminster system" (Plaid Cymru) and "Imagine the end of cronyism, corruption and the 'Westminster bubble'" (the Greens).

Based on pretesting our conceptualization of antiestablishment rhetoric as outlined earlier, and through this in-depth analysis of the 2015 British and 2016 Irish elections, we created the following coding scheme, which we used to train the human coders. It develops a rubric of antiestablishment rhetoric that includes four elements: antisystem, anti–political elite, antitechnocratic, and generic anti-elite. The sentences in the subset of manifestos used to hand code and train the computer model were coded in the following way:

> **Antisystem:** When a sentence either explicitly states or more implicitly conveys the message that the political system as it

currently stands not only needs reform but is broken—or rigged—by the players of the game, code the category "antisystem" as 1, and otherwise 0. The implication—or even the stated idea—is that the political system as it stands is undemocratic and abusive and facilitates patronage. Examples include: "UKIP wants far reaching political reform to ensure that government answers properly to Parliament and that Parliament is accountable to the people," and "Too much power is unaccountable, concentrated in the market and the state, at the expense of individuals and their communities."

Anti–political elites: When a sentence either explicitly states or more implicitly conveys the message that political elites are insiders or part of a cartel; only look after their own interests; are irresponsible, dishonest, or guilty of cronyism, code the category "anti–political elites" as 1, and otherwise 0. The implication—or even the stated idea—is that the current political elite is not serving the people. Examples include: "Politicians in Britain have become part of a cartel," and "Elected representatives must be answerable to the people. We support a right to recall Members of Parliament, and other elected representatives, who have broken the law or otherwise brought their role into disrepute."

Antitechnocratic: When a sentence either explicitly states or more implicitly conveys the message that the elites, which constitute a broader group than just national politicians, are portrayed as insiders, part of a cartel, only looking after their own interests, irresponsible, dishonest, or guilty of cronyism, code the category "antitechnocratic" as 1, and otherwise 0. The text can also refer to the European Union, International Monetary Fund, World Trade Organization, or other international organizations or (bureaucratic) agencies. The implication—or even the stated idea—is that the current elites are just serving their own interests at the expensive of the people. Examples include: "Until we leave, we are forced to abide by the EU's founding, unshakable principle of the 'free movement of people,' meaning we cannot prevent the flow of citizens from all EU member states into Britain," and "The inconvenient truth for our Europhile political class is that political union offers no advantages to trade, although it may inhibit it."

Generic anti-elite: When a sentence either explicitly states or more implicitly conveys the message that the nonpolitical elites are insiders, part of a cartel, only looking after their own interests, irresponsible, dishonest, or guilty of cronyism, code the category "generic anti-elite" as 1, and otherwise 0. The text can also refer to big money, big business, the 1 percent, greedy (bankers), the superrich, millionaires, the powerful, and the media being above the law. Examples thereof are: "For 40 years the rich and powerful have forced us to live in their fantasy world—a world that suits the minority not the majority," and "The public lost £1 billion, while George Osborne's best man's hedge fund pocketed £36 million."

On the basis of the computer model that was trained using hand coding by the rules outlined above, we coded a manifesto of a political party in a country in a given election year as antiestablishment. Our measure ranges theoretically between 0 and 1 and thus gives us the proportion of a party's manifesto that consists of antiestablishment rhetoric. A value of 0 indicates that none of the sentences can be classified as antiestablishment, and 1 indicates that all sentences in the manifesto can be classified as antiestablishment.

The Antiestablishment Rhetoric of Challenger Parties

We now turn to the empirical examination of our expectation that challenger parties are more likely to employ antiestablishment rhetoric compared with dominant parties. We also expect that antiestablishment rhetoric will be quite pronounced across the entire time period under investigation, and should not be limited to the

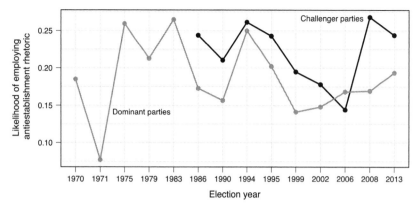

FIGURE 6.1 Antiestablishment rhetoric of dominant and challenger parties in Austria
Source: Authors' own calculations based on MARPOR data

rise of populist parties on the left and right of the political spectrum. We empirically test these expectations by examining the extent of antiestablishment rhetoric of challenger and dominant parties in each of the six countries under investigation. We rely on our own novel measure of antiestablishment rhetoric and cross-validate it with the CHES data from 2014 and 2017 that tap into the importance parties attach to antiestablishment rhetoric, based on expert judgments.

Figure 6.1 plots the average level of antiestablishment rhetoric in the manifestos of challenger and dominant parties in Austria across time. Three key findings stand out from the figure. First, on average, the likelihood of classifying parties as using antiestablishment rhetoric is rather low. On a scale from 0 (not employing any antiestablishment rhetoric) to 1 (relying fully on antiestablishment rhetoric), we find that the average for challenger and dominant parties in Austria hovers between 0.10 and 0.25. This is not entirely surprising, given that political parties pay most attention to specific policy proposals in their manifestos. Yet, our analysis suggests that between 10 and 25 percent of sentences in the manifestos can be classified as explicitly antiestablishment. Viewed in this light, the proportion of antiestablishment rhetoric is quite considerable. Second, except for 2006, challenger parties in Austria are considerably more likely to employ antiestablishment rhetoric than their dominant competitors. The exception for the early 2000 period can most likely be explained by the fact that the Austrian Freedom Party entered a government coalition in 1999, and subsequently toned down some of its antiestablishment rhetoric. This is a point we will return to later in our case-study evidence. The fact that dominant parties in Austria also engage in antiestablishment rhetoric, albeit to a lesser extent than challenger parties, suggests that, in line with previous research on party competition in Europe, parties compete not only over differing policy stances, but also over questions of competence.[50] Third, in line with our idea that antiestablishment rhetoric is a more general phenomenon in party competition, because it is in the strategic interest of parties engaging in issue entrepreneurship, we find that antiestablishment rhetoric is not a recent phenomenon.

Figure 6.2 presents the difference between challenger and dominant parties in terms of the importance they were attaching to antiestablishment rhetoric in 2014. Austria was not included in the 2017 round of the CHES, so we rely on the 2014 data. This figure supports the idea that challenger parties are more likely to employ this type of rhetoric. The average importance challenger parties attached to antiestablishment rhetoric was around 6.5 on a 10-point scale, while the average for dominant parties was about 2.5. Note that the results also show that the dominant parties in Austria vary tremendously in how much importance they attach to antiestablishment rhetoric. This is mainly because of the Austrian Freedom Party, which counts as a dominant party owing to its government experience and is perceived by experts to attach a very high level of importance to antiestablishment rhetoric: 8 out of 10.

Figure 6.3 shows the use of antiestablishment rhetoric by challenger and dominant parties in France based on our automated text analysis measure. It displays the average level of antiestablishment rhetoric in the manifestos of the two types of parties across French elections between 1970 and 2017. Compared with Austrian parties, the overall level of antiestablishment rhetoric was higher in the 1980s,

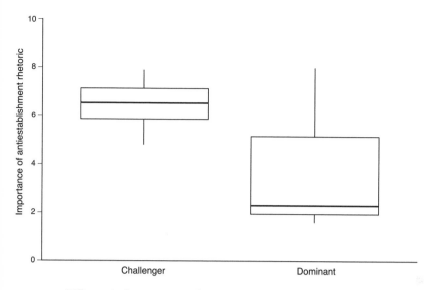

FIGURE 6.2 Difference in the importance of antiestablishment rhetoric between dominant and challenger parties in Austria
Source: Authors' own calculations based on CHES data (2014)

mainly because of the strong antiestablishment rhetoric of the Communist party. In contrast, the electoral manifestos of the dominant parties in France hardly include any sentences that can be classified as antiestablishment, especially in recent years. But, as with Austria, we do find that challenger parties in France are more likely to employ antiestablishment rhetoric compared with dominant parties. The highest level is over 35 percent in 1988, which coincides with the breakthrough of the National Front under the leadership of Jean-Marie Le Pen, the father of Marine Le Pen. Although he founded the party in 1972, the party first won seats in local elections in 1983 and European parliamentary elections in 1984 with a fiercely antiestablishment rhetoric.[51] Interestingly, the time trend displayed in figure 6.3 suggests that in recent elections this difference has narrowed. By the end of the time frame under investigation, challenger parties were displaying very similar levels of antiestablishment rhetoric to dominant parties. The fact that one of the key challenger parties in France, the National Rally, underwent a significant change over

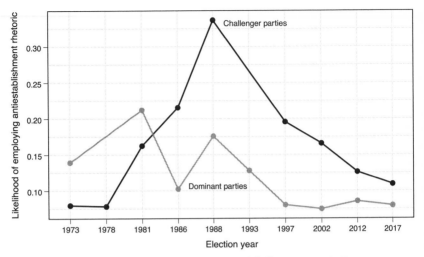

FIGURE 6.3 Antiestablishment rhetoric of dominant and challenger parties in France
Source: Authors' own calculations based on MARPOR data

the last few years may not be entirely surprising. The new leader of the party, Marine Le Pen, worked hard to make the National Front more socially acceptable and electorally successful while serving under her father, and attempted to make the party more mainstream from the moment she took over the helm in 2011.[52] This may at least in part account for the recent decline in the use of antiestablishment rhetoric by challenger parties in France.

Figure 6.4 uses the 2017 CHES data for the importance of antiestablishment rhetoric for French parties. The figure supports our argument that challenger parties in France attach a higher level of importance to antiestablishment rhetoric compared with dominant parties. The average level of importance attached to antiestablishment rhetoric by challenger parties was roughly 7 on the 10-point scale, while it was roughly 4 for dominant parties. In France we see much more variation in the importance attached to antiestablishment rhetoric by different challenger parties, while dominant parties displayed more variation in Austria. The variation in the use of antiestablishment rhetoric by French parties stems largely from the fact that the La République En Marche! party of French president Em-

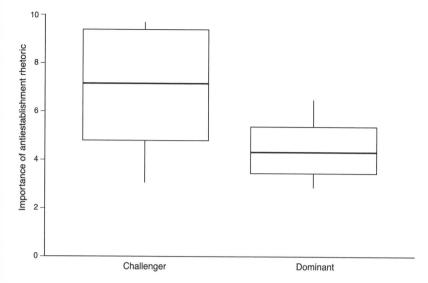

FIGURE 6.4 Difference in the importance of antiestablishment rhetoric between dominant and challenger parties in France
Source: Authors' own calculations based on CHES data (2017 round)

manuel Macron attached less importance to antiestablishment rhetoric compared with, for example, Marine Le Pen's National Rally.

Figure 6.5 displays the average level of antiestablishment rhetoric employed by dominant and challenger parties in Germany in their electoral manifestos between 1970 and 2017. In common with Austria and France, challenger parties in Germany are much more likely to employ antiestablishment rhetoric compared with dominant parties. The figure shows a striking spike in antiestablishment rhetoric in the early 1980s. This coincides with the entry of the German Green Party on the political scene in the former West Germany. As we described in the case study of the Greens in Germany in chapter 5, the party shook up German politics by introducing and mobilizing the environment as an issue, as well as employing a very different style of politics that set it apart from the dominant parties. For example, one of its leaders, Joschka Fischer, broke a parliamentary taboo in the regional parliament of Hessen in the 1980s by wearing sneakers to his swearing-in ceremony. A pair of his sneakers even went on display

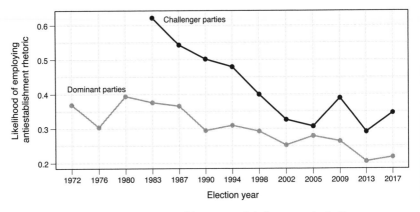

FIGURE 6.5 Antiestablishment rhetoric of dominant and challenger parties in Germany
Source: Authors' own calculations based on MARPOR data

in the German Leather Museum in Offenbach.[53] Figure 6.5 suggests that this unconventional style also translated into the electoral manifesto of the challenger party in the 1980s and early 1990s. Since then, as in France, we see a decline in the antiestablishment rhetoric of German challenger parties, although it has picked up again in recent elections. This decline and then rise again is most likely because of the Green Party entering a government coalition in 1998, becoming a dominant party, and toning down its antiestablishment rhetoric, and then the recent rise of the right-wing populist Alternative for Germany in the 2017 election. The fact that antiestablishment rhetoric was the highest in German politics in the early 1980s when the Greens as a challenger party shook up the party system underscores our argument that this type of rhetoric is part of a more general pattern of innovation, and not just an attribute of the rise of far-right or far-left populist parties.

Figure 6.6 shows the difference in the average importance attached to antiestablishment rhetoric between challenger and dominant parties in Germany, using the 2017 CHES data. The figure suggests that challenger and dominant parties in Germany are more cohesive when it comes to the importance they attach to antiestablishment rhetoric, and that challenger parties are clearly more likely than dominant parties to think that antiestablishment rhetoric is important. This difference is also statistically significant.

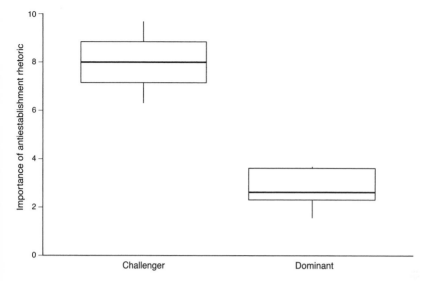

FIGURE 6.6 Difference in the importance of antiestablishment rhetoric between dominant and challenger parties in Germany
Source: Authors' own calculations based on CHES data (2017 round)

Figure 6.7 displays the average level of antiestablishment rhetoric employed by dominant and challenger parties in Ireland in their electoral manifestos since the early 1970s. Traditionally, Irish political parties have displayed lower levels of antiestablishment rhetoric compared with Austrian, French, and German parties. Yet, this has changed in recent elections, with a steady increase in antiestablishment rhetoric, mainly due to the more antiestablishment turn taken by Sinn Féin in recent years, especially during the Eurozone crisis and deep recession that hit the Irish economy. As with the other countries we examine, challenger parties have employed more antiestablishment rhetoric compared with dominant parties, and this difference has increased in Ireland in recent years. Figure 6.8 shows a similar pattern, with challenger parties attaching more importance to antiestablishment rhetoric compared with dominant parties, when we look at the data for 2014.

Figure 6.9 provides an overview of antiestablishment rhetoric in Dutch elections from the 1970s onward. Ever since the late 1970s, challenger parties have displayed more antiestablishment rhetoric

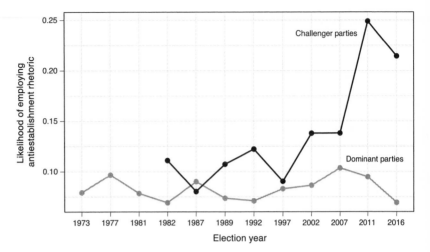

FIGURE 6.7 Antiestablishment rhetoric of dominant and challenger parties in Ireland
Source: Authors' own calculations based on MARPOR data

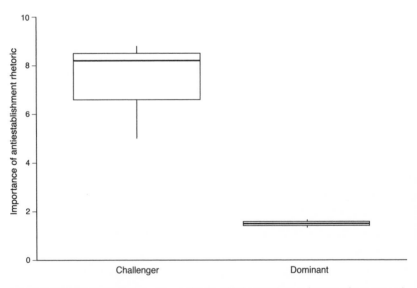

FIGURE 6.8 Difference in the importance of antiestablishment rhetoric between dominant and challenger parties in Ireland
Source: Authors' own calculations based on CHES data (2014 round)

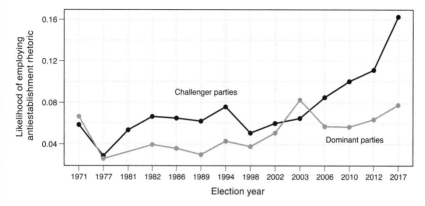

FIGURE 6.9 Antiestablishment rhetoric of dominant and challenger parties in the Netherlands
Source: Authors' own calculations based on MARPOR data

compared with dominant parties. Interestingly, the figure also shows that the number of party manifestos that include antiestablishment rhetoric doubled between 1977 and 2017. This is mostly because of the type of rhetoric employed by right-wing political entrepreneurs like Geert Wilders and Thierry Baudet, leaders of the Party for Freedom and Forum for Democracy respectively. Figure 6.10 shows that while challenger parties in Dutch politics on average display more antiestablishment rhetoric compared with dominant parties, there is also huge variation across challenger parties. This is perhaps not entirely surprising, as the Dutch system also includes small religious parties whose actions are very much driven by their religious ideology rather than electoral competition with other parties.

Finally, figure 6.11 shows the average level of antiestablishment rhetoric of dominant and challenger parties in the United Kingdom. The evidence from the British case underscores the patterns we found in Austria, France, Germany, Ireland, and the Netherlands. Challenger parties in the United Kingdom employ more antiestablishment rhetoric compared with dominant parties. This pattern is supported when we look at figure 6.12, which shows the difference in the importance attached to antiestablishment rhetoric between challenger and dominant parties. The average importance attached to antiestablishment rhetoric by challenger parties is just below 6 on the 10-point scale, while it is just below 4 for dominant parties.

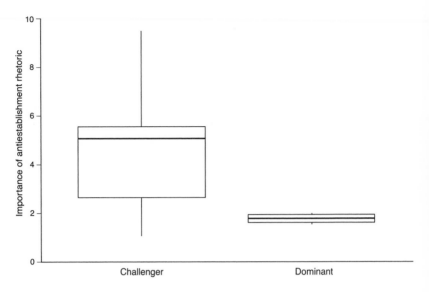

FIGURE 6.10 Difference in the importance of antiestablishment rhetoric between dominant and challenger parties in the Netherlands
Source: Authors' own calculations based on CHES data (2014)

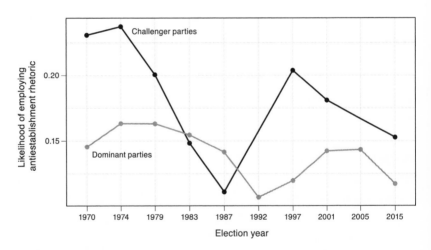

FIGURE 6.11 Antiestablishment rhetoric of dominant and challenger parties in the United Kingdom
Source: Authors' own calculations based on MARPOR data

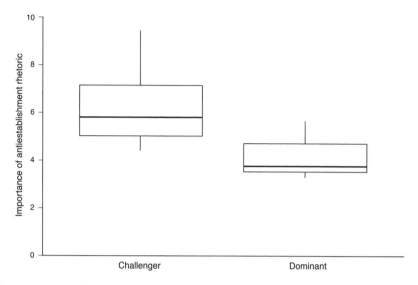

FIGURE 6.12 Difference in the importance of antiestablishment rhetoric between dominant and challenger parties in the United Kingdom
Source: Authors' own calculations based on CHES data (2017)

Our results thus far support the idea that challenger parties are more likely to engage in antiestablishment rhetoric compared with dominant parties. That said, the data also show that dominant parties attack the competence of competitors and the political system, albeit to a lesser extent. This finding supports the idea that party competition is not only about competing over policy stances, but also about aiming to devalue the brand of competitors, and that such strategies are used by all parties.[54]

Next, we examine the antiestablishment rhetoric of challenger parties in greater depth. We do so in two ways. First, we explore possible differences in antiestablishment rhetoric between challenger parties on the left and those on right of the political spectrum. This allows us to provide an additional test of our idea that antiestablishment rhetoric is not a feature only of right-wing populist parties. Second, we delve deeper into the content of the antiestablishment rhetoric that is employed by political parties in the six countries under investigation by presenting an overview of the kinds of words that are most frequently used in manifestos that can be classified as strongly antiestablishment. We provide this information via word clouds.

Figure 6.13 shows the average level of antiestablishment rhetoric used by challenger parties on the left and the right of the political spectrum across the time period under investigation for the six different countries. To classify challenger parties as left or right, we use the MARPOR classification based on electoral manifestos, as we did in the previous chapter. The figure suggests that the antiestablishment rhetoric of challenger parties is most pronounced in Austria and Germany, but no clear pattern emerges when it comes to ideology. Both left- and right-wing challenger parties employ antiestablishment rhetoric. This evidence, together with the fact that in Germany the Green Party engaged very much in antiestablishment rhetoric, suggests that this type of rhetoric is definitely not the preserve of populist parties as is sometimes suggested.

In order to examine what antiestablishment rhetoric consists of, we provide information via word clouds of the words that are most frequently used in this type of rhetoric. The larger the font of the word in the figure, the more frequent the use of that word. Figure 6.14 shows a word cloud using the Austrian data and suggests that the word "government" (*Regierung*) is frequently used in antiestablishment rhetoric. Figure 6.15 shows the data from French parties. The words "political" (*politique*) and "against" (*contre*) are among the more frequently used in the antiestablishment rhetoric of French political parties.

Figure 6.16 shows the German data. The words "society" (*Gesellschaft*) and "Germany" (*Deutschland*) are among the most frequently used in the antiestablishment rhetoric of German political parties. The word "green" (*Gruenen*) is also frequently used. Given the prominent use of antiestablishment rhetoric by the Green Party in the 1980s, this is not surprising. A similar pattern in the frequency of words used can be found in the Irish data displayed in figure 6.17. Irish parties engaging in antiestablishment rhetoric frequently use the words "government," "political," and "public." Figure 6.18 shows that in the Netherlands, the words "party cartel" (*partijencartel*) and "democracy" (*democratie*) are the most frequently used in parties' antiestablishment rhetoric.

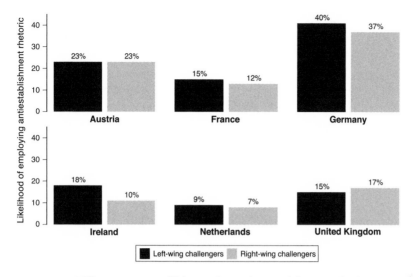

FIGURE 6.13 Differences in antiestablishment rhetoric between left-wing and right-wing challenger parties

Source: Authors' own calculations based on MARPOR data

FIGURE 6.14 Frequency of words used in antiestablishment rhetoric among Austrian parties

Source: Authors' own calculations based on MARPOR data

Note: The larger the font, the higher the frequency of the word.

FIGURE 6.15 Frequency of words used in antiestablishment rhetoric among French parties
Source: Authors' own calculations based on MARPOR data
Note: The larger the font, the higher the frequency of the word.

FIGURE 6.16 Frequency of words used in antiestablishment rhetoric among German parties
Source: Authors' own calculations based on MARPOR data
Note: The larger the font, the higher the frequency of the word.

FIGURE 6.17 Frequency of words used in antiestablishment rhetoric among Irish parties
Source: Authors' own calculations based on MARPOR data
Note: The larger the font, the higher the frequency of the word.

FIGURE 6.18 Frequency of words used in antiestablishment rhetoric among Dutch parties
Source: Authors' own calculations based on MARPOR data
Note: The larger the font, the higher the frequency of the word.

FIGURE 6.19 Frequency of words used in antiestablishment rhetoric among British parties

Source: Authors' own calculations based on MARPOR data

Note: The larger the font, the higher the frequency of the word.

Finally, figure 6.19 displays the frequency of words used in antiestablishment rhetoric for political parties in the United Kingdom. Here we find a similar pattern. The words "government," "power," and "people" are used very frequently, as well as the word "EU." The fact that the European Union plays a significant role in the antiestablishment rhetoric of political parties in the United Kingdom may not be surprising in light of the electoral rise of the challenger party UKIP, and more recently the Brexit Party.

A Case Study of Antiestablishment Rhetoric

After having empirically established the importance of antiestablishment rhetoric across six countries over four decades, we now delve a little deeper, with examples from a country case study. Specifically, we discuss the antiestablishment rhetoric of two Austrian challenger parties: one that was electorally successful, the Freedom Party, and one that was not, Team Stronach. One reason for this difference in electoral fortunes we suggest is the reliance on anti-establishment rhetoric without a clear policy innovation by Team Stronach. This comparison serves as an illustration of our argument that issue entrepreneurship and antiestablishment rhetoric are equally important components of successful political innovation, and one rarely works without the other.

When Austria held its first democratic elections in 1945, over 800,000 former members of the German Nazi Party were not allowed to vote. In the 1949 election, this changed. In order to make sure that these former members would not all cast their ballots for the conservative Austrian People's Party, the Austrian Social Democratic Party supported the founding of a new party, the Association of Independents. This party went on to win 11 percent of the votes in the 1949 election. The following years would be marked by internal discord, and in 1955 the Carinthia branch of the party renamed itself the Freedom Party of Carinthia. This ultimately led to the dissolving of the Association of Independents, which was absorbed by the Freedom Party and took part in elections under a new name—the Austrian Freedom Party—in 1956.[55] The Austrian Freedom Party rose to international fame when Jörg Haider was elected as its leader in 1986.

The roots of the Austrian Freedom Party therefore are to be found in the postwar period, when former national socialists were looking for a new political home. By basing its ideology on the pan-Germanic and anti-Semitic views of the Nazi regime, the party remained a niche political force. Under Jörg Haider, the Austrian Freedom Party started to intensify its antiestablishment rhetoric. Haider placed emphasis in the party's rhetoric on the "little guy" (*kleinen Mann*) who had been ignored by an arrogant political class, especially by the Social Democrats. In his books, entitled *Die Freiheit, die ich meine* (My idea of freedom) and *Befreite Zukunft jenseits von rechts und links* (A liberated future beyond left and right),[56] Haider paints a picture of a working class that needs to be rescued from self-serving elites. For example, he writes: "In a democracy, the people must be taken seriously! Commandments from the ivory tower of the ruling political class, whose contempt for the common people thus becomes visible, have nothing in common with a system of freedom."[57] At the same time, Haider mobilized fierce anti-immigrant sentiment. He eventually had to resign as the prime minister of Carinthia in 1991 because of his notorious far-right and antiestablishment rhetoric. In one of his statements against the government in Vienna, he played down the atrocities of the Third Reich when he said: "Well, that did not happen in the Third Reich, because in the Third Reich they had proper employment policies, which one cannot say of your [social democratic] government in Vienna."[58]

Although it initially had a negative effect on his political career, this switch in rhetorical emphasis in the longer term proved successful. It was only when Haider took on the leadership of the party and propagated strong anti-immigrant sentiments discrediting the ruling political elite that the party experienced electoral success. Within a decade, its share of the vote rose from 5 to over 25 percent. Under Haider's leadership, the party reached its peak in the parliamentary election of 1999 when it received over 26 percent of the vote. It became the second-strongest party in Austria, behind the Social Democrats. The Austrian Freedom Party would go on to enter a coalition with the conservative Austrian People's Party after the election. Yet, this coalition did not last long as it was plagued by infighting and, following its demise, internal disputes intensified and ultimately led to the Austrian Freedom Party to split in 2005 into two factions, the Austrian Freedom Party and the Alliance for the Future of Austria. The Austrian Freedom Party eventually became a dominant party in Austrian politics, and reentered government in 2017 in a coalition with the Austrian People's Party under prime minister Sebastian Kurz. This coalition, however, also proved short-lived because of scandals involving the leader of the Austrian Freedom Party at the time, Heinz-Christian Strache.[59]

However, not all disruptive political entrepreneurs who want to distinguish themselves from the status quo through antiestablishment rhetoric are as successful as the Austrian Freedom Party under Haider. Take Team Stronach, founded by Frank Stronach, an Austrian-Canadian businessman who made his fortune as founder of Magna, an automobile supplier. One of the main drivers for Stronach entering politics was his outrage that the Austrian parliament had agreed to support the European Stability Mechanism, an EU institution set up to safeguard the Euro in the midst of the Greek debt crisis. Mobilizing Euroskepticism within Austrian politics was not new—many other parties, like the Austrian Freedom Party and the Alliance for the Future of Austria, campaigned on the same theme.[60] Yet, one of the central messages of Stronach and his party was that the political elites, as well as the national news media, were part of a corrupt system that did not listen to the needs of ordinary people and businesses. He claimed that he wanted to serve Austria, instead of "the ruling political elite who are in politics to serve their own interests and wallet."[61] In opposition to the dominant parties, Stronach positioned himself repeatedly as the (only) independent candidate not compromised by the system, and he made a point of the fact that he was using his own money to pay for his campaign. Although many of Stronach's comments gained public attention, probably his most well-known and notorious statement was on public television when he said that he would like to bring back the death penalty for serial killers.[62] His party members did not agree. While his party initially got traction in local and national parliamentary elections mainly through his strong antiestablishment rhetoric, internal quarrels led to Stronach resigning in 2016 and his party was officially dissolved in 2017.[63] The example of Team Stronach illustrates that antiestablishment rhetoric without issue entrepreneurship is unlikely to be successful in the long run.

Conclusion

This chapter has examined the use of antiestablishment rhetoric as an innovation strategy through which political parties aim to attack the competence of their competitors. We have argued that challenger parties are more likely to employ antiestablishment rhetoric for two reasons. First, to prevent imitation of their policy innovation. When imitation is quick and widespread, the electoral gains of innovation will be jeopardized. Second, antiestablishment rhetoric is advantageous for challenger parties because it may allow them to turn the competence advantage of incumbents into a liability. Dominant parties, because of their office-holding experience, are able to showcase their competence. Yet, challenger parties, through attacking the competence of dominant parties, can try to reduce the brand of dominant parties and question their ability and integrity to lead.

Developing a novel and unusually rich measure of antiestablishment rhetoric based on a machine learning approach has allowed us to examine the use of this type of rhetoric across time and countries. The long time frame of our analysis is important as it suggests that antiestablishment rhetoric is not the preserve of the populist parties that have been on the rise in recent years. Rather, it is a more general feature of party competition that can be found in previous decades as well, when challenger parties aimed to mobilize issues with high appropriability, such as the environment, immigration, or European integration. We have also delved deeper into the use of antiestablishment rhetoric by presenting qualitative evidence from two case studies, the Austrian Freedom Party and Team Stronach in Austria.

Our findings have important implications for our understanding of how political change comes about. Existing work explaining the prevalence of antiestablishment rhetoric in European party systems has focused very much on the emergence of populist parties, especially those on the far right. Although we do not contest that these parties often employ antiestablishment rhetoric, we suggest that this is not the entire story. Challenger parties who engage in policy innovation more broadly need to distinguish themselves from the dominant parties and question their ability to deal with the policy at hand. If challenger parties do not discredit their dominant competitors, they run the risk that their policy innovation will be imitated and co-opted into the political programs of dominant parties or new entrants into the system. This reduces the possible electoral gains associated with issue entrepreneurship. In this chapter we suggest that antiestablishment rhetoric is not necessarily, or at least not only, a recent phenomenon associated with a particular party family, but is at the heart of the different strategic incentives that political parties have on the political marketplace. Attempts to discredit dominant parties by attacking their brand through antiestablishment rhetoric are an integral element of political party competition.

PART IV

Transformation

7

Changing Voter Appeal

Issue salience is neither an inherent property of a topic, nor . . . a direct reflection of the characteristics and conditions of society. Rather the importance of an issue dimension is subject to manipulation.

—BONNIE MEGUID, AMERICAN POLITICAL SCIENTIST[1]

You can't just ask customers what they want and then try to give that to them. By the time you get it built, they'll want something new.

—STEVE JOBS, COFOUNDER, CHAIRMAN AND CEO OF APPLE INC.[2]

Social media platforms are the entry point into the world of digital advertising, and Facebook has become one of the world's leaders in social media advertising. Yet, after many years of growth, Facebook has been experiencing a decline in popularity among its younger users since 2017. Millennial and Generation Z social media users began to decrease their time on the platform, and headed for newer competitors such as Instagram and Snapchat. In the American market in 2018, for example, Instagram gained 1.6 million users under the age of 25 and Snapchat welcomed 1.9 million new users of the same age group, while Facebook faced a decline of about 6 percent in users between the ages of 18 and 24.[3] This migration from Facebook was partly due to the more visually appealing content of the newer social platforms,[4] and partly that it was simply seen as old technology used by "old people." Younger users preferred messaging on WhatsApp, for example. And it was not coincidental that the migration away from Facebook occurred at a time when the company was embroiled in scandals relating to its failure to safeguard private data content that severely impacted its carefully constructed image as being a socially responsible and inclusive brand. These factors combined created a perfect storm for Facebook.[5] When Facebook published its second quarterly report in July 2018, which showed weaker than expected revenue as well as disappointing global daily active users, a key metric for Facebook, it sparked off the largest one-day loss in market value by any company in US stock market history.[6]

Safeguarding a brand is as important for political parties as it is for social media giants. While dominant parties can command a core following, competitors aim to chip away at their dominance. Changes in the electoral appeal of dominant and challenger parties, as with companies like Facebook, Instagram, and Snapchat, are a combination of the popularity of what the brand has to offer and its ability to adapt to changing consumer demands. Firms are able to deal with changes in consumer demand through a strategy of mergers and acquisitions.[7] Facebook, for example, paid an astounding one billion US dollars to acquire Instagram. Mergers of political parties do sometimes happen, but they are very rare.[8] Changing patterns in voter demand leave dominant parties vulnerable to the political innovation of challengers, as we have shown in previous chapters. Challenger parties innovate by mobilizing high appropriability issues that are difficult to handle for dominant parties because they risk splitting their rank and file. Challenger parties also aim to protect their innovation and first-mover advantage by discrediting rivals. This twofold approach based on policy and rhetoric is aimed at increasing electoral appeal and thus breaking the brand loyalty of voters to dominant parties.

In this chapter, we examine whether the innovation strategies of challenger parties are successful in terms of extending their voter base and generating more votes. Two expectations can be derived from our theory of political change. First, challenger parties that innovate want to attract new voters, and by doing so break the market power of dominant parties. Second, when choosing a challenger over a dominant party, voters should be voting on the basis of high appropriability issues and motivated by antiestablishment considerations. We empirically test our expectations by combining data for over 200 parties between 1950 and 2017 in 18 West European countries with survey data for over 18,000 individuals in 17 West European countries in 2014.[9]

Voter Appeal

We have demonstrated that brand loyalty to dominant parties, either understood as formal party membership or more informally as the psychological ties people feel toward particular parties, has been declining significantly (albeit not uniformly) across Western Europe. Election outcomes have become more unpredictable as voters have become much more willing to switch parties (see chapter 3). Citizens are acting more and more like critical consumers who constantly reevaluate the political marketplace and decide if there is something more appealing on offer. This, we have shown, creates clear opportunities for challenger parties to enter the market or to enhance their market share. Challenger parties aim to break the market power of dominant parties through a strategy of innovation. We have also shown in previous chapters that this innovation strategy is twofold. First, challengers engage in policy innovation by introducing issues that pose a threat to dominant parties because they are not easily integrated into the left–right dimension. Positioning themselves clearly on the left–right dimension is the source of the success of dominant parties. So, in contrast, challenger parties will attempt to "own" high appropriability issues and enjoy a first-mover advantage based on their policy innovation (see chapter 5). Second, challenger parties aim to prevent rivals from copying their policy innovation through a strategy of discrediting the competence of dominant parties through antiestablishment rhetoric. This is what we have termed *rhetorical innovation* (see chapter 6).

Ultimately, the success of these innovation strategies employed by challenger parties is based on the positive response of voters, something we call *voter appeal*. Voter appeal is analogous to customer appeal in the economic market for goods and services, which is generally defined as the attractiveness of a product and its supplier.[10] One can think, for example, of the popularity of the iconic Air Jordan sneakers, named after the famous basketball player Michael Jordan, in the 1980s and its supplier Nike. Voter appeal is defined as the attractiveness of a political party and its product. It includes two aspects: First, the degree to which voters think that the issues and policy solutions raised by the political party are important enough to inform their ballot choice. Second, the popularity of the party among voters, captured by voters' support for the party at election time (the party's market share). In this chapter we examine both aspects of voter appeal.

Crucial to understanding the success of innovation is the extent to which the introduction of a divisive (high appropriability) issue ultimately leads to a change in the behavior of voters at the ballot box. American political scientists Edward Carmines and James Stimson outlined the conditions under which a policy issue may come to redefine the political landscape.[11] A key element of the success of a policy innovation is the degree to which voters care enough about the issue raised to let it change their vote choice, something we refer to here as *issue importance*.[12] Issue importance is thus the individual voter's subjective sense of what is the most important issue in politics. The way political scientists typically go about measuring issue importance of citizens is through a direct, self-reported measure in a survey, asking respondents which issue is the most important one facing their country.[13] Issue importance does not involve heroic assumptions about the cognitive abilities of voters or their overall interest in politics. Quite the contrary, people need to care only about a single policy issue, or a small subset of issues, to act politically. If they care about an issue, they are more likely to pay attention to it, and to inform themselves about it.[14] Issue importance is consequential precisely because it determines the preferences according to which people process political information and make decisions, such as who to vote for.[15] Shaping and influencing issue importance is thus essential if political entrepreneurs want to change a dominant party's market share.

Over the past decades, scholars of elections and public opinion have painted starkly contrasting pictures of the degree to which citizens have stable and consistent political preferences and the extent to which they need to be knowledgeable about political issues to cast their ballot. One group of scholars has argued that because citizens appear to be largely uninterested in politics, and the level of general political knowledge is low, electoral democracy functions based on the interest and behavior of a small subset of politically sophisticated citizens.[16] Another group has argued that, despite individual idiosyncrasies, a collective rationality exists because the sum of awareness of the electorate as a whole is greater than the sum of its parts.[17] People are able to compensate for their general lack of knowledge or interest by relying on information shortcuts, such as their identification with political parties who do the thinking for them about particular policy issues.[18]

A third perspective seeks to combine both approaches. It suggests that the electorate is made up of small groups of people who are intensely concerned about particular issues.[19] Citizens do not resemble the pundits you see on television or read about online, but have special interests and are passionately concerned about particular things, like the environment or immigration. They might not even care about any other issue besides the one or two they really focus on. Most people have neither the resources nor the will to pay close attention to each and every issue confronting society—only the highly educated, time rich, and politically interested will try to become fully informed about everything.[20] What matters for most voters is the extent to which they find an issue important. Only to the extent that they do will that issue inform the choices they make at the ballot box.

Many factors influence the importance people attach to issues. Large-scale societal events, reported through the media or experienced personally, are likely to have an effect, such as terrorist attacks, for example. Issues that immediately affect an individual's material well-being, such as job loss or illness, are unsurprisingly also likely to be viewed as important. Yet, people also care about issues that do not directly affect them. An example is the so-called "halo effect" when it comes to opposition to immigration and support for the far right in Europe. This is the idea that anti-immigration sentiment and support for far-right parties is the highest in places that are close to immigrant-dense areas, but not necessarily within these areas.[21]

As we have previously argued, in common with firms, a large part of the activities of political parties are focused on "branding." One way in which parties can protect their brand is by making sure that voters think that the issues they mobilize are the most important ones. This idea is central to the notion of "issue ownership" introduced by the American political scientist John Petrocik.[22] Issue ownership is the idea that political parties are more than just the set of policy positions that they promote in their campaign or political manifesto. Political parties have *issue reputations*, which are images that voters have based on the issues that the parties highlight. This type of branding plays a crucial role in attracting new and retaining old voters. Political parties thus have an interest in cultivating their brand by focusing their campaign activities around the issues they "own." They aim to raise the importance that voters attach to the issues they own, while downplaying the importance of issues that their competitors own. When it comes to the economy, for example, left-wing parties in European countries are traditionally associated with the expansion of welfare state policies, while right-wing parties are associated with free market policies.[23]

As we highlighted in chapter 4, dominant parties hold a strategic advantage that is directly linked not only to the issues they mobilize, but also to their experience in office. Being in office allows dominant parties to showcase their ability to deliver on their promises. Like Facebook, dominant parties are well-known brands, and voters know what to expect of them in terms of reliable and consistent "product delivery" while in government.[24] Dominant parties often have a competence advantage that they will try to use to their benefit. Competence advantages are important for voters. Voters often cast their ballots for issue owners and support the parties that they think will be best able to handle the issues they care about.[25] Voting on the basis of brand reputations and issue importance requires less information.[26] It is less demanding in terms of time and other resources than having to carefully review all the issues that parties mobilize. Voters need only to pay attention to the issues they care about most and to determine which party is the owner of that issue. This incentivizes political parties to cultivate their branded issue reputation. They will try to appear as the "genuine supplier," while branding their competitors as copycats. Voters associate parties with certain issues and, as a result, other parties de-emphasize issues that voters connect to their rivals. Party competition perceived in this way is less a direct confrontation of opposing views on the same issues, but rather a competition over the importance of different issues.[27] Political parties compete by strategically nurturing their brand through the mobilization of the issues they own.[28]

It is therefore in the interest of political parties to try to change people's issue priorities in order to improve their electoral fortunes.[29] The importance parties attach to issues affects the importance voters give to those issues.[30] At the same time, however, there are limits to the ability of political parties to mobilize the issues they want. This is especially true for dominant parties, who, thanks to their overall advantageous position in the system, have an incentive to reinforce existing patterns of political competition and highlight the issues that underlie them. In order to appear credible to voters, a dominant party will tend to mobilize left–right issues, consistent with the party's long-standing image.[31] Left–right issues are those on which dominant parties, because of their time in government, have policy reputations and relationships with coalition partners to protect.[32]

Challenger parties are less constrained and seek to break the issue ownership of dominant parties by mobilizing other issues. They can mobilize issues that they expect to be beneficial to them but problematic for dominant parties, in that they may divide the latter's voter base. Since challenger parties do not have policy records or relationships with previous coalition partners to protect, they have a higher degree of flexibility when it comes to mobilizing issues. Challenger parties may also have more leeway in the eyes of voters to stake out different issues and abandon them when they feel they are not (or no longer) appealing for votes. The Spanish challenger party Podemos is a case in point. It is a relatively new party, which emerged on the Spanish political scene in 2011. It made considerable electoral gains by vocalizing anti-austerity, anti-EU, and anticorruption sentiments.[33] Yet, even in spite of the austerity measures linked to Spain's membership in the European Monetary Union, Spanish support for EU membership remained high. As a result, Podemos toned down, and largely abandoned, its initial Euroskeptic message.[34] It was much more advantageous to focus instead on an anticorruption message as the Spanish government became more and more embroiled in a large-scale corruption scandal involving the Popular Party, as discussed in chapter 4.[35] Arguably, making this type of shift in issue importance is much more difficult for parties that have longstanding reputations as issue owners to protect or a government track record to defend.

In chapter 5, we demonstrated that challenger parties are more likely to mobilize high appropriability issues, specifically the environment, European integration, and immigration, in their political manifestos. Challenger parties aim to innovate politically by emphasizing high appropriability issues in order to reap electoral gains and ultimately break the market dominance of dominant parties. Now we examine whether this innovation strategy is indeed successful and increases voter appeal.

The Electoral Effects of Innovation

In the first step of this analysis, we examine the extent to which the policy and rhetorical innovation strategies of issue entrepreneurship and antiestablishment rhetoric generate the desired voter appeal. We explore the importance that voters attach to the issues that challenger parties mobilize—notably, the environment, European integration, and immigration, as well as antiestablishment sentiment—and determine how these factors influence people's choice to vote for a challenger party versus a dominant party. In the second step, we examine whether challenger parties have been able to increase their voter appeal over the last few decades because of these innovation strategies, and the extent to which this has undermined the market power of dominant parties.

THE VOTER APPEAL OF CHALLENGER PARTIES

To test whether voting for a challenger party is more strongly affected by the importance of high appropriability issues and antiestablishment sentiment than is voting for dominant parties, we make use of the European Election Study (EES) 2014.[36] The 2014 EES is a post-election survey with representative samples of the voting population from the member states of the European Union. Here we focus on 17 Western European countries, with a sample of around 18,000 individuals in total. Our decision to rely on the EES instead of national election surveys stems from the breadth and comparability cross-nationally of the EES and the nature of the questions included. This cross-national survey allows us to examine both people's views on the importance of three high appropriability issues—the environment, European integration, and immigration—and their antiestablishment sentiment in many countries using identical questions. The EES administers comparable surveys in member states across the European Union, which allows us to analyze the way voters respond to political innovation strategies across a diverse set of institutional and political contexts. Moreover, the timing of the survey—2014—makes for a very conservative test of our hypotheses, since low appropriability issues relating to the left–right dimension were made salient by the Eurozone crisis that crippled economic growth in most of the countries under investigation until 2013.

The dependent variable is whether a voter is intending to vote for a dominant or challenger party in the upcoming national election. It is constructed using the following question: "Which party will you vote for in the next general election in [year]?" Based on respondents' vote choice, we created a dichotomous variable, with 1 denoting a vote for a challenger party and 0 a vote for a dominant party. In line with previous chapters, we define challengers as those parties that have not participated in a governing coalition in the postwar period (see, specifically, chapter 2). In our data set, 3071 respondents voted for challengers, while 14,704 voted for dominant parties.

Our independent variables, through which we aim to explain people's vote choices for challenger parties versus dominant parties, are the importance people attach to high appropriability issues and antiestablishment sentiment. In our analysis, we aim to determine whether vote choice for challenger parties is affected more by the importance voters attach to high appropriability issues compared with vote choice for dominant parties. We capture this differential impact by including in our analysis of vote choice a measure of how important voters think certain issues are. The EES 2014 includes a question asking voters "what [they] think the most important issue or problem is facing their country today." On the basis of voters' answers to this question, we construct a measure called the *importance of high appropriability issues*, which takes a value of 1 if voters think that the environment, European integration, or immigration is among the most important issues in their country, and a 0 if they think other issues are more important. We also construct a measure that taps into the importance voters attach to issues that relate to left–right dimension, which we label the *importance of left–right issues*. This measure takes a value of 1 if voters think that economic growth, inflation, or unemployment is among the most important issues in their country, and a 0 if they think other issues are more important.

Figure 7.1 shows the distribution of issue importance of high appropriability issues (displayed as dots) versus left–right issues (displayed as triangles) across the countries under investigation as a share of respondents. Values range between 0 (none of the respondents find the issues important) and 1 (all respondents find the issues important). The figure shows that in 2014 in Austria, Denmark, Germany, the Netherlands, Sweden, and the United Kingdom, the share of people who thought high appropriability issues were the most important in their country is higher than the share of people who viewed left–right issues as most important. In Finland and Malta, the share of those who thought left–right issues were most important only slightly exceeds the share of respondents who viewed high appropriability issues as most important. In countries like Cyprus, Greece, Italy, Ireland, and Spain the importance of left–right issues clearly surpasses that of high appropriability issues. Given that the survey was taken in the midst of the Eurozone crisis, this may not be entirely surprising. All these countries experienced a severe economic downturn and received international bailouts. This finding

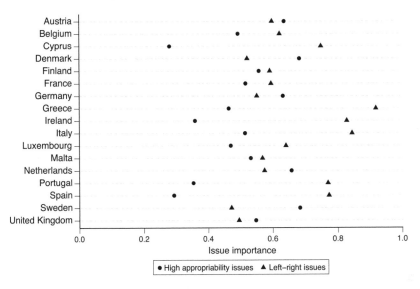

FIGURE 7.1 Importance of high appropriability and left–right issues
Source: Authors' calculations based on Schmitt et al., European Parliament Election Study 2014

suggests that external events are sometimes more powerful than parties in terms of making certain issues salient.

We capture the success of the antiestablishment rhetoric of challenger parties by tapping into people's thoughts about the degree that parliament considers citizens' interests as important.[37] This antiestablishment measure varies from 1 to 4, where 4 indicates that people think that parliament does consider citizens' interests important, and 1 that parliament does not. We recoded the measure whereby values 3 and 4 indicate high antiestablishment sentiment (parliament does not consider citizens' interests important), and values 1 and 2 low antiestablishment sentiment (parliament does consider citizens' interests important). Figure 7.2 shows the distribution of antiestablishment sentiment across the countries under investigation as a percentage. Antiestablishment sentiment is most pronounced in Greece, Italy, Portugal, and Spain, closely followed by France. In Denmark, Malta, and Sweden, we find the lowest level of antiestablishment sentiment.

To determine whether the effects of importance of high appropriability issues and antiestablishment sentiment on vote choice occur independently of other sources of voting behavior, we control

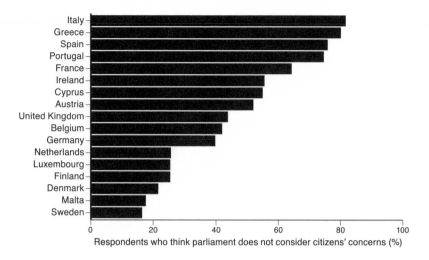

FIGURE 7.2 Antiestablishment sentiment
Source: Authors' calculations based on Schmitt et al., European Parliament Election Study 2014

for other political preferences as well as for the socioeconomic characteristics of respondents. Specifically, we include respondents' left–right ideological position, ranging from 0 (left) to 10 (right). We also include controls for people's socioeconomic status, such as if someone is unemployed, identifies as working class, is a professional, or has experienced economic hardship. We also include gender and education. We include these variables to control for dominant models explaining vote choice, such as economic and cleavage-based voting. To test the effects of the importance voters attach to high appropriability issues and their antiestablishment sentiment on their vote choices, we employ a linear probability model and include country fixed effects to account for differences across countries.

Table 7.1 shows the results of our analysis. We find that voters who view high appropriability issues as the most important for their country are more likely to vote for challenger parties than for dominant parties. Those who consider left–right issues the most important are less likely to vote for challenger parties. The results indicate that when they do vote for challenger parties it is mostly the result of the importance voters attach to immigration and European integration, rather than the environment. Moreover, the findings also

TABLE 7.1 Issue Importance and Voting for Challenger Parties

	Vote for Challenger Party			
Importance of high appro- priability issues	0.033*** (0.004)			
Immigration		0.075*** (0.008)		
EU			0.022*** (0.008)	
Environment				0.013 (0.010)
Parliament does not con- sider citizen concerns	0.073*** (0.005)	0.070*** (0.005)	0.073*** (0.005)	0.073*** (0.005)
Importance of left–right issues	– 0.030*** (0.008)	– 0.033*** (0.008)	– 0.027*** (0.008)	– 0.028*** (0.008)
Working class	0.041*** (0.013)	0.037*** (0.013)	0.034*** (0.013)	0.039*** (0.013)
Unemployed	0.031** (0.015)	0.029** (0.015)	0.030** (0.015)	0.030** (0.015)
Professional	0.017 (0.013)	0.021 (0.013)	0.019 (0.013)	0.020 (0.013)
Female	– 0.027*** (0.0067)	– 0.026*** (0.007)	– 0.025*** (0.007)	– 0.026*** (0.007)
Education	0.012** (0.005)	0.017*** (0.005)	0.015*** (0.005)	0.016*** (0.005)
Adverse effect crisis	0.027*** (0.005)	0.026*** (0.005)	0.027*** (0.005)	0.027*** (0.005)
Constant	0.386*** (0.021)	0.375*** (0.021)	0.395*** (0.021)	0.395*** (0.021)
N (observations)	11,442	11,442	11,442	11,442
R^2	0.154	0.156	0.151	0.151

Source: Authors' calculations based on Schmitt et al., European Parliament Election Study 2014.
Notes: Table entries are coefficients based on a linear probability model with intended vote for challenger versus dominant party as the dependent variable. Standard errors in parentheses.
**Significant at $p < 0.05$.
***Significant at $p < 0.01$.

suggest that those who do not think that parliament takes the concerns of ordinary citizens into consideration are more likely to vote for challenger parties compared with those who think that parliament is responsive to citizens. The effect of antiestablishment sentiment is quite substantial. While the predicted probability of casting

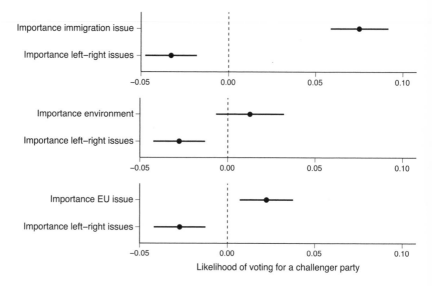

FIGURE 7.3 The effect of the importance of high appropriability issues on challenger-party vote
Source: Authors' calculations based on Schmitt et al., European Parliament Election Study 2014

a ballot for a challenger party is 9 percentage points among respondents who think that parliament takes citizens' concerns very much into account, it is 31 percentage points among those who think that parliament does not take citizens' concerns into consideration at all.

It is important to raise a caveat here. Based on this analysis we are not able to establish what comes first: issue priorities, antiestablishment sentiment, or challenger vote intention. That said, overall, we find strong empirical support for our expectations.

Figure 7.3 displays the sizes of the effects and plots them against those of the importance of left–right issues, based on table 7.1. It shows the association between the importance people attach to the immigration, environment, and European integration issues and their likelihood to vote for a challenger party. Taken together, the figures underscore the fact that while the importance of high appropriability issues is associated with the increased likelihood of voting for a challenger party, the opposite is the case for the importance people attach to left–right issues. Those respondents who viewed economic growth, inflation, or unemployment as the most important issue facing their nation were much more likely to state that they intended to cast a ballot for dominant parties versus challenger parties. Attaching importance to the immigration issue increases the likelihood of voting for a challenger party by about eight percentage points. Attaching importance to the European integration issue increases the likelihood of voting for a challenger party by about roughly three percentage points. Attaching importance to the environmental issue does not affect the likelihood of voting for a challenger party at all. While viewing European integration as important corresponds to a similar increase in vote intention for challenger parties compared with the importance of left–right issues for dominant parties, the effect size of the importance of the immigration issue for challenger-party vote intention is in fact larger than that of left–right issues for dominant parties.

THE ELECTORAL SUCCESS OF CHALLENGER PARTIES

In our second analysis, we explore whether challengers benefit electorally from their innovation strategies. Introducing new products on the political market is a risky strategy because the innovation may not catch on with voters or, worse, may even backfire. But if the innovation does catch on, does it really increase the challenger's electoral market share? In chapters 5 and 6, we demonstrated that innovation is primarily the prerogative of challenger parties. Now, we wish to examine whether challenger parties are able to increase their appeal with voters by innovating. Our first set of analyses demonstrated that voters who view the high appropriability issues that challenger parties mobilize, specifically European integration and immigration, as important, and hold more antiestablishment views, are more likely to cast a ballot for challenger parties. Respondents who care more about left–right issues are more likely to vote for dominant parties. Now, in our second set of analyses, we examine whether challenger parties are indeed able to increase their vote share through innovating, and break the market dominance of dominant parties. In order to do this, we employ a longitudinal perspective and bring together data on the electoral gains and losses of parties from 18 European countries between 1950 and 2018. We do so in two steps. First, we look at whether the electoral success of challenger parties is indeed influenced by their issue entrepreneurship strategy. Second, we examine the changes in market share of challenger and dominant parties using a classical measure from the study of business, the *Herfindahl index*, which we will explain later.

In the first step of our analysis, the dependent variable is the change in the vote share of a party between consecutive national elections. The main independent variable captures whether or not a party is a challenger party. This variable is operationalized as a dummy variable indicating whether or not a party has been part of a government coalition in the postwar period (see chapter 2 and the list of challenger parties in the online appendix at http://catherinedevries.eu /challenger_party_list.pdf). In order to examine whether challenger parties that engage in issue entrepreneurship are more electorally successful than those who do not, we interact this challenger party measure with the extent to which a party mobilizes high appropriability issues. We use the same measures as in chapter 5, but now create a scale that adds the attention that a party pays to the environment, European integration, and immigration in its manifestos, based on the MARPOR data. We recode this variable in such a way that higher values indicate more attention given to high appropriability issues. The scale ranges from 0 to 22.

Our models also include control variables. This is to make sure that issue entrepreneurship is not capturing some other characteristic of a party. First, we control for party family. We classify parties based on the party family membership indicated in existing databases (MARPOR and CHES trend file, and party handbooks).[38] We differentiate between parties belonging to the radical right, conservative, liberal, Christian democratic, socialist, radical left, green, regionalist, confessional, and agrarian party families. Adding party family dummies allows us to isolate the plausibility that a possible positive effect of being a challenger party on increasing vote share is in fact driven by other factors, such as broad-based party reputations. Second, we include a variable capturing the extremity of a party's left–right position by including a squared term as a control. This is to rule out the possibility that our explanation of challenger parties is not simply a function of occupying an extreme position on

TABLE 7.2 The Electoral Success of Challenger Parties

	Increase in Vote Share	
Intercept	0.707	2.795*
	(1.132)	(1.615)
Challenger party	0.889**	−1.702
	(0.438)	(1.397)
Issue entrepreneurship		− 0.128**
		(0.062)
Challenger party × issue entrepreneurship		0.186*
		(0.099)
Left–right extremity	0.0002	0.0002
	(0.0002)	(0.0002)
Party family dummies	✓	✓
Country dummies	✓	✓
R^2	0.04	0.04
N (observations, groups)	1972, 267	1917, 267

Source: Authors' calculations based on own party data set.

Notes: Table entries are regression coefficients with standard errors in parentheses based on a panel GLS estimation with random effects varying across parties and country dummies (not shown).

*Significant at $p \leq 0.10$ (two-tailed).

**Significant at $p \leq 0.05$ (two-tailed).

the left–right ideological dimension.[39] Finally, we turn to our statistical modelling choices. We have data on the vote shares of political parties across countries and time, so we need to deal with possible country and time effects. We do this by employing a panel data GLS regression.[40]

Table 7.2 provides an overview of our empirical findings. The results in the second column show that within the 1950–2017 time frame and within the 18 West European countries under investigation, challenger parties indeed gained more electorally compared with dominant parties. Challenger parties were able to increase their market share in each election by a factor of 0.889, which equates to an increase of one percentage point on average, significantly better electorally than dominant parties in the postwar period. This figure, however, constitutes an average and masks considerable variation between countries and parties. The results in the second column indicate that challenger parties who engage in issue entrepreneurship

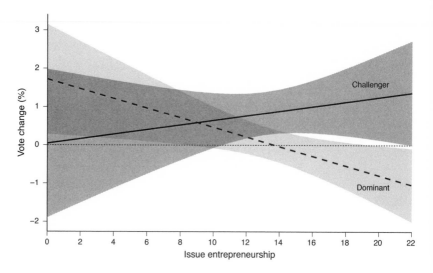

FIGURE 7.4 Vote changes due to issue entrepreneurship by party type
Source: Authors' calculations based on own party data set.

are more electorally successful than those who do not. Figure 7.4 plots the results from the interaction between being a challenger party versus not being one and the extent to which a party mobilizes high appropriability issues. It shows that challengers engaging in issue entrepreneurship gain electorally, while dominant parties do not.

In a second step, we examine the market shares of challenger and dominant parties. Within the study of competition between firms, from which this book takes its inspiration, economists have developed measures of the concentration of competition between firms by relating the market share of individual firms to the overall industry. This measure is called the *Herfindahl index*.[41] The Herfindahl index is defined as the sum of the squares of the market shares of the firms within the industry, where the market shares are expressed as fractions. The result captures the average market share, weighted by market share. It ranges from 0 to 1, where 0 corresponds to a market with a huge number of very small firms and 1 to a market where a single producer holds a monopoly. Increases in the Herfindahl index generally indicate a decrease in competition and an increase in the market power of a few dominant players, whereas decreases indicate the opposite. The index thus provides a simple way to describe the competition between firms, and is sensitive to both the number of firms competing as well as the market shares they occupy.

We apply this measure to the political market for votes as a way to capture both the number of parties that compete in a system and the support they have among the electorate—their market share. The index involves taking the market share of an individual party, squaring it, and adding them together for all parties. To give a concrete example of how the measure works, consider two cases in which the three largest parties command 90 percent of the electoral market, while the remaining 10 percent of votes are equally divided among two smaller parties. In scenario A, the three largest parties have 30 percent of votes each, while in scenario B, the largest party gets 60 percent and the two next-largest parties get fifteen percent each. The three largest parties' market share would be equal to 90 percent in both scenarios, but the first case would promote significant competition, where the second case approaches monopolistic competition. The Herfindahl index makes the difference between the two scenarios strikingly clear:

Scenario A: Herfindahl index = $(0.30^2 + 0.30^2 + 0.30^2) + (0.05^2 + 0.05^2) = 0.29$

Scenario B: Herfindahl index = $0.60^2 + (0.15^2 + 0.15^2) + (0.05^2 + 0.05^2) = 0.42$

This difference is because the market shares are squared prior to being summed, giving additional weight to parties of a larger size. Economists view an index above 0.25 as indicating a market with high concentration; that is to say, where a small set of firms have a high market share and the competition among firms is low. This is a situation in which a couple of firms are thought to have a high market power. A small index value of below 0.01 indicates a competitive industry with no dominant players.

We calculate the Herfindahl index to get a sense of political market concentration in Europe using our data of vote shares of parties between 1950 and 2017 in elections in the 18 Western European countries under investigation.[42] The result of this analysis is shown in figure 7.5, which displays the Herfindahl index per year averaged

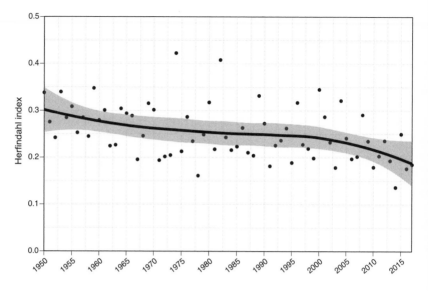

FIGURE 7.5 Political market concentration in Europe
Source: Authors' calculations based on ParlGov data

across countries. Across the period of investigation, the average Herfindahl index is around or markedly above the 0.25 cutoff point for high concentration and little competition. This further illustrates our observation from the introductory chapter that a small group of dominant parties have had considerable market power over the postwar period. The figure also shows, however, that competition has increased over time, especially over the last decade. By the end of the time period under investigation, the Herfindahl index is below 0.20.

Figure 7.5 averages the Herfindahl index for 18 different countries and thus masks variation between countries. In order to delve deeper into cross-national patterns, figure 7.6 provides the same information, but now presented separately for the 18 different countries. The figure shows interesting variation. For example, in Austria, Belgium, Luxembourg, the Netherlands, Norway, Sweden, and more recently in Portugal and Spain, we see very clear steady declines in market concentration over time. In these countries an increasing number of parties compete, occupying smaller market shares over time. In Denmark, Iceland, Ireland, and the United Kingdom, we see a similar

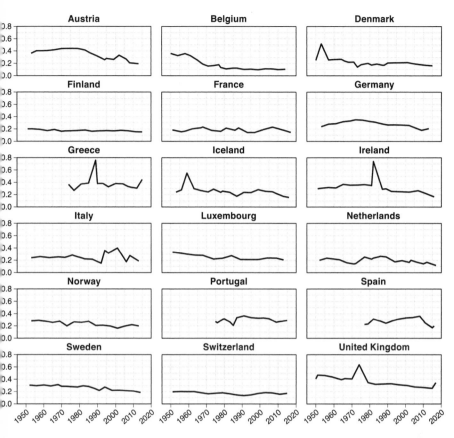

GURE 7.6 Political market concentration across countries
urce: Authors' calculations based on ParlGov data

downward trend, yet with some spikes upward in the 1970s or 1980s, and in the recent British election. In Finland, France, Germany, and Switzerland, we see less change over time, although the recent trend seems to be also downward. Finally, in Greece and Italy, we see changes in both directions over time, which partly reflects that the market power of dominant parties was threatened and challenger parties emerged that obtained large shares of the vote—think of Silvio Berlusconi's Forza Italia (Forward Italy), or Syriza in Greece.

In virtually all countries in Western Europe dominant parties have lost some of their market power, especially over the last decade. By 2017, Greece, Portugal, and the United Kingdom are showing the highest levels of market concentration, all having a Herfindahl index higher than 0.25. In Portugal and the United Kingdom, this signifies the market power of traditionally dominant parties: the Socialist Party and the right-wing electoral alliance of the Social Democratic Party and People's Party in Portugal; the Labour Party and the Conservative Party in the United Kingdom. In Greece this captures the fact that two former challenger parties became dominant—namely, Syriza and the Independent Greeks. These parties gained electorally during the Eurozone crisis and formed a coalition government in 2015.[43]

Market concentration is the lowest in Belgium and the Netherlands,[44] indicating that the Belgian and Dutch political markets are highly competitive, with very limited market power for dominant parties. Here, the Herfindahl index is close to or even below 0.1. As a result of the limited concentration in the political market, both countries have witnessed longer government formation periods, as we will discuss in chapter 8. The political markets in Finland and Sweden are also highly competitive. In these countries the Herfindahl index is about 0.15. In the remaining countries—Austria, Denmark, France, Germany, Iceland, Ireland, Italy, Luxembourg, Norway, Spain, and Switzerland—we find moderate levels of market concentration and lower competition between parties by 2017. Here, the Herfindahl index ranges between 0.15 and 0.25. Overall, in the vast majority of countries in Western Europe we see at least a moderate degree of competition in the political marketplace by 2017. The market power of dominant parties seems to be waning. Yet, there are also real consequences resulting from low market concentration for governability and feelings of representation, as we will discuss further in chapter 8.

Conclusion

The market power of dominant parties, just like that of tech giants like Facebook, is not a given. It is under constant threat from challengers. In recent decades, challenger parties, like Facebook's rivals Instagram and Snapchat, have been increasingly successful at chipping away at the market power of dominant parties. Unlike Facebook, dominant parties in Western Europe cannot easily acquire their rivals. Rather, they have to compete with them. They have to deal with the fact that challenger parties through their innovative strategies are trying to win over voters and gain market share. This chapter has demonstrated that challenger parties in most countries in Western Europe have been very successful in enhancing their voter appeal. The mobilization of high appropriability issues and use of antiestablishment rhetoric have proven to be powerful tools in shoring up voter appeal.

The consequence of the rise of challenger parties is that a larger number of market players have secured a smaller share of the political market space. This fragmentation has weakened the market dominance of dominant parties and arguably made elections less easy to predict. On the face of it, such reduced dominance of established parties and a more competitive political marketplace sounds like an improvement: challenger parties can be more responsive to voters' concerns over new political issues, they feel less compelled to adopt positions near the political center, and therefore can offer voters more choice. The antiestablishment rhetoric of challenger parties may also encourage dominant parties to govern better: to be more efficient and responsive as well as less corrupt. The lesson from classical economics is that more competition is a good thing, although nuances of this argument of course exist (see our discussion in chapter 9). However, when it comes to the political marketplace, more competition and greater volatility may also have clear negative consequences. In the next chapter, we will discuss the consequences of the rising success of challenger parties for government formation, government stability, and representation.

8
Representation and Government

Political parties become more like governors than representatives, at least within the mainstream or core of the party system. Representation itself either moves out of the electoral channel altogether or, when it remains within the electoral channel, becomes the primary preserve of so-called "niche" or "challenger" parties, which may downplay a governing ambition or which may lack a governing capacity.
—PETER MAIR, IRISH POLITICAL SCIENTIST[1]

If you open up the mind, the opportunity to address both profits and social conditions are limitless. It's a process of innovation.
—JERRY GREENFIELD, COFOUNDER OF
BEN & JERRY'S HOMEMADE HOLDINGS[2]

In 1977, childhood friends Ben Cohen and Jerry Greenfield completed a correspondence course in ice-cream making. This would mark the beginning of one of the most well-known and innovative ice cream brands: Ben & Jerry's. Because of Ben Cohen's anosmia (a lack of the sense of smell and near loss of the sense of taste), the founders introduced chunks in their ice cream for added texture and "mouth feel." They opened their first ice-cream shop in a renovated gas station in Burlington, Vermont, in 1978. A key aspect of Ben & Jerry's appeal was not just the product itself, but the brand value of "linked prosperity": a business model that promised that the wider community of stakeholders, suppliers, local community, and employees would benefit as well from the success of the business. The company's marketing was also different. In 1986, Ben & Jerry's launched its "Cowmobile," a modified mobile home used to distribute free scoops of ice cream, driven and served by Cohen and Greenfield themselves, in a unique cross-country marketing drive. In the world of ice cream, Ben & Jerry's was the ultimate challenger: an innovative ice-cream brand with funky new flavors and textures as well as a social consciousness. It was therefore not entirely surprising that some people felt Ben and Jerry had abandoned their principles and morally sold out when the founders sold the company to the multinational conglomerate Unilever for over 300 million US dollars in 2000. Although, unlike other Unilever brands, it retained an independent board of directors to preserve the social mission, brand integrity, and product quality of Ben & Jerry's. As a subsidiary of a large multinational firm, Ben & Jerry's was given considerable resources for research and development, and innovation continued in many areas, in terms of both novel ice-cream flavors and names, and promoting a progressive, liberal agenda and marketing drive. In 2008, the company renamed a flavor "Yes, Pecan!" to celebrate Barack Obama's presidential election victory, and donated the proceeds from the sale of that flavor to the Common Cause Education Fund. But Ben & Jerry's has also grown globally since its acquisition by Unilever, having nearly tripled its revenue and doubled its sales and added production plants in outposts ranging from Nevada to the Netherlands.[3]

The rise of Ben & Jerry's from its humble origins suggests that a fragmented market structure with relatively low barriers to entry, such as the food industry, may have several advantages, as it allows different firms to tailor different products for specific local and regional consumer demands.[4] This also encourages innovation to meet a range of consumer tastes. One might also argue that the rise of challenger parties in a changing political market allows for a type of innovation and enhanced choice that can cater to the entire range of electoral preferences, and thus make citizens feel better represented. This raises the question: does a more fragmented and polarized political market with stronger challenger parties produce better outcomes for citizens?

Just as there is a debate in economics as to whether oligopoly encourages more resource-intensive, innovative, and efficient production or stifles innovation to protect profits and status quo,[5] political scientists have identified a tension between systems that produce strong and stable governments that can deliver consistent and clear-cut politics and responsive political systems that represent a wide range of preferences.[6] The political market, however, differs from the economic market in one important respect: the delivery of the product. When it comes to competition between companies, even small start-ups, such as Ben & Jerry's in the late 1970s, can deliver their product to customers. However, in politics, product delivery depends on holding the levers of power—being in office. A small challenger party cannot deliver its product (policy promises) to voters without forming part of a government (or exerting considerable influence upon parties in government). That means that there is often a tension, as Peter Mair pointed out in the above quote, between enhancing representation and enabling strong government that can deliver the product to voters. Mair argued that political parties have two fundamental roles in modern democracies: first, to act as representatives, articulating interests, aggregating demands, translating collective preferences into distinct policy options, and giving a voice to the citizenry; second, to govern by giving coherence to the institutions of government and implementing policy programs that serve the interests of their supporters and of the wider polity.[7] But as the party system evolves, the tension grows between these roles. Previous chapters have shown that the nature of the political market is changing: barriers to entry are lowering, as voters have become less attached to the dominant parties and more volatile (chapter 3). The rise of challenger parties has led to a more fragmented, atomistic market (chapter 7). These trends suggest that we are moving away from a model of oligopoly, with power concentrated among a few dominant party families, toward a reality of greater competition. Is that a good thing? What are the consequences of greater competition and greater fragmentation?

We argue that while the rise of challenger parties may have contributed to making the system more representative of a range of voter preferences, it is also a hindrance to responsible government. On the one hand, challenger parties facilitate representation by widening the available choice and thus mobilizing voters with shared preferences, raising issues that voters care about, and holding the political establishment to account. On the other hand, the delivery of products in the political market is concentrated in the hands of the executive. Efficient and responsible government thus requires a certain degree of stability among a set of parties that can agree on a number of core policy issues. If the political system is too fragmented and/or polarized, and if competition is diffused along a number of cross-cutting dimensions, then it becomes difficult to form such stable coalitions, and responsible government is thus at risk.

This chapter examines the impact of the rise of challenger parties on both representation and responsible government. The first part of the chapter examines whether voters are more mobilized and feel more represented in systems with greater choice and more challenger parties. We also look at how the rise of a new challenger, the Alternative for Germany, on the far right in German politics has had a mobilizing effect on citizens. Thereafter we turn to the effect on government stability. We firstly show that it is more difficult to form a government as the share of challenger parties rises and, importantly, the governments that are formed are less stable. We discuss the specific examples of government formation in Belgium and government instability in the Netherlands.

Representation

A long-standing debate in modern liberal democracies is the tension between two competing visions of the democratic ideal: a majoritarian and a proportional one. The majoritarian principle emphasizes that democracy is majority rule and is based on a concentration of power. Majoritarian democracy not only tends to create sharp divisions between those who hold power and those who do not, it also creates high barriers of entry for challengers (as discussed in chapter 3). In contrast, the proportional, or consensus, principle promotes the idea that democracy should represent as many citizens as possible. Consensus democracy disperses power so that there are multiple decision makers and checks and balances, thus limiting the power of the central government while providing for the representation of a broader array of interests.

There are clear parallels to the business world: in majoritarian democracies, market power is concentrated in the hands of a few firms and barriers to entry are high. In proportional democracies, on the other hand, the market is more fragmented, as barriers to entry are lower. In political science, much of the debate has focused on the effect of electoral institutions on democratic practices, in particular the distinction between majoritarian and proportional electoral systems. American political scientist G. Bingham Powell has famously argued that two constitutional features determine whether a democracy is tilted toward the majoritarian or proportional principle. Firstly, the electoral system: a low district magnitude is favorable to a majoritarian design, increasing the likelihood of a single-party majority government, while proportional electoral systems with large district magnitudes promote multipartisan and proportional democracy. Secondly, legislative rules in majoritarian democracies give the parliamentary majority the more or less unconstrained capacity to implement its policies, while rules in proportional democracies favor the dispersion of power and enhance the opposition's influence.[8] Electoral and legislative institutions are undoubtedly important in shaping party systems, and more proportional systems offer much lower barriers to entry for challenger parties, as discussed in chapter 3. Yet, as we have also shown in this book, even when institutions have remained stable both within and across countries there has been considerable variation in the concentration and fragmentation of the party system. Here we focus on the effects of these variations in "market structures."

We argue that the degree of concentration or dispersion in the party system influences both the choice offered to citizens and the ability of parties to govern. We start by exploring the effect of choice on citizen representation and then we turn to governability. When it comes to representation, political choice is seen as crucial to democracy and lies at the heart of what distinguishes democratic systems from nondemocratic ones. Party systems with greater dispersion of market power, such as so-called proportional democracies, also have lower barriers to entry for challenger parties, and provide a greater range of choice to voters. As we have seen in previous chapters, the rise of challenger parties has also resulted in greater political choice as voters can choose between parties with distinct positions on issues that are important to them. What are the effects of such changing market structures on representation?

Greater choice in the political marketplace may have a number of effects on citizens' engagement with the democratic process. More choices may make citizens more likely to turn out to vote. If voters perceive no difference between parties, they will feel there is little point voting, turnout at elections will be low, and abstention more likely. As we saw in chapter 4, dominant parties tend to converge in the center, thus offering limited distinct choice to voters. In contrast, greater perceived polarization of the parties, such as with the arrival of challenger parties, may encourage more voters to participate in elections.[9] It may be not only the difference between the parties, but simply the ability to vote for a party that represents a person's ideology, issue positions, or group identity that encourages citizens to turn out.[10] Finally, more choice may increase citizens' sense of representation and political efficacy within the system. Again, we would expect that when citizens have the opportunity to choose a party that represents their views, and thereby enter their preferences into the public realm, they will feel better represented and may feel that their vote matters more in elections.[11]

The rise of challenger parties can affect the political choice available to citizens in different ways. First, it is likely to result in a polarization of choice—that is, a greater range of ideological positions offered to voters. We focus on how voters perceive this choice. Second, it may also result in the offering of a viable government alternative to the dominant parties, depending on the size of the challenger parties. We are thus interested in the size of challenger-party competition. We expect that both the range of the political offering and the degree of challenger-party competition will have a positive effect on voters' willingness to participate in the democratic process and to vote in elections, and will increase their feeling that elections present them with a party that represents their views and that their vote makes a difference. In contrast, we expect that a more oligopolistic political market structure that offers a limited range of ideological choices and with insignificant challenger party competition will depress turnout and lower the sense of representation and political efficacy.

THE EFFECT OF CHOICE ON TURNOUT AND PERCEPTIONS OF REPRESENTATION

To test the impact of the different components of choice on turnout and perceptions of representation, we adopt a two-pronged approach. First, we use the Comparative Study of Electoral Systems (CSES),[12] which combines postelectoral surveys from democracies across the world to examine the effect of political choice in a cross-national multilevel analysis. Second, we discuss the entry of a new party in Germany, the Alternative for Germany, to examine the mobilizing effect of the party on the far right by comparing turnout within regions before and after this new challenger entered the electoral arena.

The CSES is a comparative postelectoral survey, which allows us to examine the factors that drive turnout and feelings of representation across very different party systems. CSES respondents are asked to indicate whether they have cast a ballot in the most recent election in their country. Our analysis focuses on the West European countries in the CSES, covering 50 legislative elections in 17 countries between 1996 and 2016. Turnout is operationalized as a categorical variable, which takes the value of 1 if the respondent voted and 0 if he or she abstained.[13] As mentioned above, we focus on two components of political choice: ideological polarization and the proportion of challenger parties. Polarization is measured as the standard deviation of party placements perceived by a respondent on the left–right dimension. Importantly, this is a measure of how much choice each individual perceives there to be in the party system. For example, if a respondent places party A at 3 and party B at 7 and party C at 9, the standard deviation would be 3.06. Ideally, we would have a measure of ideological polarization and choice on more issues than just left–right, which is the dominant dimension of contestation, to effectively measure the choice provided by challengers, but unfortunately CSES does not allow us to capture that directly. Second, we measure the size of the challenger party alternative to the dominant bloc by simply including the vote share of challenger parties going into the election. The idea is that larger challenger parties offer a more realistic government alternative, and may thus have a greater mobilization effect than we can measure by looking just at fragmentation or polarization. We also control for compulsory voting rules.[14] At the individual level, we control for a number of sociodemographic characteristics that have been shown to be correlated with turnout: income, education, political knowledge, and gender. As our data set has a multilevel structure, with individual citizens in different countries interviewed at different times (after each national election), we fit multilevel logistic regression models with random intercepts at the level of country-elections.[15] The results are shown in table 8.1.

Table 8.1 shows that both the perception of party-system polarization and greater challenger-party competition have a mobilizing effect on voters. The size of the challenger-party effect is quite small, which is not surprising given that it is measured at the party-system level, where many other factors determine the national cultures of high or low electoral participation. But it is nonetheless interesting to note that the degree of choice available to voters appears to have a positive effect on their willingness to participate in elections. Moreover, there is also a substantive and significant effect of polarization on turnout: the greater the difference that voters perceive between parties, the more likely they are to turn out.

The effects of polarization and challenger-party competition could be due to the fact that there is more is at stake when parties adopt more divergent positions and challengers seek to upset the

TABLE 8.1 The Effect of Party Choice on Turnout

	Effect of Polarization on Turnout	Effect of Challenger-Party Competition on Turnout
Age	0.34**	0.34**
	(0.01)	(0.01)
Gender	0.09**	0.09**
	(0.02)	(0.02)
Education	0.11**	0.11**
	(0.01)	(0.01)
Income	0.12**	0.12**
	(0.01)	(0.01)
Political knowledge	0.45**	0.45**
	(0.01)	(0.01)
Compulsory voting	− 0.38	− 0.81
	(0.38)	(0.38)
Polarization	**0.17****	**0.17****
	(0.01)	(0.01)
Challenger-party competition		**0.03****
		(0.01)
Constant	−1.01**	−1.56**
	(0.15)	(0.23)
N (country elections)	50	50
N (observations)	72,566	72,566

Source: Comparative Study of Electoral Systems, CSES Modules 1–5 1996–2016.
Notes: Table entries are logistic regression coefficients with standard errors in parentheses based on multilevel logistic regression with random effects varying across country-elections. Bold entries highlight the significant effects of polarization and challenger-party competition.
**Significant at $p < 0.05$.

status quo. It may also be because greater ideological polarization and the presence of challenger parties make voters feel that there is a party that better represents their specific preferences, and thus voting for them makes a difference. By contrast, in a system with limited ideological competition, there is a danger that people may feel that the choice is between Tweedledum and Tweedledee,[16] as shown in chapter 4, and that turning out to vote will make little difference because there is no party that represents their interests and preferences. We examine this empirically in table 8.2 by look-

TABLE 8.2 The Effect of Party Choice on Feelings of Representation

	A Party that Represents You	Who People Vote for Makes a Difference	Satisfaction with Democracy
Age	0.15**	0.01**	− 0.01**
	(0.01)	(0.00)	(0.00)
Gender	0.03	0.06**	− 0.01
	(0.03)	(0.01)	(0.01)
Education	0.03**	0.02**	0.01**
	(0.01)	(0.00)	(0.00)
Income	0.02	0.02**	0.03**
	(0.01)	(0.00)	(0.00)
Political knowledge	0.32**	0.07**	0.04**
	(0.02)	(0.01)	(0.00)
Polarization	**0.20**	**0.12**	0.00
	(0.02)	(0.00)	(0.00)
Challenger-party competition	**0.02**	**0.003**	− 0.004**
	(0.004)	(0.001)	(0.000)
Constant	− 0.50**	3.10**	2.65**
	(0.15)	(0.04)	(0.04)
N (country elections)	29	49	51
N (observations)	29,293	67,656	73,785

Source: Comparative Study of Electoral Systems, CSES Modules 1–5 1996–2016.
Note: Table entries are logistic regression coefficients with standard errors in parentheses. Models include fixed effects for country. Bold entries highlight the significant effects of polarization and challenger-party competition.
**Significant at $p < 0.05$.

ing at the effect of ideological polarization on whether citizens think "there is a party that represents them" and that "who people vote for makes a difference." Again, we use CSES data to analyze the effect.

In line with our predictions, we find that greater polarization and challenger-party competition are associated with a greater sense of representation by the party system and a greater feeling of political efficacy. The effects of more competition are far greater when people are asked if they feel there is a party that represents them than whether they think that who people vote for makes a difference. Perhaps this is because the presence of challenger parties alone, while securing representation, does not guarantee any kind of influence on policy making.

But does more choice also give citizens a greater sense of satisfaction with democracy? In order to assess how satisfied citizens are with the democratic process in general in their country, the CSES survey contains the following classic question item: "On the whole, are you very satisfied, fairly satisfied, not very satisfied, or not at all satisfied with the way democracy works in [country]?" We recode the variable so that 1 denotes "not at all satisfied" and 4 "very satisfied,"[17] so higher values indicate more satisfaction, and the results are shown in the final column of table 8.2. These results show that neither ideological polarization nor challenger-party competition has a positive effect on satisfaction with democracy. In fact, challenger-party competition has a small but negative effect on satisfaction with democracy. This may be because the strength of challenger parties is a symptom of dissatisfaction with the democratic system, or because challenger parties highlight the weaknesses of the system through their antiestablishment rhetoric, as shown in chapter 6, and often cause problems of the delivery of stable government, as we will show next.

Overall, our comparative evidence suggests that greater choice does not necessarily make people more satisfied with the democratic system or with the performance of the system, but our findings do indicate that greater choice makes people more engaged with democracy and more likely to feel that their voices are heard. These findings give an overview of the macrolevel relationship, but still raise the question of what happens when a new challenger party enters the scene. We explore this by looking at the case of the populist right-wing Alternative for Germany.

The Mobilizing Effect of the Alternative for Germany

What happens when a new challenger party enters the political arena? Can such a party mobilize voters who do not feel their views are fully represented by the dominant parties? One recent example is the Alternative for Germany. Ever since the experience of Nazism during the Second World War, far-right positions have been discredited in Germany, and this has prevented the rise of a successful party on the extreme right of the political spectrum. This has meant that German citizens with a far-right ideology and xenophobic views could vote either for a party with a very different ideological platform or abstain. This situation changed with the emergence of the Alternative for Germany. Originally founded in opposition to Germany's involvement in Eurozone bailouts in 2013, the party quickly became successful in German federal, European, and state elections, seizing the electoral space on the right of the political spectrum. Starting out as an anti-Euro party, it moved incrementally further to the right after a change of leadership and increasingly ran on an anti-immigration platform, a change mirrored in its voter base.[18] The party has become known for its xenophobia, anti-Islam beliefs, and overt nationalism, thus raising issues that had been rejected by the dominant German parties. The Alternative for Germany has also adopted distinct antiestablishment rhetoric, such as the slogan *Lügenpresse* (the lying press), echoing slogans used during the Nazi era. In 2017, the Alternative for Germany became the most successful challenger party in German postwar history by coming third in the elections, with 12.6 percent of the vote. It was also the first far-right party to enter the German Bundestag in six decades.

The success of the Alternative for Germany, and other far-right parties in Europe, raises important questions about the appeal of explicitly xenophobic and nationalist parties. However, an aspect of the rise of challengers that has received less attention is whether they mobilize citizens who ordinarily would not vote. Here we examine whether emergence of this new challenger on the right had a mobilizing effect on citizens, especially those who share its policy preferences.[19] To measure the impact of a new challenger party on turnout, we look at the participation of the Alternative for Germany in the German regional elections. Since the federal elections in 2013, the Alternative for Germany has stood in all regional elections (*Landtagswahlen*). These elections are scattered throughout the electoral calendar, with the constitutions of different *Länder* (federal states) providing for different term lengths, and thus after its formation the

Alternative for Germany would simply field candidates in each up-coming regional election. This case thus presents us with a unique opportunity to study the effect of the emergence of a new right-wing challenger party on turnout in general and on right-wing voters in particular. With the timing of the elections being determined by the electoral calendar, rather than strategically by the party itself, we are in a position to compare turnout within several *Länder* before and after the Alternative for Germany entered the scene.

To examine the impact of the presence of the Alternative for Germany on turnout, we rely on the *Landtagswahlen* data set of the German Longitudinal Election Study (GLES).[20] For the data set, pre-election surveys were conducted for all *Landtagswahlen* since 2010. Overall, we analyze 13 election studies for the time period 2010–16. In order to keep other sources of variation constant, we focus only on *Länder* for which we have election results from before and after the Alternative for Germany decided to run and use *Land* fixed-effects. As our dependent variable, we use vote intention on a 5-point-scale ranging from 1 (very unlikely to cast a ballot) to 5 (very likely to cast a ballot). We group respondents according to their self-placement on an 11-point scale as left (1–4), centrist (5–7), and right (8–11). In addition, we control for a number of sociodemographic variables, such as age, gender, income, and education, and include a variable capturing whether a state is in the east or west of the country.

Table 8.3 shows that the coefficient for the Alternative for Germany measure is statistically significant, indicating that there is an overall mobilizing effect of the presence of this party in the party system owing to higher polarization. When the Alternative for Germany is present, voters are around 2.5 percent more likely to cast a ballot compared with the previous election in the same *Land* without the Alternative for Germany. This is also shown in figure 8.1.

In the third column in table 8.3 we analyze the effect of mobilization by the Alternative for Germany for different groups of voters. The entry of the Alternative for Germany has a significant effect on turnout for voters who place themselves on the right of the political spectrum, indicating that this group is significantly more likely to

TABLE 8.3 The Effect of Alternative for Germany (AfD) Candidates on Turnout

	Effect of AfD Presence	Conditioned by Voter Ideology
AfD	0.11**	0.11**
	(0.03)	(0.04)
Left	0.08**	0.11**
	(0.03)	(0.04)
Right	– 0.03	– 0.06
	(0.03)	(0.03)
AfD × left		– 0.06
		(0.04)
AfD × right		0.11**
		(0.05)
Age	0.01**	0.01**
	(0.00)	(0.00)
Gender	– 0.03	– 0.03
	(0.02)	(0.02)
Income	0.04**	0.04**
	(0.01)	(0.01)
Education	0.07**	0.07**
	(0.01)	(0.01)
East	– 0.14	– 0.14
	(0.07)	(0.07)
Land fixed effects	✓	✓
Constant	4.03**	4.03**
	(0.10)	(0.10)
N (observations)	5743	5743

Source: GLES (see sources listed in note in main text).
Note: OLS regression with fixed effects at the level of *Länder* (omitted). Clustered standard errors at the election level in parentheses.
**Significant at $p < 0.05$.

be mobilized by the Alternative for Germany compared with the baseline category, centrist voters. Figure 8.2 clearly shows these different levels of mobilization by the Alternative for Germany.

The mobilization effect is strongest for right-wing voters, with an increase in the likelihood of casting a ballot of about five percentage points, compared with an increase of a bit more than two percentage points for centrist voters. This suggests that mobilization

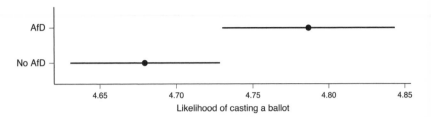

FIGURE 8.1 Mobilization effect of the Alternative for Germany
Note: Effect of the presence of the Alternative for Germany on the likelihood of casting a ballot (linear prediction). Based on table 8.3 (center column) (OLS fixed effects regression with 95% confidence intervals).

may be primarily among those who feel their views are represented by the new challenger party. Before the entrance of the Alternative for Germany, right-wing voters were the group least likely to cast a ballot, while in its presence they are the most likely to vote. It is interesting to note, however, that even for left-wing voters the likelihood of casting a ballot increases by around 1 percent. In other words, people might also turn out in larger numbers if they hold the opposite

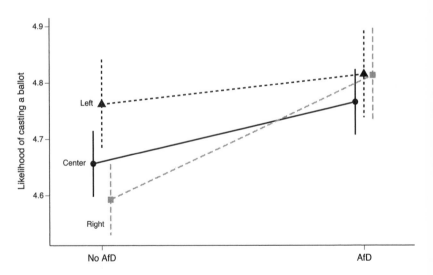

FIGURE 8.2 Mobilization effect of the Alternative for Germany by ideology
Note: Effect of the presence of the AfD on the likelihood of casting a ballot, by ideological self-placement (linear prediction). Based on table 8.3 (right-hand column) (OLS fixed effects regression with 95% confidence intervals).

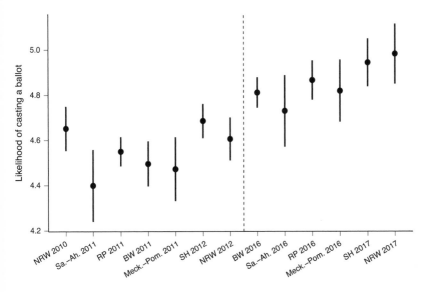

FIGURE 8.3 Likelihood of casting a ballot among right-wing voters in regional elections
Note: Average likelihood of casting a ballot for right-wing voters in different regional elections (linear prediction). The dashed line indicates the entrance of the Alternative for Germany into the party system. Based on table 8.3 (right-hand column) (OLS fixed effects regression with 95% confidence intervals). BW, Baden-Württemberg; Meck.-Pom., Mecklenburg–Western Pomerania; NRW, North Rhine–Westphalia; RP, Rhineland-Palatinate; Sa.-Ah., Saxony-Anhalt; SH, Schleswig-Holstein.

views, because they feel more is at stake when the Alternative for Germany enters the race.

We can illustrate the effect of the Alternative for Germany standing in an election by plotting the propensity to vote for right-wing voters in regional elections before and after the Alternative for Germany emerged. Figure 8.3 shows that there is a clear increase in the propensity to cast a ballot among people who identify as right wing since the Alternative for Germany stood for the first time in September 2013.

These findings suggest that there is a mobilizing effect of the entry of a new challenger party. In particular, we find a strong and significant effect for right-wing voters, who now have an option that is close to their own position but not so radical as to be socially unacceptable. These findings are supported by data from exit polls, which reveal that the Alternative for Germany gained significantly among former nonvoters.[21]

Overall, when focusing on representation, the evidence suggests that challenger parties do have a mobilizing effect on citizens and make it more likely that they feel there is a party that represents their views. To use an analogy from the world of ice cream: new flavors and textures may satisfy a wider range of customer tastes. It may even encourage people who have not eaten ice cream for a long time to try it again. However, politics is not simply about the range of products offered by parties. It is also about product delivery in office. In the next section, we turn to the issue of challenger parties and governability.

Government

For ice-cream lovers in Vermont, the sale of Ben & Jerry's to Unilever made little real difference to the ice cream experience. They were still able to enjoy their tub of Half-Baked Ben & Jerry's ice cream, regardless of whether it was made by two hippies in a dilapidated former gas station or on the production line of a multinational conglomerate. In the world of ice cream, and in business more generally, the product is delivered to the consumer whether it is produced by a challenger or a dominant player. However, in politics the product is no more than a set of promises when voters put their cross in the ballot box. Only those parties that enter government are directly able to deliver their product to voters, although other parties in parliament may, of course, exert policy influence. The political equivalent of Ben & Jerry's in the late 1970s, a minor political outsider, would have little chance of ever delivering textured ice cream to consumers. Small challenger parties may add to a sense of representation among their followers and raise the stakes for voters who take part in elections. Yet, if the political market becomes too fragmented, this may also have implications for the delivery of the product, the policy promises that people vote for. To ensure policy delivery, stable and efficient government is necessary. Hence, if we are going to assess the implications of challenger parties, we need to look not just at representation, but also at responsible government: do challenger parties help or hinder responsible government?

We look at two aspects of responsible government: first, the ability of parties to form governments, and second, the duration of governments. The ability of governments to be formed is the very first hurdle of delegation in a parliamentary system: for parties in parliament to be able to appoint an executive after elections. When government formation is delayed, it is a clear indication that the system of translating voter preferences into parliamentary seats, and by extension implementing policy preferences, is not functioning optimally. Long deadlocks, such as in the Belgian case discussed in the next section, are a clear failure of the system to produce accountable and responsible government. Second, we are interested in the stability of government once formed. Frequent government turnover and elections are signs of system instability, because parties are unable to deliver their policy programs to voters. In other words, we argue that the ability of a government to form and remain relatively stable is the starting point for good governance in parliamentary democracies.

So, how might the rise of challenger parties influence government formation and stability? The literature has long suggested that there is a relationship between the characteristics of a party system and government stability. As early as 1896, the American political science professor, and later president of Harvard University, A. Lawrence Lowell argued that having more than one party in government is problematic for government stability, since "the larger the number of discordant groups that form the majority, the harder the task of pleasing them all, and the more feeble and unstable the position of the cabinet." He was equally concerned about a fragmented opposition, since "the parliamentary system will give the country a strong and efficient government only [when] the majority consists of a single party. But this is not all. The opposition must also be united."[22] Of course, when Lowell was writing, very few European governments actually fit the ideal of strong and stable single-party-majority governments. And with the rise of challenger parties, party systems have become more fragmented, as we showed in chapter 1, and often more ideologically polarized.

Our expectation is that these changes to European party systems have also reduced the ability to form and sustain governments. Existing work on government formation tells us that a key hindrance is bargaining complexity, which comprises two key elements: the number of parties in parliament and the degree of ideological polarization.[23] The expectation is that the greater the number of parliamentary parties, the greater the number of potential players involved in any bargaining process with the power to veto, and the more difficult it is to form a government.[24] Similarly, ideological polarization among parties increases complexity because there are more potential policy domains in which there are significant disagreements between the parties.[25] Studies have shown that party fragmentation can have a negative effect on the ability of parliaments to form governments, and particularly in postelection periods, rather than interelection periods.[26] These findings suggest that significantly longer delays are more common in more complex and polarized legislative party systems. Since challenger parties tend to increase both the number and polarization of parties, we would expect this to make government formation more difficult, with the added complication that challenger parties have no experience of forming governments.

Importantly, fragmentation and polarization should make it more difficult for governments not only to form, but also to survive. The Italian political scientist Giovanni Sartori is famous for his work on stable and unstable party systems. In his empirical work, he found that party fragmentation can lead to government instability if combined with ideological polarization.[27] More recent work has also found that it is ideological diversity within governments specifically that leads to a higher risk of governments falling.[28] But the problem is not only that the rise of challenger parties leads to more polarization and fragmentation; it often also brings with it a different approach to government. As we saw in chapter 6, challenger parties tend to employ explicit antiestablishment rhetoric that makes coalition building and consensual policy making more difficult. For parties that have been successful on the back of such an anti-elite strategy, it is also often less appealing to enter, or remain in, government and be held accountable for actual policy delivery. As Peter Mair noted, "[challenger parties] are often characterized by a strong populist rhetoric. They rarely govern and also downplay office-seeking motives. On the rare occasions when they do govern, they sometimes have severe problems in squaring their original emphasis on representation and their original role as a voice of the people with the constraints imposed by governing and by compromising with coalition partners."[29] Mair argued that while challenger parties represent but do not govern, dominant parties increasingly govern but no longer represent. Our expectation is therefore that party systems with stronger challenger parties make it more difficult for governments to survive.

We now examine this expectation empirically by looking at quantitative data on government formation and survival, as well as two case studies of how challenger parties have affected government formation and stability in Belgium and the Netherlands.

SURVIVAL MODELS OF GOVERNMENT FORMATION AND STABILITY

To examine the impact of challenger parties on responsible government in a quantitative way, we measure the impact of how the size of challenger parties influences the time it takes to form government and the duration of these governments. We focus on elections in Western Europe from 1950 to 2014.[30] Table 8.4 shows the average number of days of government formation and government survival by decade.

On average, government formation takes a little over a month. However, table 8.4 shows a sharp increase in the time it took for governments to form in the early 2010s, where it almost doubled compared with earlier decades. Governments survive on average just over one-and-a-half years, indicating that most do not survive an entire electoral cycle. Again, we observe a drastic fall in average government duration during the last decade. What influences variation

TABLE 8.4 Government Formation and Survival

Decade	Government Formation (days)	Government Survival (days)
1950s	33	534
1960s	35	656
1970s	39	586
1980s	35	722
1990s	31	875
2000s	35	814
2010s	64	460
Average	37	678
N	315	581

Source: Updated version of Party Government data set (Seki and Williams, "Updating the Party Government").

in government formation and stability? Has the increasing popularity of challenger parties in recent years contributed to more protracted coalition discussions and less stable governments?

We start by examining the time it takes to form a government, using a so-called survival model, which is a statistical method for analyzing the expected length of time until government formation happens. Survival analysis allows us to answer the question of how likely it is for a government to form (or fall) on a given date. To examine the effect of challenger parties, we look at two types of systems: ones where challenger parties are strong (the top 25 percent of challenger-party strength of all parliaments) and ones where challenger parties are weak (the bottom 25 percent of challenger-party strength). We use seat shares of challenger parties as a measure of challenger-party strength, expecting that when challenger parties hold more seats, it will be more difficult for governments to form for the reasons of fragmentation, polarization, and antiestablishment posturing outlined above. The survival graph is plotted in figure 8.4.

The figure shows Kaplan-Meier estimates of government formation, which estimate the percentage of governments that are likely

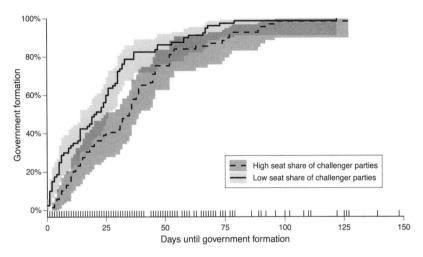

FIGURE 8.4 Government formation, by challenger parties' seat share
Note: The figure plots Kaplan-Meier estimates of the survival function with 95% confidence intervals.

to have been formed at a certain time after an election. This "success plot" is shown for both systems with strong and systems with weak challenger-party representation. So, for example, on day 1 after an election, the likelihood of forming a government is close to zero in both types of systems. But the rate of success is steeper in systems with weaker challenger parties, meaning that it takes less time to form a government. The average time it takes for a new government to form is 34 days, and after around two months, most governments will have been formed. Importantly, the analysis clearly shows that in party systems with stronger challenger parties it takes significantly longer to form a government. The difference between the two types of systems is not large, however.

How about the survival of the governments once they are formed? We operationalize government survival as duration in office—that is, the difference between investiture dates for two governments.[31] Again, we show how survival depends on the strength of challenger-party competition. Figure 8.5 shows the results (Kaplan-Meier estimates) from a survival analysis, indicating the probability for a government of surviving to time *t* or beyond.

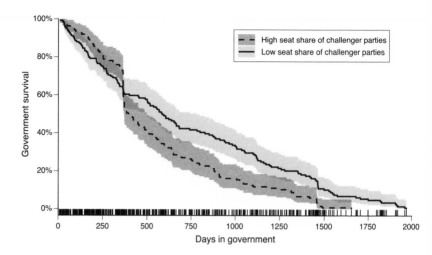

FIGURE 8.5 Government survival, by challenger party competition
Note: The figure plots Kaplan-Meier estimates of the survival function with 95% confidence intervals.

The average time that a government survives in office is just under two years. Figure 8.5 shows that the difference is quite stark between systems with strong challenger-party competition versus those with weak competition. In countries with a low vote share for challenger parties, governments survive longer. In contrast, governments in countries with a high vote share for challenger parties collapse earlier and at an increasing rate after about 400 days.

These findings indicate that governments are significantly more fragile when challenger parties are strong. This suggests that while voters can be mobilized by challenger parties, and feel represented by their policy messages, the fragmentation and polarization that they bring make it more difficult to govern responsibly. Next, we discuss how the rise of challenger parties has affected government formation and stability in two specific case studies, Belgium and the Netherlands.

Government Formation in Belgium

On January 6, 2011, Johan Vande Lanotte, a Belgian socialist politician, submitted his resignation from the position as mediator in the government formation process to the king of Belgium, Albert II, claiming that there was a lack of political will to reach an agreement. The king, however, rejected his resignation. At this point, six months had passed since the general election in June 2010, and Belgium was still without a working government. The election had produced a very fragmented political landscape, with 11 parties elected to the Chamber of Representatives, none of which had won more than 20 percent of the seats. The Belgian party system has long been split by language into two parts, a Flemish and a Francophone, both of which were themselves fragmented. Following the 2010 election, a then challenger party, the New Flemish Alliance, emerged as the largest party, controlling 27 of 150 seats in the lower chamber. The New Flemish Alliance, a Flemish nationalist party, had been founded only a decade previously with the aim of securing the gradual secession of Flanders from Belgium, but its ascendency was swift. Of the dominant parties, the winners were the two socialist parties, with 39 of the 150 seats between them. As the king rejected Vande Lanotte's resignation he asked him to work with the leaders of the two largest political parties, Di Rupo of the Francophone socialists and De Wever of the Flemish nationalists, to break the deadlock in coalition negotiations. This attempt to from a government did not work out, however, and on January 26, 2011, the king accepted Vande Lanotte's second request to be relieved of his task. It was not until December 6, 2011, after a record 589 days without an elected government, that a new government was finally sworn in, with Elio Di Rupo named prime minister of the Di Rupo I Government. The Di Rupo I Government was a six-party coalition including the liberal, socialist, and Christian democratic parties from both Flanders and Wallonia, but excluding the New Flemish Alliance.

Forming a government in Belgium has never been easy. In its postwar history the country has often experienced long delays in government formation, occasionally more than 100 days. However, more recently, government formation has proven to be unusually protracted: after the 2007 election it took 194 days to form a government, while the 2010 election led to a record-breaking 541 days. This has coincided with the fragmentation of the Belgium party system and the rise of challenger parties. This unfortunate record is also related to the strength of the cross-cutting "communitarian" dimension in Belgium politics. While most West European party systems are organized along the left–right dimension, left–right politics is combined in Belgium with an entrenched linguistic cleavage between Francophone and Dutch-speaking citizens, resulting in an effectively divided party system.[32] This process started in the late 1960s, as Belgium moved from a unitary to a federal system. In the 1970s, new parties were formed on both sides of the language border. This division and the cross-cutting linguistic dimension have unsurprisingly increased the complexity of bargaining over government formation.

Another complication is the strength of challenger parties in Belgium. The Vlaams Blok (Flemish bloc) was one of the first examples of a successful far-right anti-immigration party in postwar Western Europe. It gained 10 percent of the vote in 1999 and 12 percent in 2003 on a platform of Flemish nationalism, separatism, and anti-immigration. Other Belgian political parties were reluctant to enter coalitions with the Vlaams Blok, and the party was effectively prevented from entering any level of government. In 2004, after the party reorganized itself as the Vlaams Belang (Flemish interest), it was supported by about one in four of the Flemish electorate. Nonetheless, most other parties have continued the cordon sanitaire, effectively blocking the Vlaams Belang from taking part in government at any level.[33] A more serious threat to the dominance of the established socialist, Christian democratic, and liberal party families was the establishment of the more moderate Flemish nationalist New Flemish Alliance. As discussed, the New Flemish Alliance won a plurality of votes in the 2010 elections. It was not only its secessionist platform, but also its inexperience in forming coalitions that complicated the coalition formation process. At the time, participation in federal government was not a goal in itself.[34] In 2014, the New Flemish Alliance did join a center-right coalition government, with the Flemish Christian democrats and liberals and the French reformist movements. The coalition was formed and able to function because it focused on socioeconomic issues first and avoided "community-related" issues or constitutional reform plans.

Belgium is a good example of how problems in forming a government are related not only to fragmentation of the party system but also to ideological polarization, especially if such polarization cuts across multiple salient dimensions.

A Fragile Government in the Netherlands

The 2002 Dutch parliamentary election held on May 15 was a political earthquake. A new party, the List Pim Fortuyn, made a stunning electoral breakthrough. Out of nowhere the party become the second-largest political force in the Dutch parliament, securing 26 out of 150 parliamentary seats. In fact, the Netherlands had never before experienced such a significant voter shift in its modern electoral history.[35] In terms of volatility, the election result was also significant in the context of other West European elections: only the Italian elections of 1994, the German elections of 1920, and the French elections of 1906 had shown greater electoral volatility than the Dutch result from 2002.[36]

The 2002 election is tied to the life and death of one of the most flamboyant political entrepreneurs in Dutch history, Pim Fortuyn. The former sociology professor founded a political party in March of that year, called the List Pim Fortuyn. "It was clear from the start that Fortuyn was the party, and the party was Fortuyn. He was the party's only founder, only leader, and only spokesperson, and openly denounced the other candidates of his own party."[37] Fortuyn was known for his rule breaking, controversial policy positions, and provocative political style. One of his policy positions, his leniency toward the fur industry, sparked an animal rights activist, Volkert van de Graaf, to plan and execute his assassination, just nine days before the election.[38] His party decided to participate in the election, regardless of having lost its leader, in part as a tribute to the memory of its founder. The party then pulled off the biggest electoral upset in the postwar period, commanding 17 percent of the vote in the first nationwide election it had participated in. This was a result never before seen for a new Dutch political party.

Another special feature of the party's rapid rise to success was its entry to government. List Pim Fortuyn entered a coalition with the Christian democrats and liberals in the first government under the leadership of Jan-Peter Balkenende. The party obtained four ministerial posts and five state secretariats. Eduard Bomhoff, List Pim Fortuyn's minister of health, welfare and sport, also became deputy prime minister.[39] The coalition agreement was met with skepticism by the rank and file of List Pim Fortuyn.[40] Many within the party felt that the leadership had moved away from Pim Fortuyn's ideas in the pursuit of power. This was exactly the kind of mainstream political move they felt Fortuyn would have rebelled against. Party members also felt that Minister Eduard Bomhoff, a former economics professor and university executive, was too much of a system insider. Some preferred the more flamboyant entrepreneur Herman Heinsbroek, who was the minister of economic affairs. Heinsbroek did not care much for protocol or custom in The Hague, openly criticized other cabinet members, including those of List Pim Fortuyn, and launched plans on his own without informing others. The growing support for Heinsbroek was perceived by Bomhoff as a threat to his position. Both ministers had little fondness for the other and their relationship became increasingly acrimonious.[41]

The constant bickering between List Pim Fortuyn ministers, and within the party itself, increasingly worried its mainstream coalition partners. After weeks of argument between Bomhoff and Heinsbroek, the other ministers, including their List Pim Fortuyn colleagues, insisted on their departure. The political pressure on the party increased. Both the party chairman of the liberal party, Gert Zalm, and Prime Minister Jan-Peter Balkenende of the Christian democrats announced that the quarrels between the ministers had to end, because otherwise there would no longer be a future for List Pim Fortuyn in a government coalition. Bomhoff and Heinsbroek eventually had to resign. Yet, this was not enough in the end. On October 16, 2002, the Christian democrats and liberals declared that they had lost faith in the leadership of List Pim Fortuyn and no longer saw the party as a reliable coalition partner. That afternoon, Prime Minister Balkenende announced that he would offer the resignation of his cabinet to the queen.

The coalition including the most electorally successful challenger party in Dutch history would turn out to be the shortest in terms of time served in office. After just 87 days, the leading ministers of the Christian democrats and liberals had pulled the plug. The ministers of List Pim Fortuyn were inexperienced, and constantly in conflict with one another or with ministers from other parties. What is more, the party group of List Pim Fortuyn in parliament was filled with political novices, who found it difficult to cooperate with one another or with the cabinet. While the immediate cause of the fall of the government was the conflict between Bomhoff and Heinsbroek, many in the Christian Democrats and Liberals had been wary of the conflicts within the party long before that. List Pim Fortuyn was a new party that had lost its leader just days before its breakthrough electoral victory. Shortly after the dust settled, the party leadership had to deliver cabinet ministers and capable members of parliament. This turned out to be a challenge. It is difficult to find qualified people in a short time when there is a lack of proper party organization and internal party discipline. Also, virtually none of the cabinet members or parliamentarians had working relationships with one another, and there was limited rapport with the dominant parties within the coalition.[42] This inexperience in governing and doing business in The Hague turned out to be a huge liability. The success of List Pim Fortuyn inside and outside of government was short-lived. In the 2003 parliamentary election that followed the fall of the cabinet, the party barely made it back to parliament, and in the 2006 election it disappeared completely from the lower house.

The first Balkenende cabinet is a good example of how the participation of erstwhile challenger parties complicates government. While it is difficult to bypass challenger parties that secure a large electoral breakthrough, like List Pim Fortuyn, securing a stable and effective government coalition including them may be even more difficult. Challenger parties that make strong electoral gains often face huge organizational issues. Parliamentarians need to be recruited from a pool of people who often lack political experience. Trying to govern when most members are political novices is unlikely to be successful, as the Dutch case illustrates. From 2002 onward, after many years of stability and predictability, Dutch politics would be characterized by increasing electoral volatility and the rise of challenger parties. Creating stable government coalitions that can command majorities in both parliamentary chambers has since become quite a challenge.[43]

Conclusion

What are the consequences of a more fragmented political market, where challenger parties can more easily break through? As we have shown in previous chapters, challenger parties bring innovation to the political system: they put new issues on the agenda and are critical of the established ways of doing politics. This chapter has demonstrated that such innovation and enhanced electoral choice can mobilize citizens to be more engaged in politics. When the political system offers greater ideological choice and challenger party competition, citizens are more likely to turn out to vote. They are also more likely to feel that there is a party that represents their views in more fragmented and polarized systems.

However, this does not necessarily translate into greater satisfaction with democracy. We find no evidence that more polarized systems with stronger challenger parties lead to more satisfied citizens. This may be because challenger parties are often highly critical of the very systems that they seek to dominate. Moreover, challenger parties can make responsible government more difficult. The rise of challenger parties is often associated with greater fragmentation and polarization, which make it more difficult to form and sustain governments, in particular if polarization occurs along multiple dimensions. The antiestablishment focus of challenger parties also often makes it difficult for them to compromise in order to enter into a coalition with dominant parties. Our findings show a clear association between the strength of challenger parties and the fragility of government. Overall, this points to a tension between representation and responsible government. A more fragmented system with stronger challengers may deliver greater responsiveness and more choice to voters with different tastes, yet make it more difficult to deliver policy promises.

This raises the question of how much challenger-party competition is a good thing? Political choice is essential for any system to be a democracy, so monopolistic competition, where a single party dominates, is clearly problematic. Stable oligopolies might be more successful in delivering stable government, but people, especially on the ideological fringes, may not feel represented in such a system. Is there such a thing as too much choice in politics? Too much fragmentation and polarization across multiple issues brings about instability of government and lack of accountability. The final chapter of this book takes a closer look at the normative and policy implications of the rise of challenger parties.

9

Future Scenarios

The opening up of new markets, foreign and domestic, and the organizational development from the craft shop to such concerns as U.S. Steel illustrate the same process of industrial mutation . . . that incessantly revolutionizes the economic structure from within, incessantly destroying the old one, incessantly creating a new one.

—JOSEPH A. SCHUMPETER, AUSTRIAN ECONOMIST[1]

Being an entrepreneur . . . is about seeing connections others can't, seizing opportunities others won't, and forging new directions that others haven't.

—TORY BURCH, FOUNDER, EXECUTIVE CHAIRMAN AND CEO OF FASHION LABEL TORY BURCH[2]

European politics is undergoing a transformation. The traditional political parties of the center that used to dominate elections are struggling to remain relevant. They are being forced to confront the fact that continuing to play by the old rules may no longer work. Meanwhile, agile political entrepreneurs are defying traditional ways of doing politics by setting their own rules. They are able to adapt faster to shifting voter tastes and successfully challenge the status quo that favors their dominant competitors. Like start-up firms, many challenger parties are destined to fail. The key question is when and why some break through and what are the consequences of their success. And, of equal importance, what can dominant parties do to face off political entrepreneurs that challenge their market power?

Answering these questions is complicated by the fact that we currently find ourselves in the eye of the storm. Being in uncertain times makes it difficult to distinguish the short-term ripple effects of an unexpected election result from a political sea change that affects the overall direction of the currents guiding the political system. While there is no doubt that election outcomes in Europe have become more volatile and political fragmentation is on the rise, we have suggested that there are some key patterns in the kind of changes we have observed. These patterns may be somewhat blurred around the edges and sometimes subject to temporal or country-level idiosyncrasies, yet they are important signposts for understanding the essence of the political transformation that we are experiencing and what the future might hold. In this book, we have presented a long view of the developments in West European politics from the postwar period until today. We have shown that these developments are as much about the resilience of dominant parties as they are about the rise of challenger parties. Our objective has been to contribute to the understanding of both resilience and change, of both challenger and dominant parties, and how the tug-of-war between them transforms European politics.

Who are the dominant parties, and how are they able to face off challengers? Who are the challenger parties and which strategies have allowed them to successfully defy the market power of dominant parties? And what are the consequences of the rise of challenger parties for the stability of European democracy? By building on the literature of industrial organization in economics, we have developed a theory of political change that focuses on the interplay between the market power of the dominant mainstream parties and the disruptive innovation of challenger parties. The notion of dominant market players and disruptive political entrepreneurs is familiar in the study of industry, where dominant companies appear to be unbreakable until innovation comes along. Kodak dominated film until digital technology destroyed its market power. Nokia was unbreakable in mobile devices until smartphones emerged. The dominant forces of computing in the 1990s, Microsoft, Intel, Cisco, and Dell, were challenged by the disruptive innovators of Google, Apple, Amazon, and Facebook, which have become the new goliaths. Change in industry might occur faster than in party politics, but in this book we have argued there are important parallels between the two.

Dominant parties have long been able to maintain their dominance in most of Western Europe by employing strategies aimed at protecting their market power—namely, distinctive convergence, issue avoidance, and competence mobilization. Recently, however, they have been less successful in doing so as the ties between parties and voters have weakened. This has created opportunities for challenger parties to disrupt the political system through two types of innovation. First, challenger parties acting as issue entrepreneurs offer policy innovations by mobilizing new political issues. Second, challengers employ antiestablishment rhetoric to prevent dominant parties from imitating their innovation and to challenge the dominant "brands." By focusing on the strategies of both dominance and innovation, we can explain why European party systems have remained so stable for decades, but also why they are now increasingly under strain. We have presented a rigorous test of our arguments using a rich mixture of quantitative analysis of cross-national data from public opinion surveys, party documents, speeches and expert data (comparing over 200 parties in 19 countries in Western Europe over six decades) and qualitative evidence from in-depth case studies.

In this concluding chapter, we aim to do three things. First, we summarize the main arguments and findings of the book by defining two key principles that we argue guide political change in Europe. Second, we outline three different scenarios for the future of European politics. Third, we highlight topics that we were not able to address in this book, but nonetheless think are important areas for future research. In this final section, we also discuss important normative considerations about the stability and resilience of democratic institutions.

Principles of Political Change

In this book we have developed a new theory of political change, which we have applied to West European politics. Our theory borrows insights from the literature on party competition as well as that on industrial organization, which studies markets with imperfect competition where a limited number of firms compete.[3] We argue that party competition has many similarities with such a system, since there are a number of different parties, but only a handful of them are dominant. Just as in oligopolies, systemic and psychological barriers to entry (e.g., electoral rules and strong voter loyalties) are high for challengers in the European party systems, but when they are overcome, challenger parties can have a transformative effect. We are familiar with the disruptive influence of companies such as Apple, Dell, Facebook, and Tesla that have successfully challenged the market power of the dominant players by introducing new products and new ways of doing business, and defying the brand value of once dominant firms. We argue that there are striking similarities with the way in which challenger parties have mobilized wedge issues that do not easily fit existing lines of political conflict and challenged the competence and integrity of the dominant parties.

Our theoretical argument draws attention to the role of voter agency in the transformation of European democracy, next to the importance of societal and structural changes, which have already received much attention.[4] Our theory of political change focuses on the dynamic between *dominance* and *innovation*. Let us summarize each of these elements in turn.

> **Dominance:** Following the industrial organization literature, we argue that the political market for votes is characterized by imperfect competition where some parties tend to dominate because of their greater market power. Dominant parties are those that control the political marketplace,

while challenger parties are those that do not (yet) have dominance within the political system. How do dominant parties maintain their position within the system? We have identified three key strategies. The first is *distinctive convergence*, whereby dominant parties take positions closer to the center ground in order to appeal to the tastes of a larger share of the electorate. They strive to gain and retain an immediately recognizable brand with a broad-based and innocuous appeal to consumers, while trying to remain sufficiently distinct from their competitors. The second strategy is *issue avoidance*. Dominant parties try to keep challengers at bay by controlling the political agenda and avoiding issues that may be disadvantageous to them. Dominant parties have risen to power in political systems structured along a left–right dimension, with political programs that focus on the role of state intervention in the economy. Left–right issues are at the core of their distinctive brand. Issues that do not easily align with the left–right dimension, and have the potential to break up their loyal following, are therefore downplayed and avoided by dominant parties. This can ultimately become a form of tacit collusion whereby dominant parties keep certain policy issues that may hurt them off the political market. The third and final strategy is *competence mobilization*. A key component that makes dominant parties different from their competitors is their government experience. They benefit from the "incumbency advantage" of having been in office and the brand value associated with that. When competing with challenger parties, dominant parties aim to capitalize on this advantage and highlight their experience in office.

Innovation: Political innovation is understood as the process through which political entrepreneurs introduce a new or previously ignored issue and where they challenge the competence of dominant parties. We expect parties to engage in political innovation only when the potential benefits of doing so outweigh the costs. Challenger parties are more likely to engage in political innovation compared with dominant parties because the potential electoral and coalition costs for the latter are likely to be higher and the potential gains more uncertain. We distinguish between two types of innovation: policy and rhetorical. When it comes to *policy innovation*, parties that wish to innovate politically will choose issues with a high degree of appropriability— that is to say, issues that are not easily subsumed in the dominant dimension and may internally split mainstream parties. Political innovation allows parties to enjoy first-mover advantages and to hold on to voters who like the new product even after it is adopted by competitors. If policy innovation is successful, innovators can enjoy an effective monopoly on the issue, at least in the short term, and reap considerable electoral benefits because rival parties will react more slowly and incur switching costs. The second component of innovation is *rhetorical*. Challenger parties employ antiestablishment rhetoric with the aim of devaluing the "brand equity" of dominant parties. Innovators attempt to protect their innovation from imitation by discrediting the activities and reputation of rivals. Antiestablishment rhetoric is used to question the integrity and competence of competitors.

We argue that the interplay between these two political forces, dominance and innovation, is what determines the extent and the nature of the political change we are currently witnessing in the political marketplace in Western Europe. Based on the evidence that we have presented in this book, we develop two principles that we argue jointly drive political change: the *principle of contestability* and the *principle of appropriability*. Both principles are about the incentives for political parties to innovate. While contestability relates to the ability to innovate, appropriability relates to the likelihood that the innovation will be successful. Let us elaborate each of the principles in turn.

The **principle of contestability** focuses on the likelihood that a party can gain a larger share of the political market if it offers a product of greater value to voters. If political market shares are sticky because of institutional hurdles or strong voter loyalties to existing party brands, relatively few votes will be contestable and innovation incentives will be muted. Why is this the case? We argue it is because the parties that are dominant already enjoy a large market share and thus have no incentive to innovate, and challenger parties are unlikely to profit electorally from innovation because voters' ties to dominant-party brands are strong. As a result, the market power of dominant parties will remain untouched, and the political market will be highly concentrated among a couple of dominant players. The level of political change will be low.

Based on the wealth of evidence that we have presented in this book, we can outline three key threats to the market power of dominant parties that increase the likelihood that a challenger party can gain a larger share of the political market if it offers a product of greater value to voters:

> **Weakening of brand loyalty:** When brand loyalties weaken, the stickiness of market shares decreases. Over the past decades, political scientists and sociologists have convincingly documented that processes of economic change and social modernization have weakened key social identities—religion or class, for example—and that this has loosened the ties between political parties and groups of voters.[5]
> **Too much convergence:** If convergence among dominant parties leads voters to see elections as a choice between Tweedledum and Tweedledee where there is little real difference between the parties, they may have little incentive to vote at all. Over the past decades, dominant parties of the left and the right have converged on the center ground in most West European countries, thus offering limited political choice to voters. This has been compounded in some countries by "grand coalitions"

between the center left and the center right that have left
challengers as the only genuine opposition parties.[6]

External events: External events, like environmental disasters,
terrorist attacks, or increasing intra-European migration
flows, have increased the salience of issues that are not so
easily incorporated into the left–right dimension, and this
makes strategies of issue avoidance less credible. Moreover,
some governments have faced significant competence
shocks—think of the corruption scandals involving the
Greek and Spanish governments during the financial crisis,
for example—which lower the ability of governments to
mobilize on competence issues.[7]

These threats have made it more difficult for dominant parties in
Europe to count on a loyal following, to keep issues off the political
agenda, to transform distinctive convergence into an asset, and to
make competence mobilization credible. As a result, contestability
increases—that is to say, there is a higher likelihood that a party that
offers a product of greater value to voters will gain electorally by
doing so. This in turn provides a fertile breeding ground for challenger parties that aim to disrupt the political market. These changes
in contestability will arguably be most rapid and potentially widespread in permissive electoral systems that provide a more favorable
institutional setting for political newcomers. Yet, as we have also
shown, important differences in the timing and the degree of political change exist between political systems with similar electoral
rules. Our evidence suggests that these differences are for the most
part due to the type of political strategies that challenger parties
employ. Contestability is a necessary but not sufficient condition
for political change. The second key principle of political change is
appropriability.

The **principle of appropriability** concerns the extent to which a
successful innovator can capture the benefits resulting from its innovation. Efforts to innovate intensify with increased appropriability.
In practice, appropriability depends mainly on the extent to which
a political party can protect the competitive advantage associated

with its innovation. The long-term gains of innovation are larger when an innovator picks an issue that cuts across the dominant dimension of political competition, and when it engages in antiestablishment rhetoric to discredit competitors. If imitation is rapid, a political party that innovates is unable to differentiate its product or achieve an electoral advantage over its rivals. As a result, electoral gains are likely to be lower and innovation incentives will be muted. With rapid and effective imitation, contestability is of limited relevance.

Based on the evidence that we have presented in this book, we can distinguish two threats to the ability of political entrepreneurs to successfully appropriate their innovation:

Competition about who is first: It is difficult for two parties to own the same issue in the eyes of voters, so increased appropriability of a policy issue for one party likely reduces it for another. This may also mean that when two parties simultaneously compete over a divisive issue, the abilities of both parties to own the policy innovation and reap the electoral benefits of doing so decrease.

External developments: External developments, like increasing refugee flows, the Eurozone crisis, or climate change protests, might increase the salience of high appropriability issues like immigration, European integration, or the environment. In the short term, this might enhance the ability of innovators, as first movers, to reap benefits from their innovation; however, in the long run this might undermine their ability to appropriate. This is because the issue becomes so important that competitors will also start to engage with it. This might lead dominant parties to co-opt the issue.[8]

Both the contestability and appropriability principles relate to the incentives for innovation. The degree of change we witness on the political market is guided by both principles. Incumbent political parties often resist innovations because they threaten their advantageous position, and they are more likely stick to centrist positions, aim to keep wedge issues off the agenda, and focus on mobilizing competence as a means to differentiate their product. Political parties without a significant incumbency position may have a freer hand to innovate because they are not tied to a specific voter base or past coalition partners. Challenger parties can act as political entrepreneurs and be a potent force of innovation. They can shake up a market by bringing new issues on to the political agenda and discrediting competitors through antiestablishment rhetoric. New political parties, like start-up firms, often play the role of disruptive entrants, by introducing new products or employing novel rhetoric. But political entrepreneurs do not always need to be new entrants to the market. They can also be existing players who, having previously been unsuccessful, decide to adopt a new approach.

What is important for political change is that both principles, contestability and appropriability, are met. Only when elections are contestable because of exogenous factors (such as external shocks or changes to the electoral rules) or because the strategies of dominant parties to protect their market power fail *and* challenger parties are able to appropriate their innovation will we witness political change. It is only then, our evidence suggests, that market concentration decreases, and competition increases. Increased political competition, due to the increased market shares of the challenger parties, in turn increases electoral turnout because voters feel their views are better represented, but at the same time it decreases government stability, as we have also shown.

Future Scenarios for Political Change

So, what does the future hold for the different party systems in Western Europe? Of course, no one can predict what will happen in European party competition, as there are simply too many unknowns in politics. Yet, what we can do is outline several possible scenarios for the future, based on our theory and the historical patterns in party competition that this book has uncovered. We distinguish between three possible future scenarios:

Fragmentation: A situation in which more challenger parties will successfully compete in elections, and the market power of dominant parties will wane as many more parties are able to command a significant share of the vote.

Replacement: A situation in which challenger parties overtake the market position of the previously dominant parties and are transformed into the new dominant players on the political market.

Reinvention: A situation in which dominant parties faced with the electoral success of challenger parties revive their market power by successfully reinventing themselves to increase their voter appeal.

Let us discuss each of these future scenarios in more depth. We will do so by highlighting recent experiences in Dutch, Greek, and Spanish politics that we think may act as signposts for future developments in other European countries.

FRAGMENTATION

Market fragmentation in economics denotes the idea that markets are diverse and that with time they are likely to break up into distinct groups of customers—that is to say, different fragments. An innovation brought on to the market by a disruptive entrepreneur will initially solve the needs of most early adopters, yet over time customers will become accustomed to the new product. As more and more customers adopt the product, the need for more unique product features and benefits arises. As the novelty of the initial innovation wears off, depending on the loyalty that customers have developed towards the brand, they will either stay put or move on to the next big thing.[9]

In the political market, we might witness a similar process. In chapter 3, we demonstrated that voters have become less attached to the dominant parties and are more volatile in their choice of which party to support. Voters resemble picky consumers who are willing to substitute one product for another when they think the quality is higher. Chapters 5 and 6 demonstrated that challenger parties have used this window of opportunity to innovate politically. In chapter 7, we showed that the innovation of challenger parties has been electorally successful, especially when it comes to introducing issues such as European integration and immigration, and their antiestablishment rhetoric is associated with less market concentration. The political marketplace in virtually all West European countries has become more fragmented in recent years in the sense that more political parties compete, and a larger share of them attract a significant voter following. Echoing the work of experts on political change in Eastern Europe Tim Haughton and Kevin Deegan-Krause, politics in Western Europe seems to resemble more and more the political instability and party system fragmentation found in the eastern part of the continent.[10]

One of the clearest examples of such a fragmentation scenario is the Netherlands. Dutch politics has seen some of the most electorally successful challenger parties to date. While in the 1960s and 1970s the Netherlands witnessed the birth of a set of challenger parties on the left of the political spectrum, since the early 2000s the rise of challengers has been primarily on the right. Ever since the political entrepreneur Pim Fortuyn shocked the Dutch political establishment in 2001, with his outspoken rhetoric against immigration and Islam against the backdrop of 9/11, Dutch election results have remained highly volatile.[11] While the party of Pim Fortuyn—List Pim Fortuyn—collapsed quickly after his death and a brief, chaotic period in office, in 2006 Dutch voters moved on to the next challenger party, the Party for Freedom under the leadership of Geert Wilders. In order to trump Fortuyn's legacy, Wilders hardened his rhetoric and advocated an even more restrictive stance on immigration, now also attacking intra-EU migration, for example.[12] For a little over a decade, with his fiercely anti-Islam, anti-EU, and antiestablishment platform, Wilders was able to control the political agenda and turn Dutch party politics into a divide over a cosmopolitan versus a nationalistic world view, rather than the traditional left–right divide over economic issues.[13]

Yet, by 2017, the impact of Wilders's innovation was starting to wane. Although the Party for Freedom won 20 seats in the 2017 elections and improved on its previous seat share, the party fell short of its strongest electoral showing of 24 seats in 2010. In 2017 a new challenger, Thierry Baudet with his Forum for Democracy, entered the Dutch parliament. Thierry Baudet is a far-right populist entrepreneur and an arch Euroskeptic who gained notoriety as one of the initiators of the campaign to hold a referendum on the European Association Agreement with Ukraine. The Dutch government did not accept the result of the nonbinding referendum, although a majority voted against the agreement, because of low turnout. But as far as Baudet was concerned it did not really matter, because the campaign launched his political career.[14] The Forum for Democracy gained parliamentary representation the next year and became the largest party in the regional elections in 2018. Just as Wilders had to put distance between himself and Fortuyn, Baudet had to distinguish himself from Wilders and the Party for Freedom, by differentiating his political offer to voters. Like Wilders, Baudet and his Forum for Democracy are anti-immigrant and anti-Europe, but Baudet goes further. He is known in the Netherlands for his ultra-hard-line conservative views. In his speeches, Baudet combines a "Dutch First" message with rhetoric critical of feminists and the liberal Dutch establishment (universities, journalists, and politicians), which, according to him, have all undermined Dutch civilization. A civilization that Baudet says was "once the greatest and most beautiful civilization the world has ever known."[15]

After the initial innovation by the first successful far-right challenger party on the Dutch political market wore off, the subsequent challenger parties have needed to add new elements—such as a stronger anti-European focus and a more encompassing antiestablishment rhetoric—to be successful. Fragmentation has increased as a result. Never before in electoral history has the winning party in an election received a smaller vote margin (less than 15 percent of the vote) as during the 2018 regional election, an election that determines the composition of the upper chamber in Dutch parliament.[16] As a consequence, forming stable governments that can straightforwardly pass laws by commanding a majority in both parliamentary chambers in the Dutch context has become increasingly difficult.

These Dutch trends suggest that moving away from a model of oligopoly with power concentrated among a few dominant party families toward greater fragmentation and more political competition may also go hand in hand with more polarization and a harsher tone in the political debate. While the Dutch case is perhaps one of the clearest examples of fragmentation and its consequences, we are witnessing a "Dutchification" trend in many other countries in Western Europe as well. Dutchification refers to party systems moving from competition in which a few main parties dominate to competition between many midsized ones.[17] Indeed, party system concentration is weakening in many countries, and the market power of dominant parties seems to be waning, as we showed in chapter 7.

REPLACEMENT

While fragmentation seems a very likely future scenario for party systems in Europe, there are other possible scenarios. One is replacement. The replacement scenario comes closest to the notion of "creative destruction" as developed by Joseph Schumpeter.[18] It refers to the idea that the firms who once revolutionized product markets through innovation are themselves replaced by rivals who launch new products and improve on the design or delivery of existing ones. Think of the various cases that we have discussed throughout this book, like Dell in personal computers, Nokia in mobile phones, or Kodak in photography. All of these firms saw their profits fall dramatically and their dominance vanish as they were replaced by the likes of Apple and Samsung. On the political market, challenger parties that chip away at the market power of dominant parties through innovation strategies can become so electorally successful that they are able replace these parties and themselves become dominant.

In recent years, we have witnessed some dramatic and sudden declines in the staying power of dominant parties as they were replaced by challengers. One of the clearest examples of replacement can perhaps be found in Greece. Here, a once-dominant social democratic party, the Panhellenic Socialist Movement (PASOK), collapsed and was replaced by the challenger Syriza. PASOK as the dominant social democratic party in Greece was part of the coalition government responsible for the unprecedented austerity measures taken in response to the sovereign-debt crisis that hit Greece after the Great Recession started in 2008. During this time, the party went from being the largest in the Greek parliament, commanding over 40 percent of the popular vote, to being the smallest, with less than 5 percent in the January 2015 election. It eventually merged into a new party called Movement for Change in 2018.[19] This decline became known as "PASOKification," a term used for the more general decline of social democratic political parties in Western Europe in the 2010s and the simultaneous rise of left- and right-wing populist challengers.[20]

As the electoral fortunes of the Greek social democratic party waned, the left-wing populist challenger Syriza quickly took its place as the main party of the Greek left. The meteoric rise of Syriza occurred during the unprecedented depths of the Greek sovereign-debt crisis. In the 2012 election, the party obtained over 36 percent of the vote under the leadership of Alexis Tsipras, and became the main party of opposition. In January 2015, Tsipras led Syriza to victory in a snap legislative election, winning 149 out of 300 seats and forming a coalition with the right-wing populist party the Independent Greeks. In another snap election in the same year, Tsipras led his party to another victory, winning 145 out of 300 seats and remaining in coalition with the Independent Greeks. Unlike the latter, a party formed in 2012 in the midst of the crisis, Syriza was not a new entrant, but an existing challenger. It was originally founded in 2004 as a coalition of left-wing and radical left parties but was electorally unsuccessful before 2012. The party's tough anticorruption and overall antiestablishment rhetoric combined with a strong anti-austerity and anti-EU platform resonated with voters during the crisis.[21]

By 2015, Syriza had effectively replaced PASOK, the Greek social democrats, as the party of the left. Despite its newly pivotal position in the Greek political system, Syriza defied classical political norms and stayed true to its antiestablishment roots by deciding to enter into a government coalition with another challenger party, the Independent Greeks, in 2015, rather than forming a coalition with left-wing or centrist parties. While the two parties differed in many ways, they shared a platform that was wary of the influence of EU institutions as well as the political establishment in Greece. Despite internal turmoil because of a decades-old dispute over the naming of Macedonia, which led the junior partner, the Independent Greeks, to leave the government in January 2019, Prime Minister Tsipras remained in office—after narrowly surviving two no-confidence votes in June 2018 and January 2019—until the elections of 2019, in which Syriza lost to its right-wing competitor New Democracy.[22]

The Greek experience suggests that successful challengers can replace dominant parties. Yet, it also suggests that this may happen only in quite extraordinary times. Research by Noam Lupu regarding the breakdown of dominant parties in Latin America suggests that the implosion of once-dominant parties is most likely to occur when the brands of these parties have become blurred in the eyes of voters—for example, when politicians implement policies that are inconsistent with their party's traditional positions.[23] Brand dilution makes the electoral fortunes of parties much more vulnerable to short-term changes in voter evaluations, which may ultimately lead to voters abandon these parties altogether. The Greek experience seems to fit Lupu's conjectures as the Greek social democrats had to implement harsh austerity measures during the crisis that were not in line with their social democratic brand. Voters deserted them as a result.

Not only is replacement likely to be rare, it might pose risks for challenger parties as they transition from challenger to dominant status. When they gain in strength and enter government, challenger parties have to leave the safety of criticizing dominant parties from the sidelines. The political outsiders become the new insiders, which often sparks off internal power struggles over the direction and strategy of the party. This is what happened within the Green Party in Germany in the struggle between the "Fundis" (activists) and the "Realos" (realists) in the 1990s, as we documented in chapter 1, and with the infighting within List Pim Fortuyn in the Netherlands in the early 2000s that we discussed in chapter 8. Moreover, challenger parties that gain office may find it hard to square their antiestablishment rhetoric and their emphasis on one or a small set of issues with the broader constraints of government, such as compromising with coalition or international partners. As a result, challenger parties when in government might retain some of their disruptive traits. The confrontational and unorthodox way in which the economy minister in the first Syriza-led government in Greece, Yanis Varoufakis, operated within the EU context is a recent example of this.[24]

REINVENTION

A third and final future scenario is reinvention. Is it possible for dominant parties to face off challengers by reinventing themselves around the issues they own? Much has been made in Europe about the decline of traditional political powerhouses. Secularization and the shrinking size of the working class have led commentators to predict an inescapable decline of social and Christian democracy.[25] While structural changes are without a doubt important, in this book we have suggested that parties are not powerless. Rather, they have strategies they can use to deal with a changing electoral landscape. The obituaries of social and Christian democracy may have been written prematurely. In some countries, there seems to be something of a revival of traditional dominant forces that were once proclaimed dead. The case of Spain illustrates this type of future scenario. The Spanish parliamentary elections in 2019 saw not only the electoral breakthrough of a new challenger party on the right, VOX, but also a revival of Spain's oldest active party, the Spanish Socialist Workers' Party. The socialists had come to power in June 2018 as a result of a surprise vote of no confidence against the government of Prime Minister Mariano Rajoy of the conservative People's Party. The confidence vote was triggered by corruption charges that reached deep into Rajoy's party and administration.[26] While the government led by Prime Minister Pedro Sánchez faced an uphill battle, commanding just 84 of the 350 seats in the Spanish parliament, it did not stop the socialists from leaving their mark in office. Sánchez positioned himself as an outspoken left-wing politician aiming to create jobs, achieve greater redistribution, and eradicate social injustice. He has also presented himself as a dedicated feminist, touting his record of

65 percent women in his cabinet, the highest share among advanced industrial economies to date.[27]

After several Catalan parties withdrew their support for the government's budget bill in February 2019, Sánchez called a snap election, which was held on April 28.[28] During the election campaign, the socialists stuck to their left-wing narrative, highlighting job creation, redistribution, and the fight against social injustice, as well as tying themselves to the party's historical legacy of being the protectors of democracy in Spain. Sánchez has repeatedly warned voters against the danger of far-right parties like VOX—which, according to him, evoke the "specter of Francoism"—as well as "their enablers on the right."[29] The return to a left-wing message by the socialists, after flirting with Third Way social democracy under the previous socialist prime minister, José Luis Rodriguez Zapatero, made it difficult for the populist challenger on the left, Podemos, to make its mark on the election campaign.[30] Although the socialists' successful reinvention of their social democratic roots paved the way to electoral victory, the fragmentation of the Spanish party system (especially on the right between the traditional Popular Party and two right-wing challengers, Ciudadanos and VOX) has made it difficult to form a stable coalition government.[31] This was illustrated by the fact that in November 2019, Spanish voters went to the polls once again after Pedro Sánchez failed to form a government. The social democrats remained largest party. Nonetheless, the difficulty of forming a government coalition and the unexpected return to power of the socialists in 2018 have been celebrated by left-wing progressives across Europe as a bright light in an otherwise bleak electoral prospect for social democratic parties.[32] The social democratic recovery under the leadership of Pedro Sánchez illustrates the possibility of dominant parties regaining market share and facing off the electoral threat from challengers. Only time will tell how long Sánchez's success will last, and whether social democratic or Christian democratic parties in other European countries can follow suit, and revive their electoral fortunes to pave their way to back to political office.

Each of these future scenarios is likely to become political reality in some European party systems over the next decades. Fragmentation is perhaps the one that has already most clearly manifested itself in parliaments across Europe. Even in party systems with relatively high levels of two-party concentration, such as the Spanish one, we are now witnessing high levels of fragmentation and challenger party success. Replacement is still a relatively rare phenomenon in postwar West European party politics, but it is likely to become more common as challenger parties enter power and crowd out erstwhile dominant parties. But in cases where the brand of dominant parties has not been seriously tarnished (as was the case with the Christian democrats in Italy, for example), there is also plenty of scope for reinvention.

The development of greater fragmentation and volatility in the political market raises a number of empirical and normative questions about the implications for representation and government in Europe. The next section considers how this book might pave the way for future research into political change in Europe and beyond.

Questions for Future Research

Both normative and empirical questions are important when studying party politics in the future. The empirical questions relate to factors other than the strategies of dominance and innovation that we have outlined here, while the normative ones relate to the consequences of the rise of challenger parties that we have documented.

Starting with the empirical questions, in this book we have focused on the role of party strategy in bringing about political change. We have defined the strategies that dominant and challenger parties employ, and explained how they help us understand the timing and extent of the political change we have observed in Western Europe. Party strategy does not take place in a vacuum, however. As we have shown, it may be affected by structural changes or external events. Yet, the degree to which technological changes, such as the development of social media or the organizational features of parties, matter has not been the locus of our attention here. We do, however, think that these factors are very important for understanding the precise mechanisms of political change and thus deserve more attention in the future. Unpacking the dynamics within a party, between leaders, activists, and careerists, is important for understanding how parties may change strategies over time. Internal party dynamics are therefore an important angle for future research.[33] Developments in digital communication and social media are also important.[34] The increasing use of social media may, for example, lower barriers to entry for challenger parties as they can communicate more directly with potential supporters without needing the organizational structure and resources available to dominant parties. These technologies may also change the communication between parties and voters in fundamental ways, which should be explored further in future research.

In addition, the focus of this book has been on Western Europe, mainly because our theory starts from the assumption of established party systems that are not in constant flux, as is the case in some other parts of the world. For future research it might be worth exploring the extent to which our theory of political change is a useful tool for understanding developments in other parts of the world. The changing nature of party politics and the role of political outsiders within it may be just as relevant for understanding developments in Eastern European or Latin American politics. When moving to consolidating and developing democracies, we would also need to consider additional factors such as the ability of dominant parties to prevent challenger-party entry by relying on vote buying or forms of clientelism, for example. Latin American experts Beatriz Magaloni and Kenneth Greene suggest that the availability of state resources for vote buying is crucially important for the survival of dominant parties in Mexico.[35] Experts on East European party politics argue that, because of problems of entrenched corruption, challenger parties ousting dominant parties by mobilizing anticorruption and antiestablishment sentiment can quickly find themselves challenged by new party entrants. This causes huge party system instability.[36]

Turning to the normative consequences of the rise of challenger parties that this book has uncovered, we need to ask ourselves what it means for the stability of party systems and the quality of democracy more generally. Is there is an optimal level of competition in the political market? A monopolistic political market, with a single dominant party, is clearly far removed from the democratic ideal. But does a more fragmented market allow for greater innovation, efficiency, and consumer satisfaction than a market that is dominated by only a few parties? And what happens to challengers when they become dominant? Having more political choice might appeal to voters, but what are the consequences when the political market becomes too fragmented?

There is a long-standing debate in economics about the consequences of market structure for efficiency and innovation. Following the Scottish economist and philosopher Adam Smith, the neoclassical approach assumes that perfect competition is the ideal market structure, both for consumers and for businesses.[37] Yet, this approach has been famously challenged by Schumpeter, who argued that "perfect competition is not only impossible but inferior, and has no title to being set up as a model of ideal efficiency."[38] Schumpeter's main argument is that innovation is more likely to occur in large-scale enterprises as they have the resources to invest in innovative activities. Moreover, oligopolistic market structures reward successful innovation with the promise of greater market power. In contrast, small firms operating in atomistic markets of perfect competition have fewer incentives to innovate. This view has been challenged by the American economist Kenneth Arrow, among others, who posited that the concentration of power in the hands of a few companies does not spur innovation, but rather incentivizes the dominant firms to protect the status quo, and thus be less likely to be the instigators of disruptive new technology.[39]

This raises the question of how much challenger party competition is a good thing. Political choice is essential for any system that is a democracy, so monopolistic competition (where a single party dominates) is undesirable. Stable oligopolies might be more successful in delivering stable government, but people (especially on the ideological fringes) may not feel represented in such systems. But is there such a thing as too much choice in politics? Too much fragmentation and polarization across multiple issues might bring about government instability and lack of accountability. Is there a bliss point in political competition?

In chapter 7, we showed that the rise of challenger parties has increased competition. Yet, chapter 8 suggested that increased political competition may be something of a double-edged sword: it might increase feelings of representation, but at the same time reduce governability. We have demonstrated that as challenger parties offer more choice, they can mobilize citizens to turn out at elections and feel more represented. Yet, our analysis also revealed a tension between the choice offered at the ballot box and the delivery of policies in office. More fragmentation creates difficulties when it comes to government formation and government stability, which may in turn reduce policy performance and hinder accountability. Moreover, we have shown that the rise of challenger parties has not increased democratic satisfaction. In fact, it may have lowered it, which is in part the result of the increasing use of antiestablishment rhetoric.

Might this be a breeding ground for democratic backsliding? While democratic political institutions are resilient, the dominant players that have been seen as guarantors of democratic stability are rapidly losing ground. Within the time period that we have covered in this book (1945 to 2019), successful challenger parties in Western Europe have mostly played by the rules of liberal democracy. Yet, our qualitative evidence also points toward a situation in which increasing fragmentation may induce new challenger parties to be more aggressive and polarizing. Against this backdrop, we need to ask ourselves if this may lead some challenger parties to become more inclined to question and break with democratic norms. A question for the future is how citizens and other political parties would react to this increased political polarization and democratic backsliding if it were to happen. Only time will tell.

NOTES

Introduction

1. Hegel quoted by Dr Martin Luther King in *Strength to Love*, vol. 27 (New York: Harper and Row, 1963).

2. Christensen cited in Christoph Fuchs and Franziska J. Golenhofen, "Disruptive Innovation," in *Mastering Disruption and Innovation in Product Management* (Cham, Switzerland: Springer, 2019), 11.

3. Canovan, *Populism*; Taggart, *Populism*; Mény and Surel, "Constitutive Ambiguity of Populism"; Mudde, *Populist Radical Right Parties*.

4. Important recent structural approaches to political change in European politics include: Kriesi et al., *West European Politics*; Beramendi et al., *Politics of Advanced Capitalism*; Hooghe and Marks, "Cleavage Theory."

5. See, for example, Fetzer, "Did Austerity Cause Brexit?"; Colantone and Stanig, "Trade Origins of Economic Nationalism."

6. See, for example, Norris and Inglehart, *Cultural Backlash*.

7. Benedetto, Hix, and Mastrorocco, "Rise and Fall"; Berman and Snegovaya, "Populism"; J.-W. Müller, "End of Christian Democracy."

8. Tirole, *Theory of Industrial Organization*; Cabral, *Readings in Industrial Organization*; Belleflamme and Peitz, *Industrial Organization*.

9. Himanshu, "Rise, Dominance, and Epic Fall."

10. Lee, "Nokia."

11. Statista Research Department, "Global Market Share."

12. Schumpeter, *Capitalism, Socialism and Democracy*.

13. Schumpeter, "Creative Response in Economic History."

14. Hotelling, "Stability in Competition."

15. Downs, *Economic Theory of Democracy*. See also Adams, Merrill, and Grofman, *Unified Theory*.

16. See also the important work by Bonnie Meguid in this regard. Specifically, *Party Competition between Unequals*.

Chapter 1: The Rise of Challenger Parties

1. Riker, *Liberalism against Populism*, 209.

2. Jobs quoted in Ben Woo, "Innovation Distinguishes between a Leader and

a Follower," *Forbes*, February 14, 2003, http://www.forbes.com/sites/bwoo/2013/02/14/innovation-distinguishes-between-a-leader-and-afollower.

3. Adams et al., "Are Niche Parties Fundamentally Different"; Jensen and Spoon, "Thinking Locally, Acting Supranationally"; Meguid, *Party Competition between Unequals.*

4. Kriesi, "Populist Challenge"; Mudde, *Populist Radical Right Parties*; Pauwels, *Populism in Western Europe.*

5. Poguntke, "New Politics and Party Systems."

6. Müller-Rommel, "New Challengers"; Hino, *New Challenger Parties*; Lavezzolo and Ramiro, "Stealth Democracy."

7. Harmel and Robertson, "Formation and Success"; Hino, *New Challenger Parties.*

8. Lipset and Rokkan, *Party Systems and Voter Alignments.*

9. Inglehart and Rabier, "Political Realignment."

10. Kriesi et al., "Globalization," and *West European Politics*; Oesch, "Coming to Grips," and "Explaining Workers' Support"; Oesch and Rennwald, "Class Basis of Switzerland's Cleavage."

11. Adams et al., "Are Niche Parties Fundamentally Different"; Meguid, *Party Competition between Unequals.*

12. Stubager, "Development of the Education Cleavage," and "Changing Basis of Party Competition"; Marks et al., "Dealignment Meets Cleavage Theory."

13. There is a large body of literature that focuses specifically on individual party families, such as Christian democratic parties (e.g., Kalyvas, *Rise of Christian Democracy*), social democratic parties (e.g., Przeworski and Sprague, *Paper Stones*; Kitschelt, *Transformation of European Social Democracy*), green and left-libertarian parties (e.g., Kitschelt and Hellemans, *Beyond the European Left*; Müller-Rommel, *New Politics in Western Europe*; Spoon, *Political Survival of Small Parties*), right-wing populist and anti-immigrant parties (e.g., Akkerman, De Lange, and Rooduijn, *Radical Right-Wing Populist Parties*; Ignazi, "Silent Counter-Revolution"; Jackman and Volpert, "Parties of the Extreme Right"; Kitschelt and McGann, *Radical Right in Western Europe*; Mudde, *Populist Radical Right Parties*), and regionalist parties (e.g., de Winter and Tursan, *Regionalist Parties in Western Europe*; Jolly, *Rise of Regionalist Parties*).

14. Hino, *New Challenger Parties.*

15. Przeworski and Sprague, *Paper Stones.*

16. The influential work of Adams and colleagues and Ezrow and colleagues includes the communist, green, and nationalist parties in the niche-party category, although communist and nationalist parties emerged from the prewar cleavages described by Stein and Rokkan. See Adams et al., "Are Niche Parties Fundamentally Different"; Ezrow et al., "Mean Voter Representation." According to Adams et al., these party families are niche parties because of their "noncentrist" or extreme ideologies.

17. Meguid, *Party Competition between Unequals.*

18. Markus Wagner, for example, has defined niche parties as those that "compete primarily on a small number of non-economic issues" ("Defining and Measur-

ing Niche Parties," 845). It is noteworthy that his operationalization goes beyond the party family membership employed by Meguid and others to look at the actual programmatic content of the parties. More recently, scholars have argued that we should move beyond the dichotomous classification of parties into mainstream and niche parties and toward a measure along a mainstream–niche continuum, where "a measure of party nicheness is a relative concept of 'being distinct' from the competitors' issue emphasis" (Meyer and Miller, "Niche Party Concept," 262; see also Bischof, "Towards a Renewal."

19. See Canovan, *Populism*; Mudde, "Populist Zeitgeist."

20. Norris and Inglehart, *Cultural Backlash*.

21. This definition of dominance bears resemblance to the threshold of "relevance" of parties found in the important writings of Giovanni Sartori and Mogens N. Pedersen. As Pedersen notes in his discussion of party typologies: "The goal of any minor party is to pass the *threshold of relevance*, and, next, to become an influential, at best a ruling party. But on the other hand these thresholds are not just markers on a continuum. Quite to the contrary, they divide up the history of a party in discrete phases, each with its own dominant and different quality" (Pedersen, "Towards a New Typology," 8; see also Sartori, *Parties and Party Systems*).

22. With the exception of participation in wartime/postwar national unity governments, which is not sufficient to qualify for status as "dominant party."

23. Benedetto, Hix, and Mastrorocco, Dataset of Parties and Elections.

24. Przeworski and Sprague, *Paper Stones*.

25. Benedetto, Hix, and Mastrorocco, "Rise and Fall."

26. Przeworski and Sprague, *Paper Stones*.

27. Bartolini and Mair, *Identity, Competition, and Electoral Availability*.

28. Kirchheimer, "Western European Party Systems."

29. Przeworski and Sprague, *Paper Stones*.

30. Inglehart, "Silent Revolution in Europe," and *Silent Revolution*.

31. Müller-Rommel, "New Challengers."

32. Spoon, *Political Survival of Small Parties*; Spoon, Hobolt, and De Vries, "Going Green."

33. Kitschelt and Hellemans, *Beyond the European Left*.

34. Doherty, "Fundi-Realo Controversy."

35. Müller-Rommel, "New Challengers"; Norris and Inglehart, *Cultural Backlash*.

36. Müller-Rommel, "New Challengers."

37. Hobolt and Tilley, "Fleeing the Centre."

38. Harteveld and Ivarsflaten, "Women Avoid the Radical Right."

39. Ivarsflaten, "Immigration Policy and Party Organization," and "Reputational Shields."

40. Rydgren, *Movements of Exclusion*; Mudde, *Populist Radical Right Parties*.

41. Mudde, *Populist Radical Right Parties*, 19.

42. Rydgren, "Sociology of the Radical Right."

43. See, for example, Norris and Inglehart, *Cultural Backlash*.

44. Van de Wardt, De Vries, and Hobolt, "Exploiting the Cracks."

45. Green-Pedersen and Krogstrup, "Immigration as a Political Issue."

46. Kitschelt and McGann, *Radical Right in Western Europe.*

47. For an excellent discussion see De Lange, "New Alliances." See also Van Spanje, *Controlling the Electoral Marketplace*; Akkerman, De Lange, and Rooduijn, *Radical Right-Wing Populist Parties.*

48. A party is considered a challenger party if at the time of consideration it has not been a member of a central government since 1930. A party is considered a dominant party if at the time of consideration it has been part of a central government since 1930. None of our results substantially change if we choose a slightly different cutoff (e.g., 1925 or 1935) or if we count as challenger parties those parties that have served in only *one* government since 1930.

Only parties with ministers in cabinet are considered to be members of a central government. A party ceases to be a challenger party once it enters central government. Participation in national war/crisis cabinets (e.g., Communists in France's provisional government) does not in itself qualify a party as a dominant party. A dominant party will continue to be considered a dominant party after merging with a challenger party, whereas a party that splits from a dominant party will be considered a challenger party.

49. Döring and Manow, Parliaments and Governments Database.

Chapter 2: A Theory of Political Change

1. Carmines and Stimson, *Issue Evolution*, 9.

2. Tom Foster, "Michael Dell: How I Became an Entrepreneur Again," *Rise Networks*, July 10, 2014, https://risenetworks.org/michael-dell-how-i-became-an-entrepreneur-again/.

3. "Our History," Dell Technologies, last modified September 12, 2019, http://www.dell.com/learn/gh/en/ghcorp1/our-history.

4. Williams, "Top 10 List."

5. Simmons, *Reinventing Dell*, 91.

6. "Dell Beats Wal-Mart as 'Most Admired,'" *CNN Money*, last modified February 22, 2005, http://money.cnn.com/2005/02/21/news/fortune500/most_admired/index.htm.

7. Simmons, *Reinventing Dell*, 3.

8. Boxall, "Dell Says Goodbye."

9. Schumpeter, *Capitalism, Socialism and Democracy*, 82–83.

10. Kitschelt, *Transformation of Social Democracy*; Pontusson, "Decline of European Social Democracy"; Giddens, *Third Way*; Cronin, Ross, and Shoch, *What's Left of the Left*; Benedetto, Hix, and Mastrorocco, "Rise and Fall."

11. Jan Rovny, "What Happened to Europe's Left?" LSE EUROPP Blog, February 20, 2018, http://blogs.lse.ac.uk/europpblog/2018/02/20/what-happened-to-europes-left/.

12. Pontusson, "Decline of European Social Democracy"; Evans and Tilley, *New Politics of Class.*

13. Note that many different definitions of populism exist in the literature. For recent overviews see, for example, Mudde and Kaltwasser, *Populism*.

14. De Vries, "Cosmopolitan-Parochial Divide."

15. Clark, Lipset, and Rempel, "Declining Political Significance"; Pontusson, "Decline of European Social Democracy."

16. See, for example, Kriesi et al., *West European Politics*; Colantone and Stanig, "Global Competition and Brexit," and "Trade Origins of Economic Nationalism."

17. See for example Cramer, *Politics of Resentment*.

18. Norris and Inglehart, *Cultural Backlash*.

19. Hooghe and Marks, "Cleavage Theory."

20. See, for example, Ford and Goodwin, *Revolt on the Right*.

21. With some notable exceptions, such as Meguid, *Party Competition between Unequals*; Mudde, *Populist Radical Right Parties*; Evans and Tilley, *New Politics of Class*.

22. Kriesi et al., *West European Politics*; Oesch, "Explaining Workers' Support"; Hooghe and Marks, "Cleavage Theory"; Marks et al., "Dealignment Meets Cleavage Theory."

23. This idea is largely consistent with existing empirical evidence suggesting that parties can both influence what voters think as well as be responsive to voters. See Gabel and Scheve, "Effect of Elite Communications"; Steenbergen, Edwards, and De Vries, "Who's Cueing Whom?"

24. See, for example, Soronka and Wlezien, *Degrees of Democracy*; Canes-Wrone, *Who Leads Whom?*; Klüver and Spoon, "Who Responds?"; Matsubayashi, "Do Politicians Shape Public Opinion?"

25. Schattschneider, *Semi-sovereign People*.

26. Carmines and Stimson, *Issue Evolution*; Riker, *Liberalism against Populism*.

27. Carmines and Stimson, "Structure and Sequence," *Issue Evolution*, and "Evolution of Political Issues"; Riker, *Liberalism against Populism, Art of Political Manipulation*, and *Strategy of Rhetoric*.

28. For useful overviews see Tirole, *Theory of Industrial Organization*; Cabral, *Readings in Industrial Organization*; Belleflamme and Peitz, *Industrial Organization*.

29. While this book provides both macro and micro accounts of political change, our contribution builds mostly on microeconomic models of industrial organization aimed at understanding the dynamics of product innovation.

30. Especially in situations of minority government where government parties do not have a majority in parliament and are therefore reliant on opposition parties every time they need to pass a law.

31. Heathman, "Biggest Challenger Bank."

32. Knight Frank, *Your Future, Now*.

33. We will use the term "political issue" throughout the remainder of this book, but recognize that parties might be selling sets of ideas about which societal problems are most important and how to tackle them, which one could loosely refer to as a political ideology.

34. Downs, *Economic Theory of Democracy*; Campbell et al., *American Voter*; Budge and Farlie, *Explaining and Predicting Elections*; Enelow and Hinich, *Spatial Theory of Voting*; H. Clarke et al., *Political Choice in Britain*.

35. Müller and Strøm, *Policy, Office or Votes?*

36. Aldrich, *Why Parties?* 4.

37. Downs, *Economic Theory of Democracy*; Campbell et al., *American Voter*; Enelow and Hinich, *Spatial Theory of Voting*.

38. Adams, Merrill, and Grofman, *Unified Theory*.

39. Clarke et al., *Political Choice in Britain*; Green and Jennings, *Politics of Competence*.

40. See Gabel and Scheve, "Effect of Elite Communications"; Steenbergen, Edwards, and De Vries, "Who's Cueing Whom?"

41. Duverger, *Parties politiques*; Riker, *Liberalism against Populism*; Cox, *Making Votes Count*.

42. Belleflamme and Peitz, *Industrial Organization*.

43. Inglehart, *Silent Revolution*.

44. Bonanno and Jost, "Conservative Shift"; Hetherington and Suhay, "Authoritarianism."

45. Colantone and Stanig, "Global Competition and Brexit," and "Trade Origins of Economic Nationalism."

46. Belleflamme and Peitz, *Industrial Organization*.

47. Most notably the work by Carles Boix, "Setting the Rules."

48. Katz and Mair, "Changing Models of Party Organization."

49. Dinas, "Does Choice Bring Loyalty?"

50. Ries and Trout, *Positioning*.

51. Keller, "Customer-Based Brand Equity."

52. Campbell et al., *American Voter*.

53. Kitschelt, *Transformation of European Social Democracy*; Kalyvas and Van Kersbergen, "Christian Democracy."

54. Müller and Strøm, *Policy, Office or Votes?*

55. Katz and Mair, "Changing Models of Party Organization."

56. Shepsle, "Strategy of Ambiguity"; Rovny, "Who Emphasizes and Who Blurs?"

57. Pellikaan, Van der Meer, and De Lange, "Depolarized to a Centrifugal Democracy," and "Fortuyn's Legacy."

58. Abernathy and Utterback, "Patterns of Industrial Innovation."

59. This is known as loss aversion; see Kahneman, *Thinking Fast and Slow*.

60. Tavits, "Role of Parties' Past Behavior"; Van de Wardt, De Vries, and Hobolt, "Exploiting the Cracks."

61. Kay, *Foundations of Corporate Success*.

62. The concept of high appropriability shows affinity with the classical concept of issue ownership as it highlights the importance of the associations between certain issues and certain parties. Yet, it differs from issue ownership in some important respects. First, the degree of appropriability is a characteristic of an issue not of a party. Second, while issue ownership in essence could apply to every

issue, high appropriability applies to issues that are not easily subsumed in the dominant dimension and may internally split mainstream parties.

63. Lieberman and Montgomery, "First-Mover Advantages."

64. Meguid, *Party Competition between Unequals.*

65. Petrocik, "Issue Ownership in Presidential Elections"; Bélanger and Meguid, "Issue Salience"; Green-Pedersen, *West European Party Politics.*

66. De Vreese et al., "Populism as an Expression."

67. Canovan, *Populism*; Mudde, *Populist Radical Right Parties.*

68. Simmons, *Reinventing Dell*, 91.

69. Costello, "Worldwide PC Shipments Declined."

70. Boxall, "Dell Says Goodbye.

Chapter 3: Voter Loyalty

1. Angus Campbell, "Surge and Decline: A Study of Electoral Change," *Public Opinion Quarterly* 24, no. 3 (1960): 399.

2. Harris quoted in Charlotte Rogers, "The Big Debate: Is Becoming an 'Ecosystem' Brand the Only Way to Win Customer Loyalty?" *Marketing Week*, July 4, 2017, https://www.marketingweek.com/the-big-debate-ecosystem-brands/.

3. Kelly, "Majority of iPhone Users."

4. Keller, "Customer-Based Brand Equity."

5. Bourdieu, *Social Critique.*

6. He, Li, and Harris, "Social Identity Perspective"; Lupu, *Party Brands in Crisis.*

7. Downs, *Economic Theory of Democracy.*

8. Kriesi et al., *West European Politics*; Beramendi et al., *Politics of Advanced Capitalism*; Hooghe and Marks, "Cleavage Theory."

9. Mair, *Ruling the Void.*

10. Dalton, "Decline of Party Identifications."

11. Hernández and Kriesi, "Electoral Consequences"; Dalton, *Political Realignment.*

12. Lupu, "Brand Dilution," and *Party Brands in Crisis.*

13. Katz and Mair, "Changing Models of Party Organization."

14. Duverger, *Parties politiques.*

15. Cox, *Making Votes Count.*

16. Cox, *Making Votes Count.*

17. Hug, *Altering Party Systems*; Tavits, "Party Systems in the Making"; Carey and Hix, "Electoral Sweet Spot."

18. Rydgren, *Tax Populism*; Golder, "Far Right Parties in Europe."

19. Aron, Superti, and Teoldi, "Populist Roots."

20. Campbell et al., *American Voter.*

21. Campbell et al., *American Voter*, 151.

22. Lipset and Rokkan, *Party Systems and Voter Alignments.*

23. Lipset and Rokkan, *Party Systems and Voter Alignments*, 54.

24. Kriesi et al., *West European Politics.*

25. Hooghe and Marks, "Cleavage Theory"; Marks et al., "Dealignment Meets Cleavage Theory."

26. Franklin and Jackson, "Dynamics of Party Identification."

27. Fiorina, *Retrospective Voting*, 84. See also Gerber and Green, "Rational Learning and Partisan Attitudes."

28. Lupu, "Brand Dilution," and *Party Brands in Crisis*.

29. Mair and Van Biezen, "Party Membership"; Van Biezen, Mair, and Poguntke, "Going, Going, . . . Gone?"; Dalton, "Decline of Party Identifications."

30. Drummond, "Electoral Volatility and Party Decline"; Mair, *Ruling the Void*.

31. Van Haute, Paulis, and Sierens, "Assessing Party Membership Figures." This group of academics has conducted a comprehensive data collection on party membership in Europe. The data can be accessed at http://www.projectmapp.eu /databases/.

32. Mair and Van Biezen, "Party Membership"; Van Biezen, Mair, and Poguntke, "Going, Going, . . . Gone?"; Van Haute, Paulis, and Sierens, "Assessing Party Membership Figures."

33. In the 1990s, the Spanish Socialist Party was one of the relatively few Western European parties to adopt party primaries. Such reforms may also have been useful as a mobilizing strategy to encourage new members to join; see also Hopkin, "Bringing the Members Back In?"

34. Mair and Van Biezen, "Party Membership," 11.

35. European Commission, Eurobarometer; Schmitt et al., Mannheim Eurobarometer Trend File; European Social Survey Cumulative File.

36. Campbell et al., *American Voter*.

37. Pedersen, "Dynamics of European Party Systems."

38. Powell and Tucker, "Revisiting Electoral Volatility"; Bértoa, Deegan-Krause, and Haughton, "Volatility of Volatility."

39. Mainwaring, Gervasoni, and Espana-Najera, "Within-System Electoral Volatility."

40. Respondents who abstained in either election are excluded, as vote switching should not be conflated with mobilization, alienation, or consistent nonvoting. Voters who were ineligible to vote or refused to answer are also excluded. Voters who responded to the vote choice question with "other party" in both the current and the previous election are also excluded, as it is impossible to determine whether or not the respondent voted for the same party. However, if the voter responded to the vote choice question with "other party" in only one election and mentioned a specific party that does not belong to the "other party" category for the other election, we can say with certainty that the individual switched votes.

41. Data sources for figure 3.4 are as follows. Denmark: Borre et al., Danish Election Study 1973, Danish Election Study 1975, Danish Election Study 1977, Danish Election Study 1981, Danish Election Study 1984, Danish Election Study 1998;Nielsen, Sauerberg, and Worre, Danish Election Study 1988; Andersen, Danish Election Study 1994, Danish Election Study 2001, Danish Election Study 2005, Danish Election Study 2007; Stubager, Andersen, and Hansen, Danish National Election Study 2011; Hansen, Danish National Election Study 2015.

Germany: GESIS, German General Social Survey. The Netherlands: Aarts, To-dosijevic, and Van der Kaap, Dutch Parliamentary Election Study; Kolk et al., Nationaal Kiezersonderzoek, 2010, and Dutch Parliamentary Election Study 2012. Sweden: Särlvik and Statistics Sweden, Swedish Election Study 1970; Pe-tersson, Särlvik, and Statistics Sweden, Swedish Election Study 1973; Petersson and Statistics Sweden, Swedish Election Study 1976; Holmberg and Statistics Sweden, Swedish Election Study 1979, Swedish Election Study 1982, Swedish Election Study 1998; Holmberg, Gilljam, and Statistics Sweden, Swedish Election Study 1985; Holmberg, Oscarsson, and Statistics Sweden, Swedish Election Study 2002; Holmberg and Oscarsson, Swedish National Election Study 2010. United Kingdom: Crewe, Robertson, and Sarlvik, British Election Study, October 1974; British Election Study, May 1979. Heath, Jowell, and Curtice, British General Election Study, 1983; British General Election Study, 1987. Heath et al., British General Election Study, 1992; British General Election Study, 1997. Clarke, Sand-ers, and Whiteley, British General Election Study, 2001; British Election Study, 2005. Whiteley and Sanders, British Election Study, 2010. Fieldhouse et al., Brit-ish Election Study, 2015; British Election Study, 2017.

42. British Election Study (postelection and cross-section) surveys from 1974 to 2017 are used (see citations above). Party-switching measure is based on actual vote and vote recall from the previous election. This is a more conservative mea-sure of electoral volatility compared with relying on panel data, as respondents are more likely to "misremember" and recall that they voted for the same party that they are currently voting for. Liberals, Alliance, and Social Democrats are recorded as one party in 1983.

43. For Germany we analyze the Allbus cross-sectional pre-election surveys from 1980 to 2014. Because the survey is measured before elections and in nonelec-tion years, electoral volatility is based on vote intention and vote choice in the previous election. The Party of Democratic Socialism (PDS) and The Left (Die Linke) are recorded as the same party. The Christian Democratic Union (CDU) and Christian Social Union (CSU) are also recorded as the same party. See GESIS, German General Social Survey.

44. The Danish parliamentary election study surveys from 1977 to 2011. See data sources cited above.

45. Oskarson, "Social Structure and Party Choice."

46. Webb, "British Political Parties in Decline?"

47. Dinas and Riera, "European Parliament Elections"; Schulte-Cloos, "Euro-pean Parliament Elections."

Chapter 4: Strategies of Dominance

1. Kirchheimer, "Western European Party Systems," 192.

2. Muhtar Kent, "What I've Learned as CEO of Coca-Cola," *Fortune*, January 15, 2017, https://fortune.com/2017/01/15/coca-cola-muhtar-kent-leadership-lessons/.

3. Kirchheimer, "Western European Party Systems," 192.

4. Miller and Wattenberg, "Throwing the Rascals Out."

5. Lipset and Rokkan, *Party Systems and Voter Alignments*.

6. Pierce, "Mass–Elite Issue Linkages"; McDonald and Budge, *Elections, Parties, Democracy*.

7. Kirchheimer, "Western European Party Systems," 185.

8. Panebianco, *Political Parties*.

9. Palmer, "10 Biggest Restaurant Companies."

10. Downs, *Economic Theory of Democracy*, 135

11. Kirchheimer, "Western European Party Systems," 192.

12. See Volkens et al., Manifesto Data Collection.

13. Budge and Klingemann, *Mapping Policy Preferences*; Klingemann et al., *Mapping Policy Preferences II*.

14. For a discussion of the left–right measure in MARPOR, see Bakker and Hobolt, "Measuring Party Positions."

15. Similar findings are reported in Adams, Ezrow, and Somer-Topcu, "Is Anybody Listening?"

16. Hobolt and Karp, "Voters and Coalition Governments."

17. International IDEA, "Voter Turnout in Western Europe."

18. Kitschelt and McGann, *Radical Right in Western Europe*; Arzheimer and Carter, "Political Opportunity Structures."

19. Pierce, "Mass–Elite Issue Linkages."

20. Downs, *Economic Theory of Democracy*, 135.

21. Rovny, "Who Emphasizes and Who Blurs?"

22. Thatcher, "Speech to Conservative Party Conference."

23. Marks and Wilson, "The Past in the Present"; Hooghe, Marks, and Wilson, "Does Left/Right Structure."

24. Abou-Chadi and Wagner, "Electoral Appeal of Party Strategies."

25. Green-Pedersen and Krogstrup, "Immigration as a Political Issue."

26. De Vries, "Cosmopolitan-Parochial Divide."

27. Kirchheimer, "Western European Party Systems," 192.

28. Stokes, "Spatial Models of Party Competition," 373.

29. See e.g., Green and Hobolt, "Owning the Issue Agenda."

30. Katz and Mair, "Changing Models of Party Organization."

31. Erikson, "Advantage of Incumbency" 5; Gelman and King, "Estimating Incumbency Advantage"; Ansolabehere and Snyder, "Incumbency Advantage in US Elections."

32. Kam and Zechmeister, "Name Recognition and Candidate Support."

33. Clarke, Sanders, and Whiteley, British General Election Study, 2001; British Election Study, 2005. Whiteley and Sanders, British Election Study, 2010. Fieldhouse et al., British Election Study, 2015; British Election Study, 2017. Rattinger et al., Long-Term Panel 2002; Long-Term Panel 2009; Long-Term Panel 2013–2017.

34. See Green and Jennings, *Politics of Competence*

35. Solaz, De Vries, and De Geus, "In-Group Loyalty."

36. "Luis Barcenas: Spain Popular Party's Ex-treasurer in Jail," *BBC News*, June

27, 2013, http://www.bbc.co.uk/news/world-23088204; Tremlett, "Spanish Prime Minister"; Cué and Hernández, "Bárcenas' Secret Papers."

37. "As It Happened: Pedro Sánchez Becomes New Spanish Prime Minister," *El País*, June 1, 2018.

38. Kennedy, "Four Party System."

39. Jones, "Far Right Wins Seats."

40. Hobolt and De Vries, "Turning against the Union?"

41. Aassve, Daniele, and Le Moglie, "Never Forget the First Time."

Chapter 5: Issue Entrepreneurship

1. Schumpeter, *Capitalism, Socialism and Democracy*, 283.

2. Quoted in Richard Harroch, "99 Inspirational Quotes for Entrepreneurs," AllBusiness.com, September 3, 2017, https://www.allbusiness.com/99-inspirational-quotes-for-entrepreneurs-18398-1.html.

3. Garfield, *MINI*.

4. Bridger, "2017 Mini Sales."

5. Schumpeter, *Capitalism, Socialism and Democracy*.

6. See our previous work on issue entrepreneurship: Hobolt and De Vries, "Issue Entrepreneurship and Multiparty Competition"; De Vries and Hobolt, "When Dimensions Collide"; Spoon, Hobolt, and De Vries, "Going Green"; Van de Wardt, De Vries, and Hobolt, "Exploiting the Cracks."

7. Schattschneider, *Semi-sovereign People*, 62.

8. Franklin, Mackie, and Valen, *Electoral Change*; Mair, *Party System Change*; Dalton, *Citizen Politics*; Dalton and Flanagan, *Electoral Change*; Green-Pedersen, *West European Party Politics*.

9. Budge and Farlie, *Explaining and Predicting Elections*; Petrocik, "Issue Ownership in Presidential Elections."

10. Interestingly, recent evidence also suggests that parties often mobilize similar issues, including those they would rather ignore. See, for example, Damore, "Dynamics of Issue Ownership"; Green and Hobolt, "Owning the Issue Agenda"; Green-Pedersen, "Growing Importance of Issue Competition"; Vliegenthart, Walgrave, and Meppelink, "Inter-party Agenda Setting"; Walgrave, Lefevere, and Nuytemans. "Issue Ownership Stability and Change"; Spoon, Hobolt, and De Vries, "Going Green."

11. Green-Pedersen and Mortensen, "Who Sets the Agenda."

12. Meguid, *Party Competition between Unequals*.

13. Electoral considerations more generally have also been shown to matter for the issue mobilization strategies of parties. See Spoon, Hobolt, and De Vries, "Going Green."

14. Hobolt and De Vries, "Issue Entrepreneurship and Multiparty Competition."

15. Rovny, "Who Emphasizes and Who Blurs?"

16. Belleflamme and Peitz, *Industrial Organization*.

17. Sherman, "Top 5 Start-Up Acquirers."

18. Carmines and Stimson, *Issue Evolution*.

19. Abou-Chadi and Krause, "Causal Effect."

20. De Sio and Till Weber, "Issue Yield"; Lupu, *Party Brands in Crisis*.

21. Somer-Topcu, "Everything to Everyone"; Lupu, *Party Brands in Crisis*.

22. Schumacher, De Vries, and Vis, "Why Do Parties Change Position?"

23. Tavits, "Role of Parties' Past Behavior"; Van de Wardt, De Vries, and Hobolt, "Exploiting the Cracks."

24. Riker, *Liberalism against Populism*, 209.

25. Riker, *Liberalism against Populism*, ch. 9.

26. Kay, *Foundations of Corporate Success*.

27. Lieberman and Montgomery, "First-Mover Advantages."

28. Wernerfelt, "Brand Loyalty and User Skills."

29. Ries and Trout, *Positioning*.

30. Lupu, *Party Brands in Crisis*.

31. Pierce, "Mass–Elite Issue Linkages"; Ezrow, *Linking Citizens and Parties*; McDonald and Budge, *Elections, Parties, Democracy*.

32. König, Marbach, and Osnabrügge, "Left/Right or U?"

33. Pellikaan, Van der Meer, and De Lange, "Depolarized to a Centrifugal Democracy," and "Fortuyn's Legacy"; Kriesi et al., *West European Politics*; Spoon, Hobolt, and De Vries, "Going Green"; Hobolt and De Vries, "Issue Entrepreneurship and Multiparty Competition."

34. It is important to note that the notion of high appropriability is linked to the concept of issue ownership used in political sciences as it underlines the importance of the associations between certain issues and certain parties. Yet, it differs from issue ownership in some important respects. First, appropriability is a characteristic of an issue, not of a party. Second, while issue ownership in essence could apply to every issue, high appropriability applies to issues that are not easily subsumed in the dominant dimension and may internally split mainstream parties. Third, the degree of appropriability of an issue allows us to develop specific hypotheses about the extent to which a certain type of party, dominant or challenger, will mobilize the issue.

35. Volkens, et al., Manifesto Data Collection.

36. Austria, Belgium, Cyprus, Denmark, Finland, France, Germany, Iceland, Ireland, Italy, Luxembourg, Malta, the Netherlands, Norway, Portugal, Spain, Sweden, Switzerland, and the United Kingdom.

37. We rely on the MARPOR data set as it allows us to capture the importance parties attach to all of the three issues we are interested in, and covers a longer time span than CHES, for example. Both the MARPOR and CHES data have a very wide geographical coverage in Europe, as they cover parties in many countries, yet MARPOR covers the entire postwar period, where CHES includes data only from the 1990s onward. Several studies have cross-validated the measures of CHES and MARPOR and found that they capture similar empirical phenomena and are closely linked to mass survey data. For more information on CHES, see Bakker et al., "Measuring Party Positions in Europe."

38. Budge and Farlie, *Explaining and Predicting Elections*; Klingemann et al., *Mapping Policy Preferences II*.

39. Specifically, following the work by Will Lowe and coauthors, we use a log transformation measure: log[(per501 + 1)/total]; see Lowe et al., "Scaling Policy Preferences."

40. To capture emphasis on multiculturalism, national culture, and minorities we take the log transformation of the following items: positive and negative mention of multiculturalism (per607/per608), or minority groups (per705), positive references to a national way of life and law and order (per601 and per605). See Alonso and da Fonseca, "Immigration, Left and Right"; Abou-Chadi, "Niche Party Success."

41. The log transformation measure we use is constructed in the following way: log[(per607 + per608 + per705 + per601 + per605 + 1)/total].

42. Specifically, we use a log transformation measure of two MARPOR categories, per108 and per110: log[(per108 + per110 + 1)/total].

43. Specifically, we use a log transformation measure of the five MARPOR categories per401 (favorable mentions of the free market economy), per403 (support for market regulation), per404 (support for economic planning), per412 (support for controlled economies), and per414 (references to sound economic policy making): log[(per401 + per403 + per404 + per412 + per414)/total].

44. As explained before, a party is considered a challenger party if in any given year it *has not* been a member of a central government since 1930. A party is considered a dominant party if in any given year it *has* been part of a central government since 1930. Only parties with ministers in cabinet are considered to be members of a central government. A party ceases to be a challenger party once it enters central government (in the election immediately preceding entry into office, it is classified as a challenger party). Participation in a national war/crisis cabinet does not in itself qualify a party as a dominant party. A dominant party will continue to be considered a dominant party after merging with a challenger party, but a party will be considered a challenger party if it splits from a dominant party.

45. Switzerland is well known for the exceptional stability of its federal executive. The Swiss government system does not have a clear division between government and opposition. Instead, all significant parties share power, and the so-called "magic formula" has meant that for nearly half a century the Swiss government has been virtually unchanged in its party competition.

46. Such as the CHES trend file (see Bakker et al., "Measuring Party Positions in Europe") and party handbooks (see Nohlen and Stöver, *Elections in Europe*).

47. Lipset and Rokkan, *Party Systems and Voter Alignments*; Marks and Wilson, "Past in the Present"; Kriesi et al., *West European Politics*.

48. Enelow and Hinich, *Spatial Theory of Voting*; Adams and Somer-Topcu, "Policy Adjustment by Parties."

49. Carmines and Stimson, *Issue Evolution*; Hobolt and De Vries, "Issue Entrepreneurship and Multiparty Competition."

50. We estimate the model using a simple party-year panel setup including country dummies to control for omitted variables that may differ between countries. We do not include fixed effects for parties, since the unobserved heterogeneity is found mainly at the country rather than the party level. We do include party family dummies. Country dummies, however, do not eliminate all problems with

the panel data estimation strategy. For example, it is likely that autocorrelation exists, that is to say that observations of the dependent variable are correlated across time within panels. Inspection of panel residuals suggests that they have a first-order autoregressive, AR(1), structure. This means that the residual at time t is influenced by the size of the residual at time $t - 1$. To deal with autocorrelation, we add a lagged dependent variable to the right-hand side of the equation. Moreover, we control for the fact that we are dealing with repeated observations for the same party across time by estimating random effects varying across parties.

51. Plümper, Troeger, and Manow have shown that with trending in the independent variables and the error term, a lagged dependent variable introduces biases. Hence, to eliminate serial correlation of errors, they suggest instead to use a Prais-Winsten transformation with a panel-specific AR(1) error structure; see Plümper, Troeger, and Manow, "Panel Data Analysis." Our results remain robust when we estimate this model instead.

52. Norris, *Radical Right*.

53. Andersen and Bjørklund, "Radical Right-Wing Populism"; Rydgren, "Explaining the Emergence."

54. Green-Pedersen and Krogstrup, "Immigration as a Political Issue."

55. Andersen, "Dansk Folkeparti."

56. "Dansk Folkeparti: Principprogram, 1997," danmarkshistorien.dk, Aarhus Universitet, n.d., accessed December 30, 2019, http://danmarkshistorien.dk /leksikon-og-kilder/vis/materiale/dansk-folkeparti-principprogram-1997/.

57. Andersen, "Dansk Folkeparti."

58. Green-Pedersen and Krogstrup, "Immigration as a Political Issue."

59. Green-Pedersen, *West European Party Politics*.

60. Green-Pedersen and Krogstrup, "Immigration as a Political Issue."

61. Pellikaan, Van der Meer, and De Lange, "Depolarized to a Centrifugal Democracy"; De Vries, "Impact of EU Referenda."

62. "Wilders Stapt uit VVD-Fractie," *Trouw*, September 3, 2004, https://www .trouw.nl/home/wilders-stapt-uit-vvd-fractie~a89d177a/.

63. Van der Pas, De Vries, and Van der Brug, "Leader Without a Party."

64. "Alle peilingen van de PVV vanaf 2004," AllePeilingen.com, n.d., https:// www.allepeilingen.com/index.php/peilingen-politieke-partijen-vanaf-2004-pvv .html.

65. Aarts and Van der Kolk, *Nederlanders en Europa*.

66. De Vries, "Impact of EU Referenda."

67. Aarts and Van der Kolk, *Nederlanders en Europa*.

68. Hobolt and Brouard, "Contesting the European Union?"; Aarts and Van der Kolk, *Nederlanders en Europa*, 187–201.

69. Hobolt and Brouard, "Contesting the European Union?"; Aarts and Van der Kolk, *Nederlanders en Europa*, 195–98.

70. Aarts and Van der Kolk, *Nederlanders en Europa*, 117–20.

71. Aarts and Van Der Kolk, *Nederlanders en Europa*, 195–98.

72. De Vries, "Impact of EU Referenda."

73. "PVV en Tweede Kamerverkiezingen 2006," Parlement.com, n.d., ac-

cessed April 14, 2019, https://www.parlement.com/id/vhnnmt7mr5zr/pvv_en
_tweede_kamerverkiezingen_2006.

74. De Vries and Hofmann, *Fears and Not Values*.

75. De Vries, *Euroscepticism*.

76. Silva, "Populist Radical Right Parties."

77. Betz, "Value Change."

78. Debus, "Analysing Party Politics in Germany."

79. Klein and Falter, *Lange Weg der Grünen*.

80. Betz, "Value Change"; Jahn, "Green Politics and Parties"; Debus, "Analysing Party Politics in Germany."

81. Die Grünen, *Die Grünen*.

82. Klein and Falter, *Lange Weg der Grünen*.

83. Bürklin, "German Greens."

84. Betz, "Value Change"; Jahn, "Green Politics and Parties."

85. Veen, "Wer wählt Grun?"

86. Jahn, "Green Politics and Parties."

87. Müller-Rommel, "German Greens in the 1980s."

88. Klein and Falter, *Lange Weg der Grünen*.

89. Debus, "Analysing Party Politics in Germany."

90. Betz, "Value Change"; Jahn, "Green Politics and Parties."

91. Riker, *Liberalism against Populism*.

Chapter 6: Antiestablishment Rhetoric

1. Schnattschneider, *Semi-Sovereign People*, 1–2.

2. Elon Musk, "All Our Patent Are Belong To You," *Tesla Blog*, June 12, 2014, https://www.tesla.com/blog/all-our-patent-are-belong-you.

3. Vance, *Elon Musk*.

4. Setili, "Your Leadership Style"; Vance, "21st Century Industrialist," and "Elon Musk's Space Dream."

5. "Tesla's Mission Is to Accelerate the World's Transition to Sustainable Energy," Tesla website, https://www.tesla.com/about.

6. Marshal, "Elon Musk Reveals."

7. Elon Musk (@elonmusk), Twitter, December 15, 2017, comment on Jarrett Walker (@humantransit), December 14, 2017, https://twitter.com/elonmusk/status/941500121564332032?ref_src=twsrc%5Etfw&ref_url=https%3A%2F%2Ftwitter.com%2Fhumantransit%2Fstatus%2F941386665519595521.

8. Higgins and Pulliam, "Elon Musk Races."

9. Bariso, "Elon Musk's Presentation Style."

10. Lavietes, "Musk, Trump."

11. Glazek, "Emmanuel Macron."

12. Gruber, " Kleine Mann."

13. "Sie sind gegen ihn. Weil er für euch ist," poster in Bildarchiv Austria, 1994, Österreichische Nationalbibliothek website, http://data.onb.ac.at/rec/baal 5954497.

14. Lewis, "Rage, Rapture and Pure Populism."

15. Mudde, "Populist Zeitgeist," and *Populist Radical Right Parties.*

16. Other authors have referred to this as "valence attacks"; see Jung and Tavits, "Valence Attacks."

17. Elon Musk, "All Our Patent Are Belong To You," *Tesla Blog*, June 12, 2014, https://www.tesla.com/blog/all-our-patent-are-belong-you.

18. See, for example: Hopkin, *Anti-System Politics*; Mudde, "Anti-Party Party"; Schedler, "Anti-political-establishment Parties."

19. For a recent overview see Mudde, and Kaltwasser, *Populism.* See also Norris and Inglehart, *Cultural Backlash.*

20. De Vreese et al., "Populism as an Expression."

21. Margaret, Canovan, *Populism* (New York: Harcourt, Brace, 1981).

22. Mudde, *Populist Radical Right Parties.*

23. Hawkins, Riding, and Mudde, "Measuring Populist Attitudes."

24. Aalberg et al., *Populist Political Communication*; Mudde, "Populist Zeitgeist"; Rooduijn, De Lange, and Van der Brug, "Populist Zeitgeist?"; Jagers and Walgrave, "Populism as Political Communication Style"; Walgrave and Dejaeghere, "Surviving Information Overload."

25. See, for example, Proksch and Slapin, *Politics of Parliamentary Debate.*

26. De Vreese et al., "Populism as an Expression," 425.

27. Hawkins, "Is Chávez Populist?"; Rooduijn, "Mesmerising Message."

28. Engesser et al. "Populism and Social Media"; Groshek and Koc-Michalska, "Helping Populism Win?"; De Vreese et al., "Populism as an Expression."

29. For an overview see N. Clarke et al., *Good Politician.*

30. Clarke et al., *Good Politician*, 17.

31. Clarke et al., *Good Politician*, 210.

32. Green and Jennings, *Politics of Competence*; Stokes, "Spatial Models of Party Competition."

33. De Vreese et al., "Populism as an Expression."

34. Shapiro, "Competition and Innovation," 367.

35. Lupu, "Brand Dilution," and *Party Brands in Crisis.*

36. Budge and Klingemann, *Mapping Policy Preferences.*

37. See, for example, Canovan, *Populism*; Mudde, *Populist Radical Right Parties.*

38. See, for example, Groseclose, "Model of Candidate Location"; Stone and Simas, "Candidate Valence and Ideological Positions."

39. Erikson, "Advantage of Incumbency"; Ashworth, Berry, and Bueno de Mesquita, "All Else Equal."

40. Mayhew, "Congressional Elections"; Ansolabehere, Snowberg, and Snyder, "Television and the Incumbency Advantage."

41. Stokes, "Spatial Models of Party Competition."

42. De Vries, Hobolt, and Van der Velden, "Taking on the Establishment."

43. For establishment of competence, see Budge, "Electoral Volatility"; Green and Jennings, *Politics of Competence.* For negative campaigning, see Geer, *Tea Leaves to Opinion Polls.*

44. Green and Jennings, *Politics of Competence.*
45. Correlations are between 0.5 and 0.9 depending on the country under investigation. For more information see De Vries, Hobolt, and Van der Velden, "Taking on the Establishment."
46. De Vries, Hobolt, and Van der Velden. "Taking on the Establishment."
47. Volkens et al., Manifesto Data Collection.
48. De Vries, Hobolt, and Van der Velden, "Taking on the Establishment."
49. See Hawkins, "Is Chávez Populist?"
50. Budge and Klingemann, *Mapping Policy Preferences.*
51. DeClair, *Politics on the Fringe.*
52. Eltchaninoff, *Inside the Mind.*
53. Scheuplein, "Tabubruch in Turnschuhen."
54. Lupu, "Brand Dilution," and *Party Brands in Crisis.*
55. Wodak and Pelinka, *Haider Phenomenon in Austria.*
56. Wodak and Pelinka, *Haider Phenomenon in Austria.*
57. "In einer Demokratie muss das Volk Ernst genommen werden! Befehlsausgaben aus dem Elfenbeinturm der herrschenden politischen Klasse, deren Verachtung für das gemeine Volk somit sichtbar wird, haben mit einem System der Freiheit nichts gemein." Jörg Haider, quoted in Hartleb, "Länderportrait Österreich," 211.
58. "Na, das hat's im Dritten Reich nicht gegeben, weil im Dritten Reich haben sie ordentliche Beschäftigungspolitik gemacht, was nicht einmal Ihre [SPÖ officials] Regierung in Wien zusammenbringt. Das muss man auch einmal sagen!" Jörg Haider, quoted in Scheidl, " Schockierende Replik stoppte Jörg Haider."
59. Bell, "Young Austrian Leader."
60. De Vries, *Euroscepticism.*
61. "Ich will Österreich dienen. . . . Die Politiker, die wollen verdienen." Stronach, "Interview."
62. Settele, "Die Wahlfahrt: Bucher–Stronach."
63. "Frank und frei und fort: Das Team Stronach ist Geschichte," *Tiroler Tageszeitung,* June 28, 2017.

Chapter 7: Changing Voter Appeal

1. Meguid, *Party Competition between Unequals,* 25.
2. "The Entrepreneur of the Decade: An interview with Steven Jobs, Inc.'s Entrepreneur of the Decade," interview by Bo Burlingham and George Gendronthe, *Inc. Magazine,* April 1, 1989, https://www.inc.com/magazine/19890401/5602.html.
3. Carroll, "Rise of Snapchat and Instagram."
4. Frenkel et al., "Delay, Deny and Deflect."
5. Stewart, "Facebook's Very Bad Year."
6. Imbert and Francolla, "Facebook's $100 Billion-Plus Rout."
7. Belleflamme and Peitz, *Industrial Organization.*

8. An example is the merger of the three centrist Protestant and Catholic parties in the Netherlands in 1980 as a response to changing religious habits.

9. Party data for: Austria, Belgium, Denmark, Finland, France, Germany, Greece, Iceland, Ireland, Italy, Luxembourg, the Netherlands, Norway, Portugal, Spain, Sweden, Switzerland, and the United Kingdom. Individual data for: Austria, Belgium, Cyprus, Denmark, Finland, France, Germany, Greece, Ireland, Italy, Luxembourg, Malta, the Netherlands, Portugal, Spain, Sweden, and the United Kingdom.

10. Belleflamme and Peitz, *Industrial Organization*.

11. Carmines and Stimson, "Structure and Sequence," and *Issue Evolution*.

12. Krosnick, "Government Policy and Citizen Passion."

13. Wlezien, "Public as Thermostat."

14. Krosnick, "Government Policy and Citizen Passion"; Iyengar, "Framing Responsibility for Political Issues"; Krosnick, Berent, and Boninger, "Pockets of Responsibility." See also Converse, "Nature of Belief Systems."

15. Krosnick, Berent, and Boninger, "Pockets of Responsibility."

16. Almond, *American People and Foreign Policy*; Zaller, *Nature and Origins*.

17. Page and Shapiro, *Rational Public*; Erikson, MacKuen, and Stimson, *Macro Polity*.

18. Lupia, "Shortcuts versus Encyclopedias"; Lupia and McCubbins, *Democratic Dilemma*.

19. Iyengar, "Framing Responsibility for Political Issues"; Krosnick, "Government Policy and Citizen Passion"; Krosnick, Berent, and Boninger, "Pockets of Responsibility." See also Converse, "Nature of Belief Systems."

20. Krosnick, Berent, and Boninger, "Pockets of Responsibility."

21. Rydgren and Ruth, "Contextual Explanations."

22. Petrocik, "Issue Ownership in Presidential Elections"

23. See Budge, Robertson, and Hearl, *Ideology, Strategy and Party Change*. Note that economic voting studies present a refinement of these ideas to suggest that partisan accountability makes right-wing parties benefit from inflation and left-wing parties from unemployment; see, for example, Powell and Whitten, "Cross-National Analysis."

24. For the importance of policy delivery for voting behavior generally, see Kedar, *Voting for Policy, Not Parties*.

25. See Budge and Farlie, *Explaining and Predicting Elections*; Nadeau and Lewis-Beck, "National Economic Voting"; Bellucci, "Cognitive and Affective Roots."

26. Downs, "Economic Theory of Political Action"; Merrill and Grofman, *Unified Theory of Voting*; Rabinowitz and Macdonald, "Directional Theory of Issue Voting."

27. See Haughton, "Exit, Choice and Legacy"; Green-Pedersen, *West European Party Politics*.

28. Budge and Farlie, *Explaining and Predicting Elections*; Budge and Klingemann, *Mapping Policy Preferences*.

29. Peffley and Williams, "Attributing Presidential Responsibility"; Rudolph,

"Who's Responsible for the Economy?"; Tilley and Hobolt, "Is the Government to Blame?"; De Vries and Giger, "Holding Governments Accountable?"

30. Bélanger, and Meguid, "Issue Salience."

31. Bowler, "Voter Perceptions and Party Strategies."

32. Green and Jennings, *Politics of Competence*; Sartori, *Parties and Party Systems*.

33. Solaz, De Vries, and De Geus, "In-Group Loyalty."

34. Errejon, Mouffe, and Jones, *Podemos*.

35. Solaz, De Vries, and De Geus, "In-Group Loyalty."

36. Schmitt et al., European Parliament Election Study 2014.

37. The question was worded in the following way: "For the following statement, please tell me to what extent it corresponds or not to your attitude or opinion. 'The European Parliament takes into consideration the concerns of European citizens.'"

38. Nohlen and Stöver, *Elections in Europe*.

39. We use the market economy/government regulation of the economy items from the MARPOR data in order to capture parties' economic left–right positions.

40. When it comes to the panel data analysis, our model structure requires specific attention to both differences between countries and parties, panel differences, and time-series dependencies, autocorrelation. We estimate the model using a simple party-year panel setup, but we still need to account for the possible existence of unobserved differences between countries. We thus include country dummies to control for omitted variables that may differ between countries. We do not include fixed effects for parties, since the unobserved heterogeneity is found mainly at the country rather than the party level. We do include party family dummies. Country dummies, however, do not eliminate all problems with the panel data estimation strategy. For example, it is likely that autocorrelation exists, which is to say that observations of the dependent variable are correlated across time within panels. Inspection of panel residuals suggests that they have a first-order autoregressive, AR(1), structure. This means that the residual at time t is influenced by the size of the residual at time $t - 1$. To deal with autocorrelation, scholars recommend adding a lagged dependent variable to the right-hand side of the equation, and this is what we do here. Moreover, we control for the fact that we are dealing with repeated observations for the same party across time by estimating random effects varying across parties.

41. Herfindahl, "Concentration in the Steel Industry."

42. Austria, Belgium, Denmark, Finland, France, Germany, Greece, Iceland, Ireland, Italy, Luxembourg, the Netherlands, Norway, Portugal, Spain, Sweden, Switzerland, and the United Kingdom.

43. Smith, "Syriza's Tsipras Sworn In."

44. It is important to note that, although we treat Belgium here as a single case, it essentially consists of two party systems: the Francophone and the Flemish. A voter cannot vote for both sets of parties. Hence, effectively, the political market is half as competitive as it appears in these figures.

Chapter 8: Representation and Government

1. Mair, "Representative versus Responsible Government," 6.

2. Greenfield quoted in Yvonne Daley, *Going Up the Country: When the Hippies, Dreamers, Freaks, and Radicals Moved to Vermont* (Lebanon, NH: University Press of New England, 2018), 137.

3. Edmondson, *Ice Cream Social*.

4. Gehlhar, "Regional Concentration."

5. See, e.g., Schumpeter, *Capitalism, Socialism and Democracy*; Arrow, "Economic Welfare."

6. See, e.g., Mair, *Ruling the Void*.

7. Mair, "Representative versus Responsible Government."

8. Powell, *Elections as Instruments of Democracy*. See also Lijphart, *Patterns of Democracy*.

9. Downs, *Economic Theory of Democracy*; Adams and Merrill, "Voter Turnout and Candidate Strategies"; Franklin, *Voter Turnout*.

10. Rosenstone and Hansen, *Mobilization, Participation, and Democracy*; Brennan and Hamlin, "Expressive Voting and Electoral Equilibrium"; Hamlin and Jennings, "Expressive Political Behaviour."

11. Rohrschneider and Whitefield, *Strain of Representation*.

12. Comparative Study of Electoral Systems, CSES Modules 1–5 1996–2016.

13. If respondents could not remember which party they voted for, but reported casting a ballot, and vice versa, we count these respondents as having casted a ballot.

14. Voting is compulsory in three West European countries today: Belgium, Luxembourg, and Greece. In Cyprus, voting was compulsory until recently (although not enforced), but this was abolished in May 2017.

15. We use multiple imputation to deal with missing data.

16. Anderson and Just, "Tweedledum and Tweedledee?"

17. Some election studies and modules also include a neutral middle category. For these countries, we recoded the middle category as "not very satisfied." The results are identical when we count the middle category as "fairly satisfied."

18. Schmitt-Beck, "Alternative für Deutschland," 144.

19. For a more detailed discussion on the effect of the emergence of the Alternative for Germany on turnout, see Hobolt and Hoerner, "Mobilizing Effect of Political Choice."

20. Rattinger et al., Election Baden-Wuerttemberg 2011, Election Mecklenburg-West Pomerania 2011, Election North Rhine-Westphalia 2010, Election Rhineland-Palatinate 2011, Election Saxony-Anhalt 2011, Election North Rhine-Westphalia 2012, and Election Schleswig-Holstein 2012; Roßteutscher et al., Election Baden-Wuerttemberg 2016, Election Mecklenburg-West Pomerania 2016, Election North Rhine-Westphalia 2017, Election Rhineland-Palatinate 2016, Election Saxony-Anhalt 2016, and Election Schleswig-Holstein 2017.

21. Data source: Arbeitsgemeinschaft der öffentlich-rechtlichen Rundfunkanstalten der Bundesrepublik Deutschland (German public-service broadcaster)/Infratest.

22. Lowell, *Governments and Parties* 1: 73–74.

23. Diermeier and Van Roozendaal, "Duration of Cabinet Formation Processes."

24. Tsebelis, *Veto Players.*

25. Martin and Vanberg, "Wasting Time?"

26. Golder, "Bargaining Delays," and *Logic of Pre-electoral Coalition Formation*; Laver and Benoit, "Basic Arithmetic of Legislative Decisions."

27. Sani and Sartori, "Polarization, Fragmentation and Competition," 335.

28. Warwick, "Economic Trends and Government Survival."

29. Mair, "Representative versus Responsible Government," 17.

30. These data are taken from the updated Party Government data set. See Seki and Williams, "Updating the Party Government."

31. The end date of a government is the day before the start of the next government. The start of a government's tenure is the date of investiture, or the first day of the parliamentary session if no investiture vote is required. A government represents any administration formed after an election, and continues in the absence of a change in prime minister, change in party composition of the cabinet (i.e., parties may move in or out, but no changes in the cabinet composition of government parties), or resignation of the government within the electoral cycle (even if it is replaced by the exact same parties and prime minister, it is still a government change).

32. Deschouwer, *Politics of Belgium.*

33. Van Spanje, *Controlling the Electoral Marketplace.*

34. Louwerse and Van Aelst, "Exceptional Belgian Case?"

35. Van Holsteyn and Irwin, "Never a Dull Moment"; Andeweg and Irwin, *Governance and Politics.*

36. Mair, "Eigenaardigheden van de Nederlanders."

37. Dinas, Hartman, and Van Spanje, "Dead Man Walking."

38. Van Holsteyn and Irwin, "Never a Dull Moment."

39. "Kabinet-Balkende I 2002–2003," Parlement.com, n.d., accessed April 16, 2019, https://www.parlement.com/id/vh8lnhrpfxup/kabinet_balkenende _i_2002_2003.

40. Boerman, "Drie maanden crisis."

41. "Kabinetscrisis 2002: LPF-crisis," Parlement.com, n.d., accessed April 16, 2019, https://www.parlement.com/id/vh8lnhrptxxl/kabinetscrisis_2002_lpf _crisis.

42. Evrengün, "LPF."

43. Andeweg and Irwin, *Governance and Politics.*

Chapter 9: Future Scenarios

1. Schumpeter, *Capitalism, Socialism and Democracy*, 83.

2. Tory Burch, "Remarks to Babson College," *Huffington Post*, May 22, 2014, https://www.huffpost.com/entry/babson-college-commencement_b_5407095 ?guccounter=1&guce_referrer=aHR0cHM6Ly93d3cuYXpxdW90ZMuY29tL3F lb3RlLzY5Njc4MA&guce_referrer_sig=AQAAAHKUMEvRJDgcmcHWH8i_-8X

_48a1f66cRvFyP98vHcHHBKsYm9fnjAYfC57J3wchYHCJyJq1RovP7sLXbb4SEc
6BxBOxcFoB9Q-Q3s67LX70_Y4P18rfrCbAe1HxOWfi4Ls7YeV9EwHhbKlI5X0b
gtFiWSPlg4UdYsMOM4lgB7RP.

3. Tirole, *Theory of Industrial Organization*; Cabral, *Readings in Industrial Organization*; Belleflamme and Peitz, *Industrial Organization*.

4. See, for example, M. Franklin, Mackie, and Valen, *Electoral Change*; Dalton and Flanagan, *Electoral Change*.

5. See, for example, Elff "Social Structure and Electoral Behavior."

6. See, for example, Arzheimer and Carter, "Political Opportunity Structures."

7. See, for example, Solaz, De Vries, and De Geus, "In-Group Loyalty"; Schleiter and Voznaya, "Party System Institutionalization."

8. Meguid, *Party Competition between Unequals*.

9. Tirole, *Theory of Industrial Organization*; Cabral, *Readings in Industrial Organization*; Belleflamme and Peitz, *Industrial Organization*.

10. Haughton and Deegan-Krause, "Hurricane Season."

11. Andeweg and Irwin, *Governance and Politics*.

12. Van der Pas, De Vries, and Van der Brug, "Leader without a Party.

13. De Vries, Hakhverdian, and Lancee, "Voters' Left/Right Identification."

14. Niels Klaasen, "'Baudet heeft sturing nodig."

15. Rusman, "Wat zei Baudet eigenlijk"; Margulies, "Why Europe Should Worry."

16. Vliegenthart, "Teveel aandacht."

17. Henley, "Real Story of Sweden's Election."

18. Schumpeter, *Capitalism, Socialism and Democracy*, 82–83.

19. See the website of the Movement for Change: https://kinimaallagis.gr/ (in Greek).

20. "It's all Greek to Them: Why Labour Is Obsessed with Greek Politics," *Economist*, June 30, 2018, https://www.economist.com/britain/2018/06/30/why-labour-is-obsessed-with-greek-politics.

21. March, "Beyond Syriza and Podemos"; Della Porta, Kouki, and Fernández, "Left's Love and Hate."

22. Kitsantonis, "Alexis Tsipras Survives Confidence Vote"; Cerulus, "Greek Government Coalition Implodes."

23. Lupu, "Brand Dilution," and *Party Brands in Crisis*.

24. See, for example, Rankin and Smith, "Yanis Varoufakis."

25. See, for example, Snegovaya and Berman, "Populism"; J.-W. Müller, "End of Christian Democracy."

26. Jones, "Pedro Sánchez Sworn In."

27. Jones, "Spanish PM Appoints 11 Women."

28. Torres, "Spain's Sánchez Calls Snap Election."

29. Minder, "Socialists Strengthen Hold in Spain"

30. Gilmartin and Greene, "Future of Podemos."

31. Jones, "Spanish Election."

32. Jones, "Spanish Election."

33. See, for example, Schumacher, De Vries, and Vis, "Why Do Parties Change Position?"

34. See, for example, Norris, *Digital Divide*.

35. Magaloni, *Voting for Autocracy*; Greene, *Why Dominant Parties Lose*.

36. Haughton and Deegan-Krause, "Hurricane Season"; Powell and Tucker, "Revisiting Electoral Volatility."

37. Smith, *Wealth of Nations*.

38. Schumpeter, *Capitalism, Socialism and Democracy*, 106.

39. Arrow, "Economic Welfare."

BIBLIOGRAPHY

Aalberg, Toril, Frank Esser, Carsten Reineman, Jens Strömbäck, and Claes H. de Vreese. *Populist Political Communication in Europe*. London: Routledge, 2016.

Aarts, Kees, and Hendrik van der Kolk. *Nederlanders en Europa: Het referendum over de Europese grondwet*. Amsterdam: Bert Bakker, 2005.

Aassve, Arnstein, Gianmarco Daniele, and Macro Le Moglie. "Never Forget the First Time: The Persistent Effects of Corruption and the Rise of Populism in Italy." Paper presented at the Causes and Consequences of Populism Workshop, Bocconi University, April 4–5, 2019.

Abernathy, William J., and James M. Utterback. "Patterns of Industrial Innovation." *Technology Review* 80, no. 7 (1978): 40–47.

Abou-Chadi, Tarik. "Niche Party Success and Mainstream Party Policy Shift: How Green and Radical Right Parties Differ in their Impact." *British Journal of Political Science* 46, no. 2 (2016): 417–36.

Abou-Chadi, Tarik, and Werner Krause. "The Causal Effect of Radical Right Success on Mainstream Parties' Policy Positions: A Regression Discontinuity Approach." *British Journal of Political Science* (2018): 1–19. doi:10.1017/S00 07123418000029.

Abou-Chadi, Tarik, and Markus Wagner. "The Electoral Appeal of Party Strategies in Postindustrial Societies: When Can the Mainstream Left Succeed?" *Journal of Politics* 81, no. 4 (2019): 1405–19.

Adams, James, Michael Clark, Lawrence Ezrow, and Garrett Glasgow. "Are Niche Parties Fundamentally Different from Mainstream Parties?: The Causes and the Electoral Consequences of Western European Parties' Policy Shifts, 1976–1998." *American Journal of Political Science* 50, no. 3 (2006): 513–29.

Adams, James, Lawrence Ezrow, and Zeynep Somer-Topcu. "Is Anybody Listening?: Evidence That Voters Do Not Respond to European Parties' Policy Statements During Elections." *American Journal of Political Science* 55, no. 2 (2011): 370–82.

Adams, James, and Samuel Merrill III. "Voter Turnout and Candidate Strategies in American elections." *Journal of Politics,* 65, no. 1 (2003): 161–189.

Adams, James, and Zeynep Somer-Topcu. "Policy Adjustment by Parties in Response to Rival Parties' Policy Shifts: Spatial Theory and the Dynamics of Party Competition in Twenty-Five Post-War Democracies." *British Journal of Political Science* 39, no. 4 (2009): 825–46.

Adams, James F., Samuel Merrill III, and Bernard Grofman. *A Unified Theory of Party Competition: A Cross-National Analysis Integrating Spatial and Behavioral Factors*. New York: Cambridge University Press, 2005.

Akkerman, Tjitske, Sarah L. de Lange, and Matthijs Rooduijn, eds. *Radical Right-Wing Populist Parties in Western Europe: Into the Mainstream?* London: Routledge, 2016.

Aldrich, John H. *Why Parties?: The Origin and Transformation of Political Parties in America*. Chicago: University of Chicago Press, 1995.

Almond, Gabriel A. *The American People and Foreign Policy*. New York: Harcourt, Brace, 1950.

Alonso, Sonia, and Sara Claro Da Fonseca. "Immigration, Left and Right." *Party Politics* 18, no. 6 (2012): 865–84.

Andersen, Johannes. "Dansk Folkeparti, demokratiet og de fremmede." PhD dissertation, Institut for Økonomi, Politik og Forvaltning, Aalborg Universitet, 2000.

Andersen, Jørgen Goul, and Tor Bjørklund. "Radical Right-Wing Populism in Scandinavia: From Tax Revolt to Neo-Liberalism and Xenophobia." In *The Politics of the Extreme Right: From the Margins to the Mainstream*, edited by Paul Hainsworth, 193–223. London: Bloomsbury, 2000.

Anderson, Christopher, and Aida Just. "Tweedledum and Tweedledee?: A Cross-National Analysis of How Voters View the Electoral Supply." Paper presented at the 114th American Political Science Association Annual Meeting, Boston, MA, August 30–September 2, 2018.

Andeweg, Rudy B., and Galen A. Irwin. *Governance and Politics of the Netherlands*. London: Macmillan International Higher Education, 2014.

Ansolabehere, Stephen, Erik C. Snowberg, and James M. Snyder Jr. "Television and the Incumbency Advantage in US Elections." *Legislative Studies Quarterly* 31, no. 4 (2006): 469–90.

Ansolabehere, Stephen, and James M. Snyder Jr. "The Incumbency Advantage in US Elections: An Analysis of State and Federal Offices, 1942–2000." *Election Law Journal* 1, no. 3 (2002): 315–38.

Aron, Hadas, Chiara Superti, and Filippo Teoldi. "Populist Roots: Variation in Grassroots Adoption of the Five Star Movement." Paper presented at the 9th European Political Science Association Annual Conference, Belfast, June 20–22, 2019.

Arrow, Kenneth. "Economic Welfare and the Allocation of Resources to Invention." In *The Rate and Direction of Inventive Activity: Economic and Social Factors*, edited by the National Bureau Committee for Economic Research and the Committee on Economic Growth of the Social Science Research Councils, 609–26. Princeton, NJ: Princeton University Press.

Arzheimer, Kai, and Elizabeth Carter. "Political Opportunity Structures and Right-Wing Extremist Party Success." *European Journal of Political Research*, 45, no. 3 (2006): 419–43.

Ashworth, Scott, Christopher R. Berry, and Ethan Bueno de Mesquita. "All Else

Equal in Theory and Data (Big or Small)." *PS: Political Science and Politics* 48, no. 1 (2015): 89–94.

Bakker, Ryan, and Sara Hobolt. "Measuring Party Positions." In *Political Choice Matters: Explaining the Strength of Class and Religious Cleavages in Cross-National Perspective*, edited by Geoffrey Evans and Nan Dirk de Graaf, 27–45. Oxford: Oxford University Press, 2013.

Bariso, Justin. "What You Can Learn from Elon Musk's Presentation Style (It's Not What You Think)." *Inc.Magazine*, May 22, 2017.

Bartolini, Stefano, and Peter Mair. *Identity, Competition, and Electoral Availability: The Stabilization of European Electorates 1885–1985.* Cambridge: Cambridge University Press, 1990.

Bélanger, Éric, and Bonnie M. Meguid. "Issue Salience, Issue Ownership, and Issue-Based Vote Choice." *Electoral Studies* 27, no. 3 (2008): 477–91.

Bell, Bethany. "The Young Austrian Leader Sharing Power with the Far Right." *BBC News*, June 30, 2018. https://www.bbc.com/news/world-europe-446 44099.

Belleflamme, Paul, and Martin Peitz. *Industrial Organization: Markets and Strategies.* Cambridge: Cambridge University Press, 2015.

Bellucci, Paolo. "Tracing the Cognitive and Affective Roots of 'Party Competence': Italy and Britain, 2001." *Electoral Studies* 25, no. 3 (2006): 548–69.

Benedetto, Giacomo, Simon Hix, and Nicola Mastrorocco. "The Rise and Fall of Social Democracy, 1918–2017." Paper presented at the American Political Science Association Annual Meeting, Boston, August 30–September 2, 2018.

Beramendi, Pablo, Silja Häusermann, Herbert Kitschelt, and Hanspeter Kriesi, eds. *The Politics of Advanced Capitalism.* Cambridge: Cambridge University Press, 2015.

Berman, Sheri, and Maria Snegovaya. "Populism and the Decline of Social Democracy." *Journal of Democracy* 30, no. 3 (2019): 5–19.

Bértoa, Fernando Casal, Kevin Deegan-Krause, and Tim Haughton. "The Volatility of Volatility: Measuring Change in Party Vote Shares." *Electoral Studies* 50 (2017): 142–56.

Betz, Hans-Georg. "Value Change and Post-Materialist Politics: The Case of West Germany." *Comparative Political Studies* 23, no. 2 (1990): 239–56.

Bischof, Daniel. "Towards a Renewal of the Niche Party Concept: Parties, Market Shares and Condensed Offers." *Party Politics* 23, no. 3 (2017): 220–35.

Boerman, Arno. "Drie maanden crisis in de LPF." *De Volkskrant*, October 4, 2002.

Boix, Carles. "Setting the Rules of the Game: The Choice of Electoral Systems in Advanced Democracies." *American Political Science Review* 93, no. 3 (1999): 609–24.

Bonanno, George A. and John T. Jost. "Conservative Shift among High-Exposure Survivors of the September 11th Terrorist Attacks." *Basic and Applied Social Psychology*, 28, no. 4 (2006): 311–23.

Bourdieu, Pierre. *A Social Critique of the Judgement of Taste.* London: Routledge, 1984.

Bowler, Shaun. "Voter Perceptions and Party Strategies: An Empirical Approach," *Comparative Politics* 23, no. 1 (1990): 61–83.

Boxall, Andy. "Dell Says Goodbye to Both Smartphones and Android, Stops International Sales." *Digital Trends*, December 13, 2012. https://www.digital trends.com/mobile/dell-says-goodbye-to-both-smartphones-and-android/.

Brennan, Geoffrey, and Alan Hamlin. "Expressive Voting and Electoral Equilibrium." *Public Choice* 95, no. 1–2 (1998): 149–75.

Bridger, Gabriel. "2017 Mini Sales Had Record Year Worldwide." *Motoring File*, December 1, 2017. http://www.motoringfile.com/2018/01/12/2017-mini-sales -hit-record-worldwide/.

Budge, Ian. "Electoral Volatility: Issue Effects and Basic Change in 23 Post-War Democracies." *Electoral Studies* 1, no. 2 (1982): 147–68.

Budge, Ian, and David J. Farlie. *Explaining and Predicting Elections: Issue Effects and Party Strategies in Twenty-Three Democracies*. Crows Nest, NSW: Stanley Unwin, 1983.

Budge, Ian, and Hans-Dieter Klingemann, eds. *Mapping Policy Preferences: Estimates for Parties, Electors, and Governments, 1945–1998*. Vol. 1. Oxford: Oxford University Press 2001.

Budge, Ian, David Robertson, and Derek Hearl, eds. *Ideology, Strategy and Party Change: Spatial Analyses of Post-War Election Programmes in 19 Democracies*. Cambridge: Cambridge University Press, 1987.

Bürklin, Wilhelm. "The German Greens: The Post-Industrial Non-Established and the Party System." *International Political Science Review* 6, no. 4 (1985): 463–81.

Cabral, Luis M. B. *Readings in Industrial Organization*. London: Wiley-Blackwell, 2000.

Campbell, Angus, Philip E. Converse, Warren E. Miller, and Donald E. Stokes. *The American Voter*. Chicago: University of Chicago Press, 1960.

Canes-Wrone, Brandice. *Who Leads Whom?: Presidents, Policy and the Public*. Chicago: University of Chicago Press, 2006.

Canovan, Margaret. *Populism*. New York: Harcourt, Brace, 1981.

Carey, John M., and Simon Hix. "The Electoral Sweet Spot: Low-Magnitude Proportional Electoral Systems." *American Journal of Political Science* 55, no. 2 (2011): 383–97.

Carmines, Edward, and James A. Stimson. *Issue Evolution: Race and the Transformation of American Politics*. Princeton, NJ: Princeton University Press, 1989.

———. "On the Evolution of Political Issues." In *Agenda Formation*, edited by William H. Riker, 151–68, Ann Arbor: University of Michigan, 1993.

———. "On the Structure and Sequence of Issue Evolution." *American Political Science Review* 80, no. 3 (1986): 901–20.

Carroll, Laura. "The Rise of Snapchat and Instagram: A Youth Movement." *Harmelin Media*, April 12, 2018. https://www.harmelin.com/media-magnified/the -rise-of-snapchat-and-instagram-a-youth-movement/.

Cerulus, Laurens. "Greek Government Coalition Implodes over Macedonia Name

Deal." *Politico*, January 13, 2019. https://www.politico.eu/article/macedonia-greece-government-implodes-over-name-deal/.

Clark, Terry N., Seymour M. Lipset, and Michael Rempel. "The Declining Political Significance of Social Class." *International Sociology* 8, no. 3 (1993): 293–316.

Clarke, Harold D., David Sanders, Marianne Stewart, and Paul Whiteley. *Political Choice in Britain*. Oxford: Oxford University Press, 2004.

Clarke, Nick, Will Jennings, Jonathan Moss, and Gerry Stoker. *The Good Politician: Folk Theories, Political Interaction, and the Rise of Anti-politics*. Cambridge: Cambridge University Press, 2018.

Colantone, Italo, and Piero Stanig. "Global Competition and Brexit." *American Political Science Review* 112, no. 2 (2018): 201–18.

———. "The Trade Origins of Economic Nationalism: Import Competition and Voting Behavior in Western Europe." *American Journal of Political Science* 62, no. 4 (2018): 936–53.

Costello, Katie. "Gartner Says Worldwide PC Shipments Declined 4.3 Percent in 4Q18 and 1.3 Percent for the Year." Gartner Newsroom, January 10, 2019. https://www.gartner.com/en/newsroom/press-releases/2019-01-10-gartner-says-worldwide-pc-shipments-declined-4-3-perc.

Converse, Philip E. "The Nature of Belief Systems in Mass Publics (1964)." *Critical Review* 18, no. 1–3 (2006): 1–7.

Cox, Gary W. *Making Votes Count: Strategic Coordination in the World's Electoral Systems*. New York: Cambridge University Press, 1997.

Cramer, Kathleen J. *The Politics of Resentment: Rural Consciousness in Wisconsin and the Rise of Scott Walker*. Chicago: University of Chicago Press, 2016.

Cronin, James E., George W. Ross, and James Shoch, eds. *What's Left of the Left: Democrats and Social Democrats in Challenging Times*. Durham, NC: Duke University Press, 2011.

Cué, Carlos E., and Jose Antonio Hernández. "Bárcenas' Secret Papers: Bárcenas Never Left PP Payroll." *El País*, February 13, 2013.

Dalton, Russell J. *Citizen Politics: Public Opinion and Political Parties in Advanced Industrial Democracies*. Los Angeles: CQ, 2014.

———. "The Decline of Party Identifications." In *Parties without Partisans: Political Change in Advanced Industrial Democracies*, edited by Dalton and Martin P. Wattenberg, 19–36. New York: Oxford University Press, 2002.

———. *Political Realignment: Economics, Culture, and Electoral Change*. New York: Oxford University Press, 2018.

Dalton, Russell J., and Scott E. Flanagan. *Electoral Change in Advanced Industrial Democracies: Realignment or Dealignment?* Princeton, NJ: Princeton University Press, 2017.

Damore, David F. "The Dynamics of Issue Ownership in Presidential Campaigns." *Political Research Quarterly* 57, no. 3 (2004): 391–97.

Debus, Marc. "Analysing Party Politics in Germany with New Approaches for Estimating Policy Preferences of Political Actors." *German Politics* 18, no. 3 (2009): 281–300.

DeClair, Edward. *Politics on the Fringe: The People, Policies and Organization of the French National Front*. Durham, NC: Duke University Press, 1999.

De Lange, Sarah L. "New Alliances: Why Mainstream Parties Govern with Radical Right-Wing Populist Parties." *Political Studies* 60, no. 4 (2012): 899–918.

Della Porta, Donatella, Hara Kouki, and Joseba Fernández. "Left's Love and Hate for Europe: Syriza, Podemos and Critical Visions of Europe During the Crisis." In *Euroscepticism, Democracy and the Media*, edited by Manuela Caiani and Simona Guerra, 219–40. London: Palgrave Macmillan, 2017.

Deschouwer, Kris. *The Politics of Belgium: Governing a Divided Society*. New York: Palgrave Macmillan, 2009.

De Sio, Lorenzo, and Till Weber. "Issue Yield: A Model of Party Strategy in Multidimensional Space." *American Political Science Review* 108, no. 4 (2014): 870–85.

De Vreese, Claes H., Frank Esser, Toril Aalberg, Carsten Reinemann, and James Stanyer. "Populism as an Expression of Political Communication Content and Style: A New Perspective." *International Journal of Press/Politics* 23, no. 4 (2018): 423–38.

De Vries, Catherine E. "The Cosmopolitan-Parochial Divide: Changing Patterns of Party and Electoral Competition in the Netherlands and Beyond." *Journal of European Public Policy* 25, no. 11 (2018): 1541–65.

———. *Euroscepticism and the Future of European Integration*. Oxford: Oxford University Press, 2018.

———. "The Impact of EU Referenda on National Electoral Politics: The Dutch Case." *West European Politics* 32, no. 1 (2009): 142–71.

De Vries, Catherine E., and Nathalie Giger. "Holding Governments Accountable?: Individual Heterogeneity in Performance Voting." *European Journal of Political Research* 53, no. 2 (2014): 345–62.

De Vries, Catherine E., Armen Hakhverdian, and Bram Lancee. "The Dynamics of Voters' Left/Right Identification: The Role of Economic and Cultural Attitudes." *Political Science Research and Methods* 1, no. 2 (2013): 223–38.

De Vries, Catherine E., and Sara B. Hobolt. "When Dimensions Collide: The Electoral Success of Issue Entrepreneurs." *European Union Politics* 13, no. 2 (2012): 246–68.

De Vries, Catherine E., Sara B. Hobolt, and Mariken A.C.G. van der Velden. "Taking on the Establishment Analyzing: Challenger Party Rhetoric." Paper presented at the American Political Science Association Annual Meeting, Washington, DC, August 29–September 1, 2019.

De Vries, Catherine E., and Isabell Hofmann. *Fears and Not Values*. Gütersloh, Germany: Bertelsmann Foundation, 2016.

De Winter, Lieven, and Huri Tursan, eds. *Regionalist Parties in Western Europe*. London: Routledge, 2003.

Diermeier, Daniel, and Peter van Roozendaal. "The Duration of Cabinet Formation Processes in Western Multi-Party Democracies." *British Journal of Political Science* 28, no. 4 (1998): 609–26.

Dinas, Elias. "Does Choice Bring Loyalty?: Electoral Participation and the Development of Party Identification." *American Journal of Political Science* 58, no. 2 (2013): 449–65.

Dinas, Elias, Erin Hartman, and Joost van Spanje. "Dead Man Walking: The Affective Roots of Issue Proximity between Voters and Parties." *Political Behavior* 38, no. 3 (2016): 659–87.

Dinas, Elias, and Pedro Riera. "Do European Parliament Elections Impact National Party System Fragmentation?" *Comparative Political Studies* 51, no. 4 (2018): 447–76.

Doherty, Brian. "The Fundi-Realo Controversy: An Analysis of Four European Green Parties." *Environmental Politics* 1, no. 1 (1992): 95–120.

Downs, Anthony. *An Economic Theory of Democracy.* New York: Harper, 1957.

———. "An Economic Theory of Political Action in a Democracy." *Journal of Political Economy* 65, no. 2 (1957): 135–50.

Drummond, Andrew J. "Electoral Volatility and Party Decline in Western Democracies: 1970–1995." *Political Studies* 54, no. 3 (2006): 628–47.

Duverger, Maurice. *Les parties politiques.* Paris: Armand Colin, 1951.

Edmondson, Brad. *Ice Cream Social: The Struggle for the Soul of Ben & Jerry's.* Oakland, CA: Berrett-Koehler, 2014.

Elff, Martin. "Social Structure and Electoral Behavior in Comparative Perspective: The Decline of Social Cleavages in Western Europe Revisited." *Perspectives on Politics* 5, no. 2 (2007): 277–94.

Eltchaninoff, Michel. *Inside the Mind of Marine Le Pen.* London: Hurst, 2018.

Enelow, James M., and Melvin J. Hinich. *The Spatial Theory of Voting: An Introduction.* Cambridge: Cambridge University Press, 1984.

Engesser, Sven, Nicole Ernst, Frank Esser, and Florin Büchel. "Populism and Social Media: How Politicians Spread a Fragmented Ideology." *Information, Communication and Society* 20, no. 8 (2017): 1109–26.

Erikson, Robert S. "The Advantage of Incumbency in Congressional Elections." *Polity* 3, no. 3 (1971): 395–405.

Erikson, Robert S., Michael B. MacKuen, and James A. Stimson. *The Macro Polity.* Cambridge: Cambridge University Press, 2002.

Érrejon, Íñigo, Chantal Mouffe, and Owen Jones. *Podemos: In the Name of the People.* London: Lawrence and Wishart, 2016.

Evans, Geoffrey, and James Tilley. *The New Politics of Class: The Political Exclusion of the British Working Class.* Oxford: Oxford University Press, 2017.

Evrengün, Hasan. "LPF: Haagse Heksenketel." *Andere Tijden,* November 16, 2006. https://www.anderetijden.nl/aflevering/375/LPF.

Ezrow, Lawrence. *Linking Citizens and Parties: How Electoral Systems Matter for Political Representation.* Oxford: Oxford University Press, 2010.

Ezrow, Lawrence, Catherine De Vries, Marco Steenbergen, and Erica Edwards. "Mean Voter Representation and Partisan Constituency Representation: Do Parties Respond to the Mean Voter Position or to their Supporters?" *Party Politics* 17, no. 3 (2011): 275–301.

Fetzer, Thiemo. "Did Austerity Cause Brexit?" *American Economic Review* 109, no. 11 (2019): 3849–86.

Fiorina, Morris P. *Retrospective Voting in American National Elections*. New Haven, CT: Yale University Press, 1981.

Ford, Robert, and Matthew Goodwin. *Revolt on the Right: Explaining Support for the Radical Right in Britain*. London: Routledge, 2013.

Franklin, Charles H., and John E. Jackson. "The Dynamics of Party Identification." *American Political Science Review* 77 (1983): 957–73.

Franklin, Mark N. *Voter Turnout and the Dynamics of Electoral Competition in Established Democracies since 1945*. New York: Cambridge University Press, 2004.

Franklin, Mark N., Thomas T. Mackie, and Henry Valen. *Electoral Change: Responses to Evolving Social and Attitudinal Structures in Western Countries*. Colchester, UK: ECPR, 2009.

Frenkel, Sheera, Nicholas Confessore, Cecilia Kang, Matthew Rosenberg, and Jack Nicas. "Delay, Deny and Deflect: How Facebook's Leaders Fought through Crisis." *New York Times*, November 14, 2018. https://www.nytimes.com/2018/11/14/technology/facebook-data-russia-election-racism.html.

Gabel, Matthew, and Kenneth Scheve. "Estimating the Effect of Elite Communications on Public Opinion Using Instrumental Variables." *American Journal of Political Science* 51, no. 4 (2007): 1013–28.

Garfield, Simon. *MINI: The True and Secret History of the Making of a Motor Car*. London: Faber and Faber, 2010.

Geer, John G. *From Tea Leaves to Opinion Polls: A Theory of Democratic Leadership*. New York: Columbia University Press, 1996.

Gehlhar, Mark. "Regional Concentration in the Global Food Economy." Paper presented at the First Biennial Conference of the Food System Research Group, June 27, 2003, Madison, WI.

Gelman, Andrew, and Gary King. "Estimating Incumbency Advantage without Bias." *American Journal of Political Science* 34, no. 4 (1990): 1142–64.

Gerber, Alan, and Donald P. Green. "Rational Learning and Partisan Attitudes." *American Journal of Political Science* 42, no. 3 (1998): 794–818.

Giddens, Anthony. *The Third Way: The Renewal of Social Democracy*. Cambridge, UK: Polity, 1990.

Gilmartin, Eoghan, and Tommy Greene. "The Future of Podemos Is at Stake Today." *Jacobin Magazine*, April 28, 2019. https://jacobinmag.com/2019/04/podemos-iglesias-spain-elections-psoe-sanchez.

Glazek, Christopher. "Emmanuel Macron Is Everything America's Democrats Are Not." *Foreign Policy*, April 25, 2017.

Golder, Matt. "Far Right Parties in Europe." *Annual Review of Political Science* 19 (2016): 477–97.

Golder, Sona N. "Bargaining Delays in the Government Formation Process." *Comparative Political Studies* 43, no. 1 (2010): 3–32.

———. *The Logic of Pre-electoral Coalition Formation*. Athens, OH: Ohio University Press, 2006.

Green, Jane, and Sara B. Hobolt. "Owning the Issue Agenda: Party Strategies and Vote Choices in British Elections." *Electoral Studies* 27, no. 3 (2008): 460–76.

Green, Jane, and Will Jennings. *The Politics of Competence: Parties, Public Opinion and Voters.* Cambridge: Cambridge University Press, 2017.

Greene, Kenneth. *Why Dominant Parties Lose: Mexico's Democratization in Comparative Perspective.* Cambridge: Cambridge University Press, 2007.

Green-Pedersen, Christoffer. "The Growing Importance of Issue Competition: The Changing Nature of Party Competition in Western Europe." *Political Studies* 55, no. 3 (2007): 607–28.

———. *The Reshaping of West European Party Politics: Agenda-Setting and Party Competition in Comparative Perspective.* Oxford: Oxford University Press, 2019.

Green-Pedersen, Christoffer, and Jesper Krogstrup. "Immigration as a Political Issue in Denmark and Sweden." *European Journal of Political Research* 47, no. 5 (2008): 610–34.

Green-Pedersen, Christoffer, and Peter B. Mortensen. "Who Sets the Agenda and Who Responds to It in the Danish Parliament?: A New Model of Issue Competition and Agenda-Setting." *European Journal of Political Research* 49, no. 2 (2010): 257–81.

Groseclose, Tim. "A Model of Candidate Location when One Candidate has a Valence Advantage." *American Journal of Political Science* 45, no. 4 (2001): 862–86.

Groshek, Jacob, and Karolina Koc-Michalska. "Helping Populism Win?: Social Media Use, Filter Bubbles, and Support for Populist Presidential Candidates in the 2016 US Election Campaign." *Information, Communication and Society* 20, no.9 (2017): 1389–407.

Gruber, Helmut. "Der kleine Mann und die alten Parteien: Ergebnisse einer Untersuchung zum Sprachgebrauch J. Haider 1983–1987." *Journal für Sozialforschung* 28, no. 19 (1988): 137–45.

Die Grünen. *Die Grünen: Wahlplattform zur Bundestagswahl 1980.* Bonn: Die Grünen, 1980. https://www.boell.de/sites/default/files/assets/boell.de/images/download_de/publikationen/1980_Wahlplattform_Bundestagswahl.pdf.

Hamlin, Alan, and Colin Jennings. "Expressive Political Behaviour: Foundations, Scope and Implications." *British Journal of Political Science* 41, no. 3 (2011): 645–70.

Harmel, Robert, and John D. Robertson. "Formation and Success of New Parties: A Cross-National Analysis." *International Political Science Review* 6, no. 4 (1985): 501–23.

Harteveld, Eelco, and Elisabeth Ivarsflaten. "Why Women Avoid the Radical Right: Internalized Norms and Party Reputations." *British Journal of Political Science* 48, no. 2 (2018): 369–84.

Hartleb, Florian. "Länderportrait Österreich." In *Jahrbuch Extremismus and Demokratie,* edited by Uwe Backes, Alexander Gallus, Eckhard Jesse, and Tom Thieme, 209–28, Baden-Baden: Nomos, 2018.

Haughton, Tim. "Exit, Choice and Legacy: Explaining the Patterns of Party Politics in Post-communist Slovakia." *East European Politics* 30, no. 2 (2014): 210–29.

Haughton, Tim, and Kevin Deegan-Krause. "Hurricane Season: Systems of Instability in Central and East European Party Politics." *East European Politics and Societies* 29, no. 1 (2015): 61–80.

Hawkins, Kirk A. "Is Chávez Populist?: Measuring Populist Discourse in Comparative Perspective." *Comparative Political Studies* 42, no. 8 (2009): 1040–67.

Hawkins, Kirk, Scott Riding, and Cas Mudde. "Measuring Populist Attitudes." Political Concepts Committee on Concepts and Methods Working Paper 55. January 2012. www.concepts–methods.org.

He, Hongwei, Yan Li, and Lloyd Harris. "Social Identity Perspective on Brand Loyalty." *Journal of Business Research* 65, no. 5 (2012): 648–57.

Heathman, Amelia. "Which Is the Biggest Challenger Bank in the UK?: An Investigation." *Verdict*, January 12, 2018. https://www.verdict.co.uk/biggest-uk -challenger-banks/.

Henley, Jon. "Real Story of Sweden's Election Is Not about March of the Far Right." *Guardian*, September 10, 2018. https://www.theguardian.com/world/2018 /sep/10/swedish-election-highlights-decline-of-europes-main-parties.

Herfindahl, Orris C. "Concentration in the Steel Industry." Unpublished PhD dissertation, Columbia University, 1950.

Hernández, Enrique, and Hanspeter Kriesi. "The Electoral Consequences of the Financial and Economic Crisis in Europe." *European Journal of Political Research* 55, no. 2 (2016): 203–24

Hetherington, Marc J., and Elizabeth Suhay. "Authoritarianism, Threat, and Americans' Support for the War on Terror." *American Journal of Political Science* 55, no. 3 (2011): 54–66.

Higgins, Tim, and Susan Pulliam. "Elon Musk Races to Exit Tesla's 'Production Hell.'" *Wall Street Journal*, June 28, 2018. https://www.wsj.com/articles/elon -musk-races-to-exit-teslas-production-hell-1530149814.

Himanshu. "The Rise, Dominance, and Epic Fall: A Brief Look at Nokia's History." *GSMArena*, August 12, 2015. https://www.gsmarena.com/the_rise _dominance_and_epic_fall__a_brief_look_at_nokias_history-blog-13460.php.

Hino, Airo. *New Challenger Parties in Western Europe: A Comparative Analysis.* London: Routledge, 2012.

Hobolt, Sara B., and Sylvain Brouard. "Contesting the European Union?: Why the Dutch and the French Rejected the European Constitution." *Political Research Quarterly* 64, no. 2 (2011): 309–22.

Hobolt, Sara B., and Catherine E. De Vries. "Issue Entrepreneurship and Multiparty Competition." *Comparative Political Studies* 48, no. 9 (2015): 1159–85.

———. "Turning against the Union?: The Impact of the Crisis on the Eurosceptic Vote in the 2014 European Parliament Elections." *Electoral Studies* 44, no. 4 (2016): 504–14.

Hobolt, Sara B, and Julian Hoerner. "The Mobilizing Effect of Political Choice." *European Journal of Political Research* (2019). doi:10.1111/1475-6765.12353.

Hobolt, Sara B., and Jeffrey A. Karp. "Voters and Coalition Governments." *Electoral Studies* 29, no. 3 (2010): 299–307.

Hobolt, Sara B., and James Tilley. "Fleeing the Centre: The Rise of Challenger Parties in the Aftermath of the Euro Crisis." *West European Politics* 39, no. 5 (2016): 971–91.

Hooghe, Liesbet, and Gary Marks. "Cleavage Theory Meets Europe's Crises: Lipset, Rokkan, and the Transnational Cleavage." *Journal of European Public Policy* 25, no. 1 (2018): 109–35.

Hooghe, Liesbet, Gary Marks, and Carole J. Wilson. "Does Left/Right Structure Party Positions on European Integration?" *Comparative Political Studies* 35, no. 8 (2002): 965–89.

Hopkin, Jonathan. *Anti-system Politics: The Crisis of Market Liberalism in Rich Democracies*. Oxford: Oxford University Press, forthcoming.

———. "Bringing the Members Back In?: Democratizing Candidate Selection in Britain and Spain." *Party Politics* 7, no. 3 (2001): 343–61.

Hotelling, Harold. "Stability in Competition." *Economic Journal* 39, no. 153 (1929): 41–57.

Hug, Simon. *Altering Party Systems: Strategic Behavior and the Emergence of New Political Parties in Western Democracies*. Ann Arbor, MI: University of Michigan Press, 2001.

Ignazi, Piero. "The Silent Counter-Revolution: Hypotheses on the Emergence of Extreme Right-Wing Parties in Europe." *European Journal of Political Research* 22, no. 1 (1992): 3–34.

Imbert, Fred, and Gina Francolla. "Facebook's $100 Billion-Plus Rout Is the Biggest Loss in Stock Market History." *CNBC*, July 26, 2018. https://www.cnbc.com/2018/07/26/facebook-on-pace-for-biggest-one-day-loss-in-value-for-any-company-sin.html.

Inglehart, Ronald. *The Silent Revolution: Changing Values and Political Styles among Western Publics*. Princeton, NJ: Princeton University Press, 1977.

———. "The Silent Revolution in Europe: Intergenerational Change in Post-Industrial Societies." *American Political Science Review* 65, no. 4 (1971): 991–1017.

Inglehart, Ronald, and Jacques-René Rabier. "Political Realignment in Advanced Industrial Society: From Class-Based Politics to Quality-of-Life Politics." *Government and Opposition* 21 no. 4 (1986): 456–79.

Ivarsflaten, Elisabeth. "Immigration Policy and Party Organization: Explaining the Rise of the Populist Right in Western Europe." Unpublished DPhil dissertation, University of Oxford, 2006.

Ivarsflaten, Elisabeth. "Reputational Shields: Why Most Anti-Immigrant Parties Failed in Western Europe, 1980–2005". Working paper. University of Oxford, 2006.

Iyengar, Shanto. "Framing Responsibility for Political Issues: The Case of Poverty." *Political Behavior* 12, no. 1 (1990): 19–40.

Jackman, Robert W., and Karin Volpert. "Conditions Favouring Parties of the Extreme Right in Western Europe." *British Journal of Political Science* 26, no. 4 (1996): 501–21

Jagers, Jan, and Stefaan Walgrave. "Populism as Political Communication Style: An Empirical Study of Political Parties' Discourse in Belgium." *European Journal of Political Research* 46, no. 3 (2007): 319–45.

Jahn, Detlef. "Green Politics and Parties in Germany." *Political Quarterly* (1997): 174–82.

Jensen, Christian B., and Jae-Jae Spoon. "Thinking Locally, Acting Supranationally: Niche Party Behaviour in the European Parliament." *European Journal of Political Research* 49, no. 2 (2010): 174–201.

Jolly, Seth K. *The European Union and the Rise of Regionalist Parties*. Ann Arbor: University of Michigan Press, 2015.

Jones, Sam. "Far Right Wins Seats in Spanish Region for First Time since Franco." *Guardian*, December 3, 2018. https://www.theguardian.com/world/2018/dec /03/spain-far-right-vox-party-wins-seats-in-andalucia-for-first-time-since -franco.

———. "Pedro Sánchez Sworn In as Spain's Prime Minister after No-Confidence Vote." *Guardian*, June 2, 2018. https://www.theguardian.com/world/2018/jun /02/pedro-sanchez-sworn-in-spain-prime-minister-socialist-psoe.

———. "Spanish Election: Socialists Win amid Far-Right Gains for Vox Party." *Guardian*, April 28, 2019. https://www.theguardian.com/world/2019/apr/28 /spain-election-socialists-to-win-most-seats-far-right-vox-resurgent.

———. "Spanish PM Appoints 11 Women and Six Men to New Cabinet." *Guardian*, June 6, 2018. https://www.theguardian.com/world/2018/jun/06/new -spanish-pm-appoints-astronaut-pedro-duque-science-minister.

Jung, Jae-Hu, and Margit Tavits. "Valence Attacks Harm the Electoral Performance of the Left but Not the Right." *Journal of Politics* (forthcoming).

Kahneman, Daniel. *Thinking Fast and Slow*. London: Penguin, 2011.

Kalyvas, Stathis N. *The Rise of Christian Democracy in Europe*. Ithaca, NY: Cornell University Press, 1996.

Kalyvas, Stathis N., and Kees van Kersbergen. "Christian Democracy." *Annual Review of Political Science* 13 (2010): 183–209.

Kam, Cindy D., and Elizabeth J. Zechmeister. "Name Recognition and Candidate Support." *American Journal of Political Science* 57, no. 4 (2013): 971–86.

Katz, Richard S., and Peter Mair. "Changing Models of Party Organization and Party Democracy: The Emergence of the Cartel Party." *Party Politics* 1, no. 1 (1995): 5–28.

Kay, John. *Foundations of Corporate Success: How Business Strategies Add Value*. Oxford: Oxford University Press, 2003.

Kedar, Orit. *Voting for Policy, Not Parties: How Voters Compensate for Power Sharing*. Cambridge: Cambridge University Press, 2009.

Keller, Kevin Lane. "Conceptualizing, Measuring, and Managing Customer-Based Brand Equity." *Journal of Marketing* 57, no. 1 (1993): 1–22.

Kelly, Gordon. "The Majority of iPhone Users Admit to 'Blind Loyalty': Why This Is a Problem for Apple." *Forbes*, March 21, 2014. https://www.forbes.com/sites /gordonkelly/2014/03/21/the-majority-of-iphone-users-admit-to-blind -loyalty-why-this-a-problem-for-apple/.

Kennedy, Paul. "Is Spain Heading for a Four Party System?: Assessing the State of Play Ahead of a Series of Key Spanish Elections." *LSE EUROPP (European Politics and Policy) blog*, March 17, 2015. http://bit.ly/1x9qZNC.

Kirchheimer, Otto. "The Transformation of Western European Party Systems." In *Political Parties and Political Development*, edited by Joseph LaPalombara and Myron Weiner, 177–200. Princeton, NJ: Princeton University Press, 1966.

Kitsantonis, Niki. "Alexis Tsipras Survives Confidence Vote in Greece's Parliament." *New York Times*, January 16, 2019. https://www.nytimes.com/2019/01/16/world/europe/greece-tsipras-confidence-vote.html.

Kitschelt, Herbert. *The Transformation of European Social Democracy.* New York: Cambridge University Press, 1994.

Kitschelt, Herbert, and Staf Hellemans. *Beyond the European Left: Ideology and Political Action in the Belgian Ecology Parties.* Durham, NC: Duke University Press, 1990.

Kitschelt, Herbert, and Anthony J. McGann. *The Radical Right in Western Europe: A Comparative Analysis.* Ann Arbor: University of Michigan Press, 1997.

Klaasen, Niels. "Baudet heeft sturing nodig, anders citeert hij de hele dag filosofen, komt er niks uit." *Algemeen Dagblad*, March 23, 2019. https://www.ad.nl/politiek/baudet-heeft-sturing-nodig-anders-citeert-hij-de-hele-dag-filosofen-komt-er-niks-uit~a6d31230/.

Klein, Markus, and Jürgen W. Falter. *Der lange Weg der Grünen.* Munich: Beck Verlag, 2003.

Klingemann, Hans-Dieter, Andrea Volkens, Michael D. McDonald, Ian Budge, and Judith Bara. *Mapping Policy Preferences II: Estimates for Parties, Electors, and Governments in Eastern Europe, European Union, and OECD 1990–2003.* Vol. 2. Oxford: Oxford University Press, 2006.

Klüver, Heike, and Jae-Jae Spoon. "Who Responds?: Voters, Parties and Issue Attention." *British Journal of Political Science* 46, no. 3 (2016): 633–54.

Knight Frank. *Your Future, Now.* Knight Frank Company report. London: Knight Frank, 2018. https://content.knightfrank.com/research/1423/documents/en/uk-retail-banking-sector-profile-2018-5188.pdf.

König, Thomas, Moritz Marbach, and Moritz Osnabrügge. "Left/Right or U? Estimating the Dimensionality of National Party Competition in Europe." *Journal of Politics* 79, no. 3 (2017): 1101–05.

Kriesi, Hanspeter. "The Populist Challenge." *West European Politics* 37, no. 2 (2014): 361–78.

Kriesi, Hanspeter, Edgar Grande, Romain Lachat, Martin Dolezal, Simon Bornschier, and Timotheos Frey. "Globalization and the Transformation of the National Political Space: Six European Countries Compared." *European Journal of Political Research* 45, no. 6 (2006): 921–56.

———. *West European Politics in the Age of Globalization.* Cambridge: Cambridge University Press, 2008.

Krosnick, Jon A. "Government Policy and Citizen Passion: A Study of Issue Publics in Contemporary America." *Political Behavior* 12, no. 1 (1990): 59–92.

Krosnick, Jon A., Matthew K. Berent, and David S. Boninger. "Pockets of Responsibility in the American Electorate: Findings of a Research Program on Attitude Importance." *Political Communication* 11, no. 4 (1994): 391–411.

Laver, Michael, and Kenneth Benoit. "The Basic Arithmetic of Legislative Decisions." *American Journal of Political Science* 59, no. 2 (2015): 275–91.

Lavezzolo, Sebastián, and Luis Ramiro. "Stealth Democracy and the Support for New and Challenger Parties." *European Political Science Review* 10, no. 2 (2018): 267–89.

Lavietes, Matt. "Musk, Trump and the Age-Old Mass Psychology Effect that Both are Successfully Exploiting." *CNBC*, July 29, 2018. https://www.cnbc.com /2018/07/28/musk-trump-and-a-mass-psychology-effect-both-successfully -exploit.html.

Lee, David. "Nokia: The Rise and Fall of a Mobile Giant." *BBC News*, September 13, 2013. https://www.bbc.co.uk/news/technology-23947212.

Lewis, Paul. "Rage, Rapture and Pure Populism: On the Road with Nigel Farage." *Guardian*, 19 May, 2019.

Lieberman, Marvin B., and David B. Montgomery. "First-Mover Advantages." *Strategic Management Journal* 9, no. S1 (1988): 41–58.

Lijphart, Arend. *Patterns of Democracy: Government Forms and Performance in Thirty-Six Countries.* New Haven, CT: Yale University Press, 1999.

Lipset, Seymour Martin, and Stein Rokkan, eds. *Party Systems and Voter Alignments: Cross-National Perspectives.* New York: Free Press, 1967.

Louwerse, Tom, and Peter van Aelst. "The Exceptional Belgian Case?: Government Formation Duration in Comparative Perspective." Paper presented at the State of the Federation/Association belge francophone de science politique conference, Louvain-la-Neuve, Belgium, October 18, 2013.

Lowe, Will, Kenneth Benoit, Slava Mikhaylov, and Michael Laver. "Scaling Policy Preferences from Coded Political Texts. *Legislative Studies Quarterly* 36, no. 1 (2011): 123–55.

Lowell, A. Lawrence. *Governments and Parties in Continental Europe.* Vol. 1. Cambridge, MA: Harvard University Press, 1896.

Lupia, Arthur A. "Shortcuts versus Encyclopedias: Information and Voting Behavior in California Insurance Reform Elections." *American Political Science Review* 88, no. 1 (1994): 63–76.

Lupia, Arthur A., and Matthew D. McCubbins. *The Democratic Dilemma: Can Citizens Learn What They Need to Know?* Cambridge: Cambridge University Press, 1998.

Lupu, Noam. "Brand Dilution and the Breakdown of Political Parties in Latin America." *World Politics* 66, no. 4 (2014): 561–602.

———. *Party Brands in Crisis: Partisanship, Brand Dilution, and the Breakdown of Political Parties in Latin America.* Cambridge: Cambridge University Press, 2016.

Magaloni, Beatriz. *Voting for Autocracy: Hegemonic Party Survival and its Demise in Mexico.* Cambridge: Cambridge University Press, 2006.

Mainwaring, Scott, Carlos Gervasoni, and Annabella Espana-Najera. "Extra- and Within-System Electoral Volatility." *Party Politics* 23, no. 6 (2017): 623–35.

Mair, Peter. "De eigenaardigheden van de Nederlanders: De verkiezingen van 2002 in een vergelijkend perspectief." *B en M: Tijdschrift voor beleid, politiek en maatschappij* 29, no. 3 (2002): 160–63.

———. *Party System Change: Approaches and Interpretations.* Oxford: Oxford University Press, 1997.

———. "Representative versus Responsible Government." MPIfG (Max-Planck-Institut für Gesellschaftsforschung) Working Paper 09/8, 2009.

———. *Ruling the Void: The Hollowing of Western Democracy.* London: Verso Trade, 2013.

Mair, Peter, and Ingrid van Biezen. "Party Membership in Twenty European Democracies, 1980–2000." *Party Politics* 7, no. 1 (2001): 5–21.

March, Luke. "Beyond Syriza and Podemos, Other Radical Left Parties Are Threatening to Break into the Mainstream of European Politics." *LSE EUROPP (European Politics and Policy) Blog,* March 24, 2015. https://blogs.lse.ac.uk/europpblog/2015/03/24/beyond-syriza-and-podemos-other-radical-left-parties-are-threatening-to-break-into-the-mainstream-of-european-politics.

Margulies, Ben. "Why Europe Should Worry about Thierry Baudet." *LSE EUROPP (European Politics and Policy) Blog,* April 24, 2019. https://blogs.lse.ac.uk/europpblog/2019/04/24/why-europe-should-worry-about-thierry-baudet/.

Marks, Gary, David Attewell, Jan Rovny, and Liesbet Hooghe. "Dealignment Meets Cleavage Theory." Paper presented at the American Political Science Association Meeting, San Francisco, August 31–September 3, 2017.

Marks, Gary, and Carole J. Wilson. "The Past in the Present: A Cleavage Theory of Party Response to European Integration." *British Journal of Political Science* 30, no. 3 (2000): 433–59.

Marshal, Aarian. "Elon Musk Reveals His Awkward Dislike of Mass Transit: The Man Trying to Build Tunnels around the Country Is Awfully Unimpressed by the Basic Concept of Shared, Public Transportation." *Wired,* December 14, 2017, https://www.wired.com/story/elon-musk-awkward-dislike-mass-transit/.

Martin, Lanny W., and Georg Vanberg. "Wasting Time?: The Impact of Ideology and Size on Delay in Coalition Formation." *British Journal of Political Science* 33, no. 2 (2003): 323–32.

Matsubayashi, Tetsuya. "Do Politicians Shape Public Opinion?" *British Journal of Political Science* 43, no. 2 (2013): 451–78.

Mayhew, David R. "Congressional Elections: The Case of the Vanishing Marginals." *Polity* 6, no. 3 (1974): 295–317.

McDonald, Michael D., and Ian Budge. *Elections, Parties, Democracy: Conferring the Median Mandate.* New York: Oxford University Press, 2005.

Meguid, Bonnie. *Party Competition between Unequals: Strategies and Electoral Fortunes in Western Europe.* Cambridge: Cambridge University Press, 2008.

Mény, Yves, and Yves Surel. "The Constitutive Ambiguity of Populism." In *Democracies and the Populist Challenge*, edited by Mény and Surel, 1–21. London: Palgrave Macmillan, 2002.

Merrill, Samuel, III, and Bernhard Grofman. *A Unified Theory of Voting: Directional and Proximity Spatial Models.* Cambridge: Cambridge University Press, 1999.

Meyer, Thomas M., and Bernhard Miller. "The Niche Party Concept and its Measurement." *Party Politics* 21, no. 2 (2015): 259–71.

Miller, Arthur H., and Martin P. Wattenberg. "Throwing the Rascals Out: Policy and Performance Evaluations of Presidential Candidates, 1952–1980." *American Political Science Review* 79, no. 2 (1985): 359–72.

Minder, Raphael. "Socialists Strengthen Hold in Spain Election." *New York Times*, April 28, 2019. https://www.nytimes.com/2019/04/28/world/europe/spain-election-socialists.html.

Mudde, Cas. "The Paradox of the Anti-party Party: Insights from the Extreme Right." *Party Politics* 2, no. 2 (1996): 265–76.

———. *Populist Radical Right Parties in Europe.* Cambridge: Cambridge University Press, 2007.

———. "The Populist Zeitgeist." *Government and Opposition* 39, no. 4 (2004): 542–63.

Mudde, Cas, and Cristóbal Rovira Kaltwasser. *Populism: A Very Short Introduction.* Oxford: Oxford University Press. 2017.

Müller, Jan-Werner. "The End of Christian Democracy: What the Movement's Decline Means for Europe." *Foreign Affairs*, July 15, 2014. https://www.foreignaffairs.com/articles/western-europe/2014-07-15/end-christian-democracy.

Müller, Wolfgang, and Kaare Strøm. *Policy, Office or Votes?: How Political Parties in Western Europe Make Hard Decisions.* Cambridge: Cambridge University Press, 1999.

Müller-Rommel, Ferdinand. "The German Greens in the 1980s: Short-Term Cyclical Protest or Indicator of Transformation?" *Political Studies* 37, no. 1 (1989): 114–22.

———. "The New Challengers: Greens and Right-Wing Populist Parties in Western Europe." *European Review*, 6, no. 2 (1998): 191–202.

———, ed. *New Politics in Western Europe: The Rise and Success of Green Parties and Alternative Lists.* Boulder, CO: Westview, 1989.

Nadeau, Richard, and Michael S. Lewis-Beck. "National Economic Voting in US Presidential Elections." *Journal of Politics*, 63, no. 1 (2001): 159–81.

Nohlen, Dieter, and Philip Stöver, eds. *Elections in Europe: A Data Handbook.* Baden-Baden: Nomos, 2010.

Norris, Pippa. *Digital Divide: Civic Engagement, Information Poverty, and the Internet Worldwide.* New York: Cambridge University Press, 2001.

———. *Radical Right: Voters and Parties in the Electoral Market.* Cambridge: Cambridge University Press, 2005.

Norris, Pippa, and Ronald Inglehart. *Cultural Backlash: Trump, Brexit, and Authoritarian Populism*. Cambridge: Cambridge University Press, 2019.

Oesch, Daniel. "Coming to Grips with a Changing Class Structure: An Analysis of Employment Stratification in Britain, Germany, Sweden and Switzerland." *International Sociology* 21, no. 2 (2006): 263–88.

———. "Explaining Workers' Support for Right-Wing Populist Parties in Western Europe: Evidence from Austria, Belgium, France, Norway, and Switzerland." *International Political Science Review* 29, no. 3 (2008): 349–73.

Oesch, Daniel, and Line Rennwald. "The Class Basis of Switzerland's Cleavage between the New Left and the Populist Right." *Swiss Political Science Review* 16, no. 3 (2010): 343–71.

Oskarson, Maria. "Social Structure and Party Choice." In *The European Voter: A Comparative Study of Modern Democracies*, edited by Jacques Thomassen, 84–105. Oxford: Oxford University Press, 2005.

Page, Benjamin, and Robert Shapiro. *The Rational Public: Fifty Years of Trends in Americans' Policy Preferences*. Chicago: Chicago University Press, 1992.

Palmer, Barclay. "The World's 10 Biggest Restaurant Companies." *Investopedia*, June 23, 2019.

Panebianco, Angelo. *Political Parties: Organization and Power*. Cambridge: Cambridge University Press, 1988.

Pauwels, Teun. *Populism in Western Europe: Comparing Belgium, Germany and the Netherlands*. London: Routledge, 2014.

Pedersen, Mogens N. "The Dynamics of European Party Systems: Changing Patterns of Electoral Volatility." *European Journal of Political Research* 7, no. 1 (1979): 1–26.

———. "Towards a New Typology of Party Lifespans and Minor Parties." *Scandinavian Political Studies* 5, no. 1 (1982): 1–16.

Peffley, Mark, and John T. Williams. "Attributing Presidential Responsibility for National Economic Problems." *American Politics Quarterly* 13, no. 4 (1985): 393–425.

Pellikaan, Huib, Tom van der Meer and Sarah de Lange. "Fortuyn's Legacy: Party System Change in the Netherlands." *Comparative European Politics* 5, no. 3 (2007): 282–302.

———. "The Road from a Depolarized to a Centrifugal Democracy." *Acta Politica* 38, no. 1 (2003): 23–48.

Petrocik, John R. "Issue Ownership in Presidential Elections, with a 1980 Case Study." *American Journal of Political Science*, 40, no. 3 (1996): 825–50.

Pierce, Roy. "Mass–Elite Issue Linkages and the Responsible Party Model." In *Policy Representation in Western Democracies*, edited by Warren Miller, Pierce, Jacques Thomassen, Richard Herrera, Soren Holmberg, Peter Esaiasson and Bernhard Wessels, 9–32. Oxford: Oxford University Press, 1999.

Plümper, Thomas, Vera E. Troeger, and Philip Manow. "Panel Data Analysis in Comparative Politics: Linking Method to Theory." *European Journal of Political Research* 44, no. 2 (2005): 327–54.

Poguntke, Thomas. "New Politics and Party Systems: The Emergence of a New Type of Party?" *West European Politics* 10, no. 1 (1987): 76–88.

Polk, Jonathan, Jan Rovny, Ryan Bakker, Erica Edwards, Liesbet Hooghe, Seth Jolly, Jelle Koedam, et al. "Explaining the Salience of Anti-elitism and Reducing Political Corruption for Political Parties in Europe with the 2014 Chapel Hill Expert Survey Data." *Research and Politics* (2017): 1–9.

Pontusson, Jonas. "Explaining the Decline of European Social Democracy: The Role of Structural Economic Change." *World Politics* 47, no. 4 (1995): 495–533.

Powell, Eleanor N., and Joshua A. Tucker. "Revisiting Electoral Volatility in Post-Communist Countries: New Data, New Results and New Approaches." *British Journal of Political Science* 44, no. 1 (2014): 123–47.

Powell, G. Bingham. *Elections as Instruments of Democracy: Majoritarian and Proportional Views.* New Haven, CT: Yale University Press, 2000

Powell, G. Bingham, and Guy D. Whitten. "A Cross-National Analysis of Economic Voting: Taking Account of the Political Context." *American Journal of Political Science* 37, no. 2 (1993): 391–414.

Proksch, Sven-Oliver, and Jonathan B. Slapin. *The Politics of Parliamentary Debate.* Cambridge: Cambridge University Press, 2015.

Przeworski, Adam, and John Sprague. *Paper Stones: A History of Electoral Socialism.* Chicago: University of Chicago Press, 1988.

Rabinowitz, George, and Stuart E. Macdonald. "A Directional Theory of Issue Voting." *American Political Science Review* 83, no. 1 (1989): 93–121.

Rankin, Jennifer, and Helena Smith. "Yanis Varoufakis: I'd Rather Cut Off My Arm than Accept Bad Deal." *Guardian*, July 2, 2015. https://www.theguardian.com/business/2015/jul/02/yanis-varoufakis-id-rather-cut-off-my-arm-than-accept-yes-vote.

Ries, Al, and Jack Trout. *Positioning: The Battle for Your Mind.* New York: McGraw-Hill, 1986.

Riker, William H. *The Art of Political Manipulation.* New Haven, CT: Yale University Press, 1986.

———. *Liberalism against Populism: A Confrontation between the Theory of Democracy and the Theory of Social Choice.* San Francisco: W. H. Freeman, 1982.

———. *The Strategy of Rhetoric: Campaigning for the American Constitution.* New Haven, CT: Yale University Press, 1996.

Rohrschneider, Robert, and Stephen Whitefield. *The Strain of Representation: How Parties Represent Diverse Voters in Western and Eastern Europe.* Oxford: Oxford University Press, 2012.

Rooduijn, Matthijs. "The Mesmerising Message: The Diffusion of Populism in Public Debates in Western European Media." *Political Studies* 62, no. 4 (2014): 726–44.

Rooduijn, Matthijs, Sarah L. de Lange, and Wouter van der Brug. "A Populist Zeitgeist?: Programmatic Contagion by Populist Parties in Western Europe." *Party Politics* 20, no. 4 (2014): 563–75.

Rosenstone, Steven J., and John Hansen. *Mobilization, Participation, and Democracy in America*. New York: Macmillan, 1993.

Rovny, Jan. "Who Emphasizes and Who Blurs?: Party Strategies in Multidimensional Competition." *European Union Politics* 13, no. (2012): 269–92.

Rudolph, Thomas J. "Who's Responsible for the Economy?: The Formation and Consequences of Responsibility Attributions." *American Journal of Political Science* 47, no. 4 (2003): 698–713.

Rusman, Floor. "Wat zei Baudet eigenlijk in zijn overwinningsspeech?" *NRC Handelsblad*, March 21, 2019. https://www.nrc.nl/nieuws/2019/03/21/de-uil-van-minerva-spreidt-zijn-vleugels-bij-t-vallen-van-de-avond-a3954103.

Rydgren, Jens. "Explaining the Emergence of Radical Right-Wing Populist Parties: The Case of Denmark." *West European Politics* 27, no. 3 (2004): 474–502.

———. *From Tax Populism to Ethnic Nationalism: Radical Right-Wing Populism in Sweden*. New York: Berghahn Books, 2006.

———. *Movements of Exclusion: Radical Right-Wing Populism in the Western World*. Hauppauge, NY: Nova, 2005.

———. "The Sociology of the Radical Right." *Annual Review of Sociology* 33 (2007): 241–62.

Rydgren, Jens, and Patrick Ruth. "Contextual Explanations of Radical Right-Wing Support in Sweden: Socioeconomic Marginalization, Group Threat, and the Halo Effect." *Ethnic and Racial Studies* 36, no. 4 (2013): 711–28.

Sani, Giacomo, and Giovanni Sartori. "Polarization, Fragmentation and Competition in Western Democracies." In *Western European Party Systems: Continuity and Change*, edited by Hans Daalder and and Peter Mair, 307–340. Thousand Oaks, CA: Sage, 1983.

Sartori, Giovanni. *Parties and Party Systems: A Framework for Analysis*. Colchester: ECPR Press, 2005.

Schedler, Andreas. "Anti-political-establishment Parties." *Party Politics* 2, no. 3 (1996): 291–312.

Scheidl, Hans Werner. "Eine schockierende Replik stoppte Jörg Haider." *Die Presse*, June 17, 2016.

Scheuplein, Isabell. "Tabubruch in Turnschuhen." N-TV.de, December 12, 2010. https://www.n-tv.de/politik/Tabubruch-in-Turnschuhen-article2123521.html.

Schleiter, Petra, and Alisa Voznaya. "Party System Institutionalization, Accountability and Governmental Corruption." *British Journal of Political Science* 48, no. 2 (2018): 315–42.

Schmitt-Beck, Rüdiger. "The 'Alternative für Deutschland in the Electorate': Between Single-Issue and Right-Wing Populist Party." *German Politics* 26. no. 1 (2017): 124–48.

Schnattschneider, Elmer E. *The Semi-sovereign People: A Realist's View of Democracy in America*. New York: Holt, Rinehart, and Winston, 1960.

Schulte-Cloos, Julia. "Do European Parliament Elections Foster Challenger Parties' Success on the National Level?" *European Union Politics* 19, no. 3 (2018): 408–26.

Schumacher, Gijs, Catherine E. De Vries, and Barbara Vis. "Why Do Parties Change Position?: Party Organization and Environmental Incentives." *Journal of Politics* 75, no. 2 (2013): 464–77.

Schumpeter, Joseph A. *Capitalism, Socialism and Democracy.* New York: Harper and Row, 1942.

———. "The Creative Response in Economic History." *Journal of Economic History* 7, no. 2 (1947): 149–59.

Setili, Amanda. "Does Your Leadership Style Destroy Agility . . . or Supercharge It?" *Leader to Leader* 78, no. 1 (2015): 56–61.

Settele, Hanno. "Die Wahlfahrt: Bucher–Stronach." *Österreichische Rundfunk*, September 11, 2013. https://tvthek.orf.at/history/Kultige-Berichte/6563743 /Die-Wahlfahrt-Bucher-Stronach/6680603.

Shapiro, Carl. "Competition and Innovation: Did Arrow Hit the Bull's Eye?" In *The Rate and Direction of Inventive Activity Revisited,* edited by Josh Lerner and Scott Stern, 361–404. Chicago: University of Chicago Press, 2011.

Shepsle, Kenneth A. "The Strategy of Ambiguity: Uncertainty and Electoral Competition." *American Political Science Review* 66, no. 2 (1972): 555–68.

Sherman, Erik. "Top 5 Start-Up Acquirers of 2012." *Inc. Magazine*, February 8, 2013. https://www.inc.com/erik-sherman/biggest-startup-acquirers-2012. html.

Silva, Bruno Castanho. "Populist Radical Right Parties and Mass Polarization in the Netherlands." *European Political Science Review* 10, no. 2 (2018): 219–44.

Simmons, Heather. *Reinventing Dell: The Innovation Imperative.* Toronto: Murmurous, 2015.

Smith, Adam. *The Wealth of Nations: Books IV–V.* Edited by Andrew S. Skinner. London: Penguin, 1999.

Smith, Helena. "Syriza's Tsipras Sworn In after Greek Government Formed with Rightwingers." *Guardian*, January 25, 2015. https://www.theguardian.com /world/2015/jan/26/syriza-forms-government-rightwing-independent -greeks-party.

Snegovaya, Maria, and Sheri Berman. "Populism and the Decline of Social Democracy." *Journal of Democracy* 30, no. 3 (2019): 5–19.

Solaz, Hector, Catherine E. De Vries, and Roosmarijn A. De Geus. "In-Group Loyalty and the Punishment of Corruption." *Comparative Political Studies* 52, no. 6 (2019): 896–926.

Somer-Topcu, Zeynep. "Everything to Everyone: The Electoral Consequences of the Broad-Appeal Strategy in Europe." *American Journal of Political Science* 59, no. 4 (2015): 841–54.

Soronka, Stuart N., and Christopher Wlezien. *Degrees of Democracy: Politics, Public Opinion, and Policy.* Cambridge: Cambridge University Press, 2009.

Spoon, Jae-Jae. *Political Survival of Small Parties in Europe.* Ann Arbor: University of Michigan Press, 2011.

Spoon, Jae-Jae, Sara B. Hobolt, and Catherine E. De Vries. "Going Green: Explaining Issue Competition on the Environment." *European Journal of Political Research* 53, no. 2 (2014): 363–80.

Statista Research Department. "Global Market Share Held by Nokia Smartphones from 1st Quarter 2007 to 2nd Quarter 2013." *Statista*, July 25, 2013. https://www.statista.com/statistics/263438/market-share-held-by-nokia-smart phones-since-2007/.

Steenbergen, Marco R., Erica E. Edwards, and Catherine E. De Vries. "Who's Cueing Whom?: Mass-Elite Linkages and the Future of European Integration." *European Union Politics* 8, no. 1 (2007): 13–35.

Stewart, Emily. "Facebook's Very Bad Year, Explained." *Vox*, December 21, 2018. https://www.businesstimes.com.sg/stocks/facebook-controversies-hit-it -where-it-hurts-most-growth.

Stokes, Donald E. "Spatial Models of Party Competition." *American Political Science Review* 57, no. 2 (1963), 368–77.

Stone, Walter J., and Elizabeth N. Simas. "Candidate Valence and Ideological Positions in US House Elections." *American Journal of Political Science* 54, no. 2 (2010): 371–88.

Stronach, Frank. "Interview." *Österreichische Rundfunk*, July 3, 2012, 04:54–05:02. https://tvthek.orf.at/history/Innenpolitik/8002278/Legendaeres-Stronach -Interview/7967720.

Stubager, Rune. "The Changing Basis of Party Competition: Education, Authoritarian–Libertarian Values and Voting." *Government and Opposition* 48, no. 3 (2013): 372–97.

———. "The Development of the Education Cleavage: Denmark as a Critical Case." *West European Politics* 33, no. 3 (2010): 505–33.

Taggart, Paul. *Populism*. London: Open University Press, 2000.

Tavits, Margit. "Party Systems in the Making: The Emergence and Success of New Parties in New Democracies." *British Journal of Political Science* 38, no. 1 (2008): 113–33.

———. "The Role of Parties' Past Behavior in Coalition Formation." *American Political Science Review* 102, no. 4 (2008): 495–507.

Thatcher, Margaret. "Speech to Conservative Party Conference" (transcript of speech given at the Brighton Conference Centre, October 14, 1988). Margaret Thatcher Foundation, n.d., accessed December 30, 2019. https://www .margaretthatcher.org/document/107352.

Tilley, James, and Sara B. Hobolt. "Is the Government to Blame?: An Experimental Test of How Partisanship Shapes Perceptions of Performance and Responsibility." *Journal of Politics* 73, no. 2 (2011): 316–30.

Tirole, Jean. *The Theory of Industrial Organization*. Cambridge, MA: MIT Press, 1988.

Torres, Diego. "Spain's Sánchez Calls Snap Election on April 28." *Politico*, February 15, 2019. https://www.politico.eu/article/spains-sanchez-calls-snap-election-on -april-28/.

Tremlett, Giles. "Spanish Prime Minister Rajoy Accused of Hiding Secret Income." *Guardian*, January 31, 2013. https://www.theguardian.com/world/2013/jan /31/spanish-prime-minister-secret-payments.

Tsebelis, George. *Veto Players*. Princeton, NJ: Princeton University Press, 2002.

Van Biezen, Ingrid, Peter Mair, and Thomas Poguntke. "Going, Going, . . . Gone?: The Decline of Party Membership in Contemporary Europe." *European Journal of Political Research* 51, no. 1 (2012): 24–56.

Vance, Ashlee. "Elon Musk's Space Dream Almost Killed Tesla." *Bloomberg*, May 14, 2015. https://www.bloomberg.com/graphics/2015-elon-musk-spacex/.

———. *Elon Musk: Tesla, SpaceX, and the Quest for a Fantastic Future*. New York: Harper Collins, 2015.

———. "Elon Musk, the 21st Century Industrialist." *Bloomberg*, September 15, 2012. https://www.bloomberg.com/news/articles/2012-09-13/elon-musk-the-21st-century-industrialist.

Van der Pas, Daphne, Catherine E. De Vries, and Wouter van der Brug. "A Leader Without a Party: Exploring the Relationship between Geert Wilders' Leadership Performance in the Media and His Electoral Success." *Party Politics* 19, no. 3 (2013): 458–76.

Van de Wardt, Marc, Catherine E. De Vries, and Sara B. Hobolt. "Exploiting the Cracks: Wedge Issues in Multiparty Competition." *Journal of Politics* 76, no. 4 (2014): 986–99.

Van Holsteyn, Joop J. M., and Galen A. Irwin. "Never a Dull Moment: Pim Fortuyn and the Dutch Parliamentary Election of 2002." *West European Politics* 26, no. 2 (2003): 41–66.

Van Spanje, Joost. *Controlling the Electoral Marketplace: How Established Parties Ward Off Competition*. New York: Springer, 2018.

Veen, Hans-Joachim. "Wer wählt Grun?" In *Die Grünen: Partei wider Willen*, edited by Helmut Berschin, Klaus Gotto, and Veen, 118–46. Mainz: v. Hase und Koehler, 1984.

Vliegenthart, Rens. "Teveel aandacht voor welke partij de grootste is." *Stuk Rood Vlees Blog*, March 25, 2019. http://stukroodvlees.nl/teveel-aandacht-voor-welke-partij-de-grootste-is/.

Vliegenthart, Rens, Stefaan Walgrave, and Corinne Meppelink. "Inter-Party Agenda Setting in Belgian Parliament: The Role of Party Characteristics and Competition." *Political Studies* 59, no. 2 (2011): 368–88.

Wagner, Markus. "Defining and Measuring Niche Parties." *Party Politics* 18, no. 6 (2012): 845–64.

Walgrave, Stefaan, and Yves Dejaeghere. "Surviving Information Overload: How Elite Politicians Select Information." *Governance* 30, no. 2 (2017): 229–44.

Walgrave, Stefaan, Jonas Lefevere, and Michiel Nuytemans. "Issue Ownership Stability and Change: How Political Parties Claim and Maintain Issues through Media Appearances." *Political Communication* 26, no. 2 (2009): 153–72.

Warwick, Paul. "Economic Trends and Government Survival in West European Parliamentary Democracies." *American Political Science Review* 86, no. 4 (1992): 875–87.

Webb, Paul D. "Are British Political Parties in Decline?" *Party Politics* 1, no. 3 (1995): 299–322.

Wernerfelt, Birger. "Brand Loyalty and User Skills." *Journal of Economic Behavior and Organization* 6, no. 4 (1985): 381–85.

Williams, David K. "Top 10 List: The Surprising Origins of 10 Major American Brands." *Forbes*, January 20, 2013. https://www.forbes.com/sites/davidk williams/2013/01/20/top-10-list-the-surprising-origins-of-10-major -american-brands/#38bc844369fa.

Wlezien, Christopher. "The Public as Thermostat: Dynamics of Preferences for Spending." *American Journal of Political Science* 39, no. 4 (1995): 981–1000.

Wodak, Ruth, and Anton Pelinka, eds. *The Haider Phenomenon in Austria*. Piscataway, NJ: Transaction, 2000.

Zaller, John R. *The Nature and Origins of Mass Opinion*. Cambridge: Cambridge University Press, 1992.

Data Sets

Aarts, Kees, Bojan Todosijevic, and Harry van der Kaap. Dutch Parliamentary Election Study Cumulative Dataset, 1971–2006. Ann Arbor, MI: Interuniversity Consortium for Political and Social Research (distributor), September 13, 2010. doi:10.3886/ICPSR28221.v1.

Andersen, Jørgen Goul. Danish Election Study 1994. Danish Data Archive, 2002. Data file DDA-2210, version 1.0.0. doi:10.5279/DK-SA-DDA-2210.

———. Danish Election Study 2001. Danish Data Archive, 2004. Data file DDA-13057, version 1.0.0. doi:10.5279/DK-SA-DDA-13057.

———. Danish Election Study 2005. Danish Data Archive, 2007. Data file DDA-18184, version 1.0.0. doi:10.5279/DK-SA-DDA-18184.

———. Danish Election Study 2007. Danish Data Archive, 2012. Data file DDA-26471, version 1.0.0. doi:10.5279/DK-SA-DDA-26471.

Bakker, Ryan, Catherine E. De Vries, Erica E. Edwards, Liesbet Hooghe, Seth Jolly, Gary Marks, Jonathan Polk, Jan Rovny, Marco R. Steenbergen, and Milada Anna Vachudova. "Measuring Party Positions in Europe: The Chapel Hill Expert Survey Trend File, 1999–2010." *Party Politics* 21, no. 1 (2015): 143–52.

Benedetto, Giacomo, Simon Hix, and Nicola Mastrorocco. Dataset of Parties and Elections in Europe, 1918–2018. London School of Economics, 2019.

Borre, Ole, Erik Damgaard, Hans Jørgen Nielsen, Steen Sauerberg, Ole Tonsgaard, and Torben Worre. Danish Election Study 1973, Danish Data Archive, 1976. Data file DDA-8, version 1.0.0. doi:10.5279/DK-SA-DDA-8.

Borre, Ole, Ingemar Glans, Hans Jørgen Nielsen, Steen Sauerberg, Torben Worre, and Jørgen Goul Andersen. Danish Election Study 1981. Danish Data Archive, 1983. Data file DDA-529, version 1.0.0. doi:10.5279/DK-SA-DDA-529.

———. Danish Election Study 1984. Danish Data Archive, 1986. Data file DDA-772, version 1.0.0. doi:10.5279/DK-SA-DDA-772.

Borre, Ole, Hans Jørgen Nielsen, Jørgen Goul Andersen, and Johannes Andersen. Danish Election Study 1998. Danish Data Archive, 2000. Data file DDA-4189, version 1.0.0. doi:10.5279/DK-SA-DDA-4189.

Borre, Ole, Hans Jørgen Nielsen, Steen Sauerberg, and Torben Worre. Danish Election Study 1975. Danish Data Archive, 1976. Data file DDA-16, version 1.0.0. doi:10.5279/DK-SA-DDA-16.

———. Danish Election Study 1977. Danish Data Archive, 1978. Data file DDA-166, version 1.0.0. doi:10.5279/DK-SA-DDA-166.

Clarke, Harold D., David Sanders, and Paul Whiteley, British Election Study, 2005. UK Data Archive, 2006. https://www.britishelectionstudy.com/data-object /2005-bes-post-election-survey/.

———. British General Election Study, 2001. UK Data Archive, 2003. https:// www.britishelectionstudy.com/data-object/2001-bes-cross-section-2/.

Comparative Study of Electoral Systems. CSES Modules 1–5 1996–2016. Ann Arbor: ICPSR, 2017.

Crewe, Ivor, David Robertson, and Bo Sarlvik. British Election Study, October 1974. UK Data Archive, 1977.

———. British Election Study, May 1979. UK Data Archive, 1981.

Döring, Holger, and Philip Manow. Parliaments and Governments Database (Parl-Gov): Information on Parties, Elections and Cabinets in Modern Democracies. Development version, 2019. http://www.parlgov.org/.

European Commission. Eurobarometer. GESIS Data Archive, 1975–2016. https:// www.gesis.org/eurobarometer-data-service/survey-series/standard-special-eb.

European Social Survey Cumulative File, ESS 1-8. Data file edition 1.0. NSD—Norwegian Centre for Research Data, Norway—Data Archive and distributor of ESS data for ESS ERIC. doi:10.21338/NSD-ESS-CUMULATIVE.

Fieldhouse, Ed, Jane Green, Geoff Evans, Hermann Schmitt, Cees van der Eijk, Jon Mellon, and Chris Prosser. British Election Study, 2015: Face-to-Face Post-Election Survey [data collection]. UK Data Service, 2019. SN: 7972. doi:10 .5255/UKDA-SN-7972-1.

———. British Election Study, 2017: Face-to-Face Post-Election Survey [data collection]. UK Data Service, 2019. SN: 8418. doi:10.5255/UKDA-SN-8418-1.

GESIS—Leibniz Institute for the Social Sciences. German General Social Survey (ALLBUS): Cumulation 1980–2016. GESIS Data Archive, Cologne, 2019. ZA4588 Data file version 1.0.0. doi:10.4232/1.13291.

Hansen, Kasper Møller. Danish National Election Study 2015. Danish Data Archive, 2017. Data file DDA-31083, version 1.0.0. doi:10.5279/DK-SA-DDA -31083.

Heath, Anthony, Roger Jowell, and John Curtice. British General Election Study, 1983. UK Data Archive, 1983.

———. British General Election Study, 1987. UK Data Archive, 1993.

Heath, Anthony, Roger Jowell, John Curtice, James Mitchell, and Jack Brand. British General Election Study, 1992. UK Data Archive, 1993.

Heath, Anthony, Pippa Norris, John Curtice, and Roger Jowell. British General Election Study, 1997: Cross-Section Survey [data collection]. UK Data Service, 1999. SN: 3887. doi:10.5255/UKDA-SN-3887-1.

Holmberg, Sören, Mikael Gilljam, and Statistics Sweden. Swedish Election Study

1985, 1988, 1994. Swedish National Data Service, 1997. https://snd.gu.se/en
/catalogue/collection/swedish-election-studies---parliamentary-elections.

Holmberg, Sören, and Henrik Ekengren Oscarsson. Swedish National Election
Study 2010. Swedish National Data Service, 2017. Version 1.0. doi:10.5878
/002905.

Holmberg, Sören, Henrik Ekengren Oscarsson, and Statistics Sweden. Swedish
Election Study 2002, 2006. Swedish National Data Service, 2012. https://snd
.gu.se/en/catalogue/collection/swedish-election-studies---parliamentary
-elections.

Holmberg, Sören, and Statistics Sweden. Swedish Election Study 1979. Swedish
National Data Service, 1986. Version 1.0. doi:10.5878/002509.

———. Swedish Election Study 1982. Swedish National Data Service, 1986. Version 1.0. doi:10.5878/002510.

———. Swedish Election Study 1998. Swedish National Data Service, 2002. Version 1.0. doi:10.5878/002515.

International IDEA (International Institute for Democracy and Electoral Assis-
tance). *Voter Turnout in Western Europe: Since 1945.* Stockholm: International
IDEA, 2004. https://www.idea.int/sites/default/files/publications/voter
-turnout-in-western-europe-since-1945.pdf.

Kolk, Henk, Kees Aarts, Jean Tillie, and Stichting Kiezersonderzoek Nederland.
Nationaal Kiezersonderzoek, 2010—NKO 2010. DANS, 2012. doi:10.17026
/dans-xvh-tghy.

Kolk, Henk, Jean Tillie, Patrick van Erkel, Mariken van der Velden, Alyt Damstra,
and Stichting Kiezersonderzoek Nederland. Dutch Parliamentary Election
Study 2012. DANS, 2012, doi:10.17026/dans-x5h-akds.

Nielsen, Hans Jørgen, Steen Sauerberg, and Torben Worre. Danish Election Study
1988. Danish Data Archive, 1990. Data file DDA-1432, version 1.0.0. doi:10.5279
/DK-SA-DDA-1432.

Petersson, Olof, Bo Särlvik, and Statistics Sweden. Swedish Election Study 1973.
Swedish National Data Service, 1984. Version 1.0. doi:10.5878/002503.

Petersson, Olof, and Statistics Sweden. Swedish Election Study 1976. Swedish
National Data Service, 1984. Version 1.0. doi:10.5878/002505.

Rattinger, Hans, Sigrid Roßteutscher, Rüdiger Schmitt-Beck, Bernhard Weßels,
Ina Bieber, Evelyn Bytzek, and Philipp Scherer. Long-Term-Online-Tracking
of State Election Baden-Wuerttemberg 2011 (GLES 2009). GESIS Data Archive, Cologne, 2015. ZA5328 Data file version 3.0.0. doi:10.4232/1.12392.

———. Long-Term-Online-Tracking of State Election Mecklenburg-Western
Pomerania 2011 (GLES 2009). GESIS Data Archive, Cologne, 2011. ZA5330
Data file version 1.0.0. doi:10.4232/1.11053.

———. Long-Term-Online-Tracking of State Election North Rhine-Westphalia
2010 (GLES 2009). GESIS Data Archive, Cologne, 2013. ZA5324 Data file
version 2.0.0. doi:10.4232/1.11504.

———. Long-Term-Online-Tracking of State Election Rhineland-Palatinate 2011
(GLES 2009). GESIS Data Archive, Cologne, 2015. ZA5327 Data file version
3.0.0. doi:10.4232/1.12391.

Rattinger, Hans, Sigrid Roßteutscher, Rüdiger Schmitt-Beck, Bernhard Weßels, Ina Bieber, Evelyn Bytzek, and Philipp Scherer. Long-Term-Online-Tracking of State Election Saxony-Anhalt 2011 (GLES 2009). GESIS Data Archive, Cologne, 2015. ZA5325 Data file version 3.0.0. doi:10.4232/1.12390.

Rattinger, Hans, Sigrid Roßteutscher, Rüdiger Schmitt-Beck, Bernhard Weßels, Jürgen Falter, Oscar Gabriel, and Tatjana Rudi. Long-Term Panel 2002-2005-2009 (GLES 2009). GESIS Data Archive, 2012. ZA5320 Data file version 2.0.0. doi:10.4232/1.11350.

Rattinger, Hans, Sigrid Roßteutscher, Rüdiger Schmitt-Beck, Bernhard Weßels, Christof Wolf, Ina Bieber, and Philipp Scherer. Long-Term-Online-Tracking of State Election North Rhine-Westphalia 2012 (GLES 2009). GESIS Data Archive, Cologne, 2015. ZA5333 Data file version 1.1.0. doi:10.4232/1.12343.

———. Long-Term-Online-Tracking of State Election Schleswig-Holstein 2012 (GLES 2009). GESIS Data Archive, Cologne, 2013. ZA5332 Data file version 1.0.0. doi:10.4232/1.11757.

Rattinger, Hans, Sigrid Roßteutscher, Rüdiger Schmitt-Beck, Bernhard Weßels, Christof Wolf, Maria Preißinger, Agatha Kratz, and Alexander Wuttke. Long-Term Panel 2013–2017 (GLES). GESIS Data Archive, 2018. doi:10.4232/1.13018.

Rattinger, Hans, Sigrid Roßteutscher, Rüdiger Schmitt-Beck, Bernhard Weßels, Christof Wolf, Tatjana Rudi, and Jan Eric Blumenstiel. Long-Term Panel 2009-2013-2017, GLES 2013. GESIS Data Archive, 2016. doi:10.4232/1.12627.

Roßteutscher, Sigrid, Rüdiger Schmitt-Beck, Harald Schoen, Bernhard Weßels, Christof Wolf, Simon Henckel, Ina Bieber, and Philipp Scherer. Long-Term Online Tracking at State Election Baden-Württemberg 2016 (GLES). GESIS Data Archive, Cologne, 2016. ZA5741 Data file version 1.0.0. doi:10.4232/1.12531.

———. Longterm Online Tracking at State Election Mecklenburg-Western Pomerania 2016 (GLES). GESIS Data Archive, Cologne, 2016. ZA5744 Data file version 1.0.0. doi:10.4232/1.12674.

———. Long-Term-Online-Tracking of State Election North Rhine-Westphalia 2017 (GLES). GESIS Data Archive, Cologne, 2017. ZA6820 Data file version 1.0.0. doi:10.4232/1.12852.

———. Longterm Online Tracking at State Election Rhineland-Palatinate 2016 (GLES). GESIS Data Archive, Cologne, 2016. ZA5743 Data file version 1.0.0. doi:10.4232/1.12533.

———. Longterm Online Tracking at State Election Saxony-Anhalt 2016 (GLES). GESIS Data Archive, Cologne, 2016. ZA5742 Data file version 1.0.0. doi:10.4232/1.12532.

———. Long-Term-Online-Tracking of State Election Schleswig-Holstein 2017 (GLES). GESIS Data Archive, Cologne, 2017. ZA6819 Data file version 1.0.0. doi:10.4232/1.12851.

Särlvik, Bo, and Statistics Sweden. Swedish Election Study 1970. Swedish National Data Service, 1986. Version 1.0. doi:10.5878/002508.

Schmitt, Hermann, Sara B. Hobolt, Sebastian A. Popa, Eftichia Teperoglou, European Parliament, Directorate-General for Communication, Public Monitoring Unit. European Parliament Election Study 2014, Voter Study, First Post-Election Survey. GESIS Data Archive, Cologne, 2016. ZA5160 Data file version 3.0.0. doi:10.4232/1.12628.

Schmitt, Hermann, Evi Scholz, Iris Leim, and Meinhard Moschner. The Mannheim Eurobarometer Trend File 1970–2002 (ed. 2.00). European Commission (principal investigator). GESIS Data Archive, Cologne, 2008. ZA3521 Data file version 2.0.1. doi:10.4232/1.10074.

Seki, Katsunori, and Laron K. Williams. "Updating the Party Government Data Set." *Electoral Studies* 34 (2014): 270–79.

Stubager, Rune, Jørgen Goul Andersen, and Kasper Møller Hansen. Danish National Election Study 2011. Danish Data Archive, 2013. Data file DDA-27067, version 1.0.0. doi:10.5279/DK-SA-DDA-27067.

Van Haute, Emilie, Emilien Paulis, and Vivien Sierens. "Assessing Party Membership Figures: The MAPP Dataset." *European Political Science* 17 (2018): 366–77.

Volkens, Andrea, Pola Lehmann, Theres Matthieß, Nicolas Merz, Sven Regel, and Bernhard Weßels. The Manifesto Data Collection. Manifesto Project (MRG/CMP/MARPOR). Wissenschaftszentrum Berlin für Sozialforschung (WZB), 2017. Version 2018a. doi:10.25522/manifesto.mpds.2017a.

Whiteley, Paul, and David Sanders, British Election Study, 2010. UK Data Archive, 2014. https://www.britishelectionstudy.com/data-object/2010-bes-cross-section/.

INDEX

A NOTE ON THE TYPE

This book has been composed in Adobe Text and Gotham.
Adobe Text, designed by Robert Slimbach for Adobe,
bridges the gap between fifteenth- and sixteenth-century
calligraphic and eighteenth-century Modern styles.
Gotham, inspired by New York street signs, was designed
by Tobias Frere-Jones for Hoefler & Co.